Architecture and Dystopia

edited by **DARIO DONETTI**

When I grow up, I wanna be
A superorganism
Superorganism, 2017

Architecture and Dystopia

The history of the Kunsthistorisches Institut in Florenz (KHI) has been shaped by many experts in medieval and Renaissance sculpture, including such distinguished scholars as Wilhelm von Bode, Friedrich Kriegbaum, Ulrich Alexander Middeldorf, Herbert Keutner, and Max Seidel. One of the founding fathers of our institute, however, dedicated his early research to how viewers move through and interact with architectural spaces. I refer to the pioneering work of August Schmarsow, whose *Antrittsvorlesung* at the University of Leipzig in 1893 (published in 1894) was entitled *Das Wesen der architektonischen Schöpfung*. In recent years, Walter Winterfeld's and Dethard von Haas's incredibly detailed critical analysis of the structure and façade of the Duomo in Siena (1999 and 2006) has confirmed the institute's commitment to the history of architecture, although the archaeological and philological approach of this monumental enterprise contrasts vividly with Schmarsow's astute observations.

Notwithstanding their importance for architectural studies in the last century, these efforts remained exceptions in the profile of KHI. Only in 2006, with the *Piazza e Monumento* project, did the institute adopt a more systematic approach to research on modern urban planning and architecture. Since then, our commitment to these issues has only grown, and a series of events and international conferences dedicated to the interaction between ethics and architecture were subsequently added to KHI's program.

This volume, *Architecture and Dystopia*, beautifully conceived and expertly realized by Dario Donetti, must be seen in this larger context. At first sight, Florence—the city of Renaissance harmony to millions of tourists from all over the world—might seem an odd place to organize a workshop on the dystopic implications of contemporary architecture. But when we recollect the projects of the Archizoom group, which operated in Florence between 1966 and 1974, and Superstudio, active here between 1966 and 1978, we understand that, for a very short period, this city was at the center of architectural experimentation in the twentieth century. These two "radical" groups—as Germano Celant defined them in his numerous writings—are even mentioned by Manfredo Tafuri in his influential essay "Per una critica dell'ideologia architettonica" published in the first issue of the journal *Contropiano* in 1969.

Having mentioned Tafuri, I would like to address a final point. At this very moment, the Kunsthistorisches Institut in Florenz is revisiting some important figures and issues of the history of twentieth century art and architecture. Not systematically, but "transversally," so to speak, with a series of seminars and conferences characterized by an intentionally critical approach. Tafuri has been a leading intellectual figure in the history of architecture of the last century, and we are particularly pleased to see that his provocative critique, formulated at the end of the 1960s, resounds so often in the essays gathered in this volume.

I would have liked to have participate in this publication with a contribution on literary dystopias: the way in which the city and society are manipulated and "distorted" in some great novels of the twentieth century, such as Yevgeny Zamyatin's *We* (1921); Aldous Huxley's *Brave New World* (1932); George Orwell's *1984* (1948); or Julio Cortázar's *62: Modelo para armar* (1968), translated with the English title *62: A Model Kit* and, in Italian, *Componibile 62*. Heavy administrative duties impeded the realization of this essay, but perhaps there will be other occasions to develop this subject with the seriousness it deserves. For the time being, I want to express my deepest gratitude to the authors and curator of this volume for engaging, in their committed contributions, with a new critical category: a "dystopian" approach to design, which might be fruitfully applied to the study of most recent developments in global architecture.

Alessandro Nova
Director of the Kunsthistorisches Institut in Florenz – Max-Planck-Institut

Architecture and Dystopia, or Negative Thinking as a Design Method

Dario Donetti

The 1973 publication of *Progetto e Utopia*—later translated as *Architecture and Utopia*—marked the synthesis of Manfredo Tafuri's reflections, already underway by the late 1960s, on the ideological experience of modern architecture **(fig. 1)**.[1] Beginning with the unsettling architectural visions of Piranesi, Tafuri traced the contradictory attempts of successive avant-gardes to spatially and productively order industrial society. He subjected the utopian tradition to rigorous dissection to reveal the ultimate exhaustion of any kind of ideology (Enlightenment rationality, positivism, or modernism) and, finally, to come to terms with architecture's new condition of crisis. Architecture had become, in his words, "obliged to return to pure architecture, to form without utopia; at best, to sublime uselessness."[2] That critical paradigm, offered by Tafuri four decades ago, served as the inspiration for the conference *Architecture and Dystopia*, organized in the autumn of 2014 at the Kunsthistorisches Institut in Florenz, whose contributions are nowgathered in the present volume. Twenty years after his death, the meeting was also meant as an homage to Tafuri's intellectual legacy, and to examine the tension between an analytical exercise addressed to the past and the critical interpretation of the present always expressed by his writings. Even when studying the Renaissance, as demonstrated by the continuity of intentions between the introductions to *L'architettura dell'umanesimo* (1969) and *Ricerca del Rinascimento* (1992),[3] and in the years of his apparent "withdrawal into philology," his exercise of historical research was meant as a militant, contemporary act. Interpretation of the past seemed valuable for Tafuri in so far as it provided an interpretive key for the extreme fragmentation of the architectural language of the twentieth century, for its "condition of doubt and anxiety," in the words of Marco De Michelis's essay presented in this book.[4]

In the time separating the conference from the present publication, recourse to the category of "dystopia" has become increasingly diffused, to the extent that one could speak of a true popularity of the term. In particular, 2017 may be remembered as the most dystopian year in recent times: from fiction to politics, the rediscovery of Margaret Wood's *The Handmaid's Tale* through television, or the need to categorize historically the new presidency of the United States, utopia's opposite has often been invoked.[5] In popular culture, this trend culminated in the highly promoted release of *Blade Runner 2049*, the sequel to Ridley Scott's celebrated 1982 science fiction movie that had already visualized an out-of-scale architecture prompting a paranoid search for individuality in a hyper-technological society of an imminent future **(fig. 2)**.[6] That imagined future had almost been reached by 2017, and its imagery has been completely absorbed by the culture, even under the guise of games, as uncovered by Simon Sadler's essay in this collection;[7] while in philosophical and literary discourse, as a response to the final waning of ideologies, cynical reason has replaced any utopian tendencies. However, as the leading utopian theorist of our day, Fredric Jameson, recently suggested, "dystopia is in reality utopia if examined more closely."[8] In short, the two categories are inextricably intertwined, since utopia has necessarily been, in the end, a negative construct **(fig. 3)**. The inherent contradictory, ambiguous nature of any utopian vision—from Plato to Le Corbusier—has always included the risk of turning into solipsistic, totalizing systems in which individual freedom would be ruthlessly erased.[9] It is revealing, for instance, that the interpretation of the last high points of the dystopian genre, from the 1960–1970s, has shifted from negative to positive, with several recent exhibitions marking the fiftieth anniversary of their first appearance—another symptom of the new fascination they are exerting on the present day.[10]

Radical artists have been expressing this widespread sentiment about the contemporary cultural condition for some time; and the present volume is devoted precisely to that experience, seen as a decisive moment of methodological elaboration for the development of contemporary architecture. Its theoretical premises—from the rediscovery of utopia in the 1960s and of its subsequent deconstruction during the following decade—are uncovered by Anthony Vidler's opening essay.[11] Calling into question the foundations of mid-century modernist utopian visions, those young architects transmuted the crisis of capitalism into a repertory of startling images that revealed the disturbing realities of the new consumer society. This was happening not only in the London of the "Second Machine Age" **(fig. 4)**,[12] or a Japan disturbed by the impact of postwar reconstruction, but even in places which still appeared resistant to the penetration of modern architecture, such as Haus-Rucker-Co's Vienna, or Superstudio and Archizoom's Florence. It was in such an apparent condition of impossibility that the conceptual obliteration of traditional architectural values could be experimentally pushed to its extreme consequences: i.e., to the silent, indifferent, and universalistic forms of the *Monumento Continuo*, or the unlimited and indistinct space of *No-stop City*, whose ironic rhetorical strategy is analyzed in this book by Marie Theres Stauffer **(figs. 5-6)**.[13]

The broader intent of this collection of essays is to offer a historiographical tool to evaluate the impact of these form makers on large-scale architectural production, instead of reducing their inventions to nothing more than a reckless use of leisure spaces, or, alternatively, to purely literary, melancholic exercises. Though conceived as eminently visual and exhausted in the space of experimentation, such models nevertheless inspired a generation of architects who sought to employ the dystopian paradigm as both a visionary and a constructive method of design. The first, almost literal applications are illustrated, for instance, in Massimiliano Savorra's study on the development of an *architecture du loisir* that was actually built resonating with the radical, ideal models.[14] Most of all, in the following decades this design method would generate unexpected possibilities for urban planning and architectural expression. After being freed from any sense of guilt toward a renegade formal order, reaching "an amoral domain, beyond good or bad," those visions would take the form of Rem Koolhaas's relativistic, process-based architectural theory **(fig. 7)**.[15] *Delirious New York* (1978), *S,M,L,XL* (1995), and *Junkspace* (2000) proposed a new urbanism of congestion and hyper-density, an accumulation of "sub-utopian fragments," in place of a coherent and rational ordering of the social space.[16] The original anti-capitalist intention was thus reversed. The architecture of liberation, complexity, and artifice had voluntarily surrendered to neoliberal economic paradigms and their proponents, and opened the metaphorical potential of metropolitan societies, under the banner of such a radical principle as "fuck the context." Also due to these methodological explorations, the *heterotopias* of the industrial metropolis—as Michel Foucault enabled us to call them[17]—have quickly evolved during the last decades of the twentieth century into an unrelenting dystopian architecture. Until the global economic crisis of 2008, this took form in great urban agglomerates and new centers of power. It reshaped, also, the landscape of cities under transformation, like Euralille, with its *éspace piranesien*, or the 1990s reconstruction of central Berlin, where the dystopian reaction was interpreted as nostalgic regression by the post-modernist experience. Our image of the city has drastically changed, and the need for new ways to represent it is exemplified by the gallery of images selected by Marco Biraghi as an appendix to this book.[18]

After all, is it truly possible to define a unified "dystopian" method of design, or does this architecture, by its very nature, resist systematization? And speaking of the most recognizable architectural expressions of this theoretical framework, characterized by brazen displays of technology and structures of overwhelming scale—such as Renzo Piano and Richard Rogers's Beaubourg, Ricardo Bofill's Antìgona, or MVRDV's Mirador **(fig. 8)**—are they merely isolated cases, albeit of particular iconic power? Or do they belong to a wider landscape of antirational architectural projects? And to what extent are these disturbing expressions premised on the utopian tradition or, better yet, on the conceptual model of negative thinking? The critical category of dystopia as applied to the study of contemporary architecture is, in fact, completely hypothetical; and so it must remain, if its legitimacy is to be verified. As an initial contribution to this goal, one can start tracing some recurring features that characterize all dystopian narratives, and have already undermined the positivity of their utopian precedents: the inherent ambiguity of their totalizing visions, and the implication of negative consequences—as a natural autoimmune reaction—implied by all visionary projects; the central role played by technology, whether embraced or denied; the inevitability of being imprisoned by architecture, sometimes willingly, more often by imposition; the out-of-scale dimensions purposely reached by utopic/dystopic expressions, a sublime bigness that visualizes the tension between individuality and the absoluteness of system; and finally, the narrative quality of such experimentations and their diagrammatic nature—illuminated respectively by Dominique Rouillard and Maddalena Scimemi[19]— which confine them to the theoretical domain, but also open up their unexpected applications. In the end, since the invention of the word by Thomas More, both utopia and its degenerate double have always been methods of possibility, instead of prefigurations of realizable environments. More than a place, dystopia is a practice when adopted as a contemporary design strategy, and an analytical category for the critical observation of architecture.

The publication of this volume has been made possible by the Kunsthistorisches Institut in Florenz – Max-Planck-Institut, and in particular its director Alessandro Nova, who enthusiastically encouraged the conference from which it stems, with no apprehension for its tentative nature, and generously sustained all of its phases. Kurt Klein and Antonina Tetzlaff have been trusted collaborators, while many colleagues and friends have rectified, steered, and enriched the project, helping to clarify its intentions and possible declinations: Lina Bolzoni, Françoise Fromonot, Stephanie Hanke, Riccardo Lami, Morgan Ng, Vittorio Pizzigoni, Maddalena Scimemi, Felicity Scott, Michael Tymkiw, and Yvonne Schweizer. The most heartfelt gratitude is extended to Hana Gründler and Brigitte Sölch, who have coordinated the *Ethik un Architektur* project over the years with unique vivacity: everyday engagement with them is what motivated the decision to question the significance of contemporary architecture in the spaces, both physical and intellectual, of our Institute.

New York, December 2017

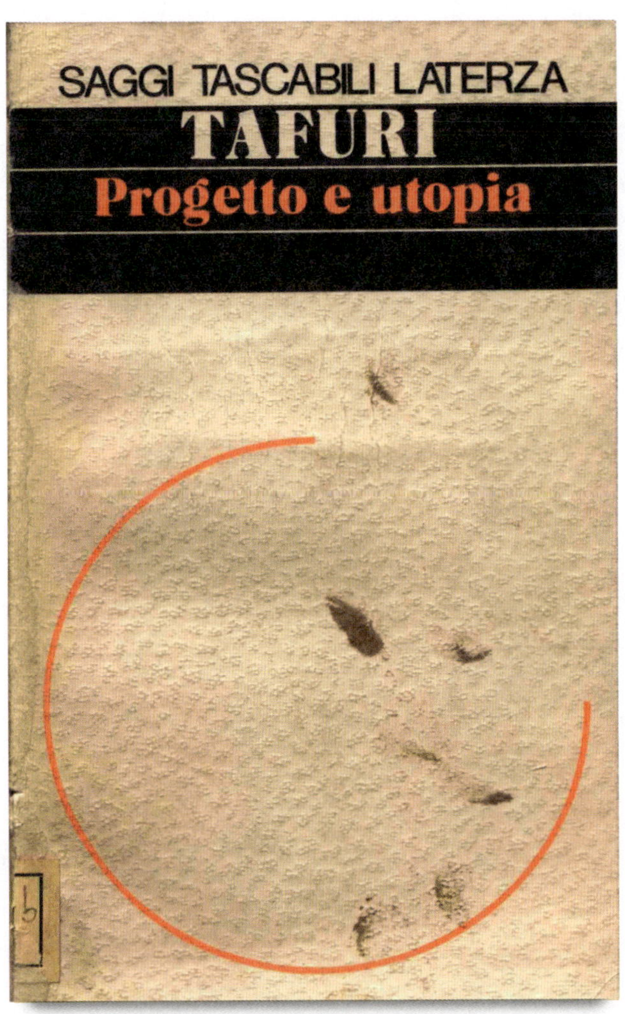

Fig. 1_ Manfredo Tafuri, *Progetto e utopia: architettura e sviluppo capitalistico,* Bari: Laterza, 1973 (book cover).

Fig. 2_ Syd Mead, *Tyrell Corporation Building for Blade Runner* (1982), directed by Ridley Scott.

Fig. 3_ Gruppo Strum, *Mediatory City*, from *Italy: The New Domestic Landscape: Achievements and Problems of Italian Design*, edited by Emilio Ambasz, New York/Florence: Museum of Modern Art/Centro Di, 1972 (exhibition catalogue).

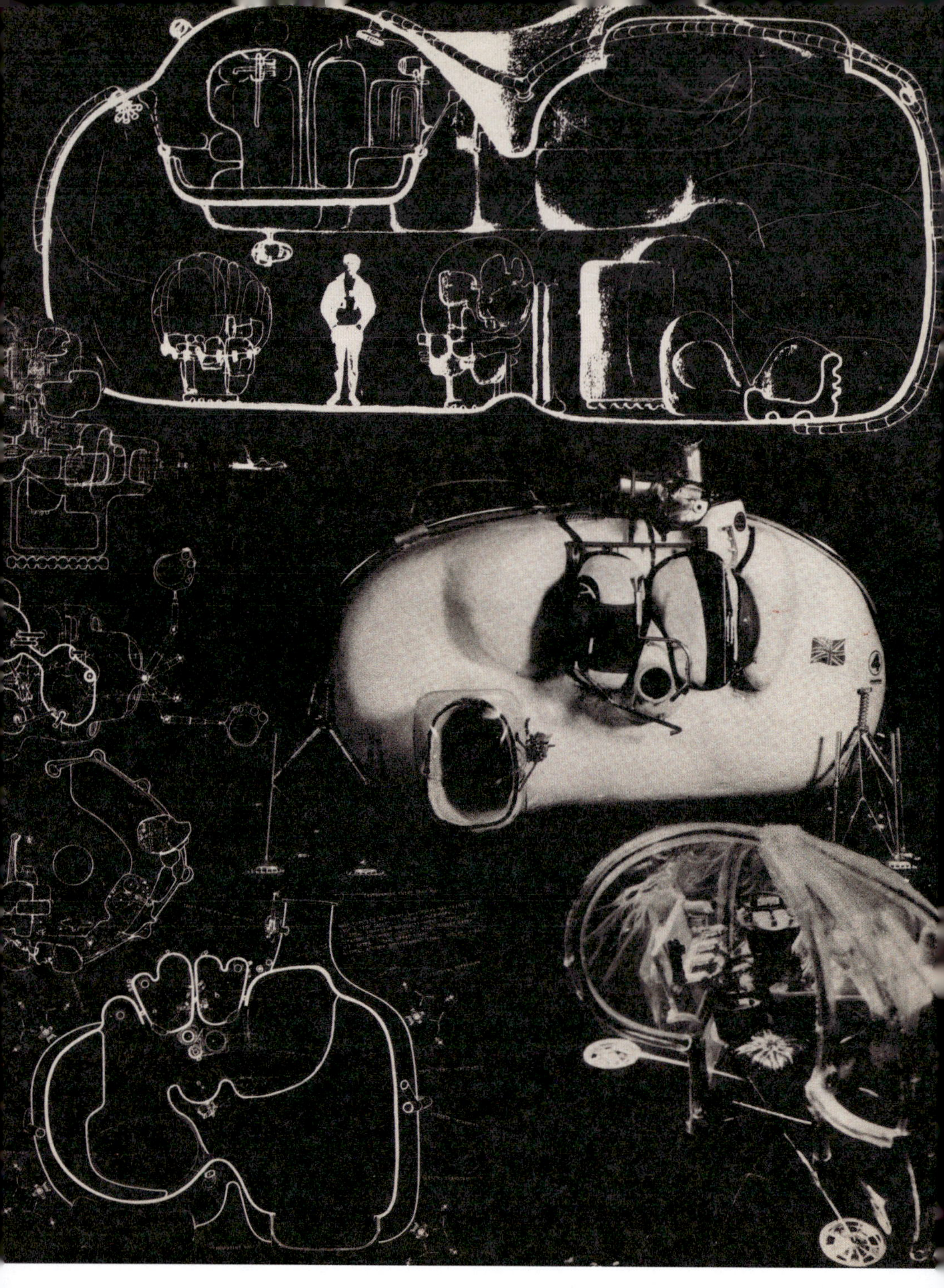

Fig. 4_ *Living Pod*, from *Archigram*, edited by Peter Cook, London: Studio Vista, 1972.

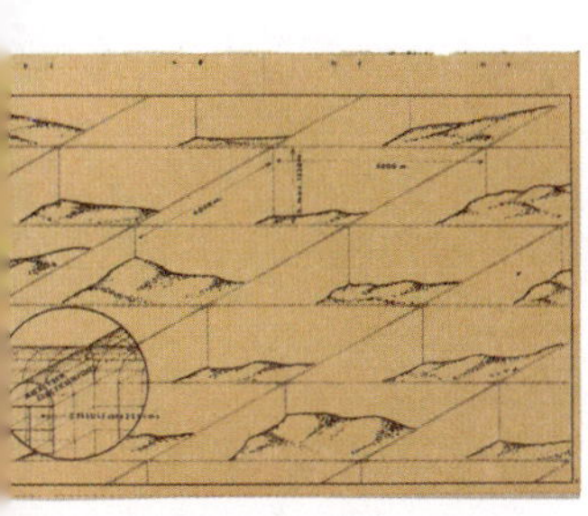
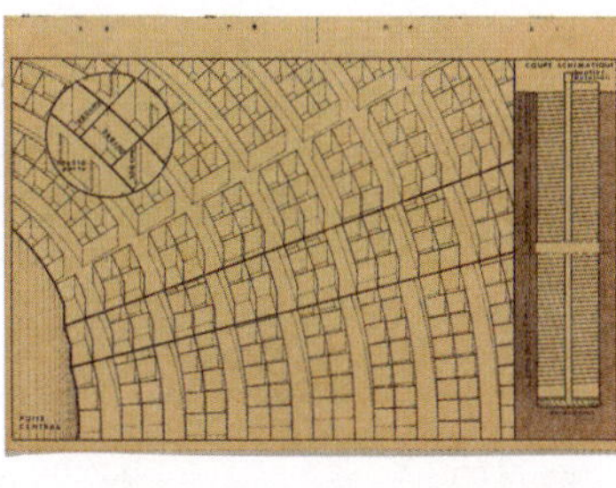
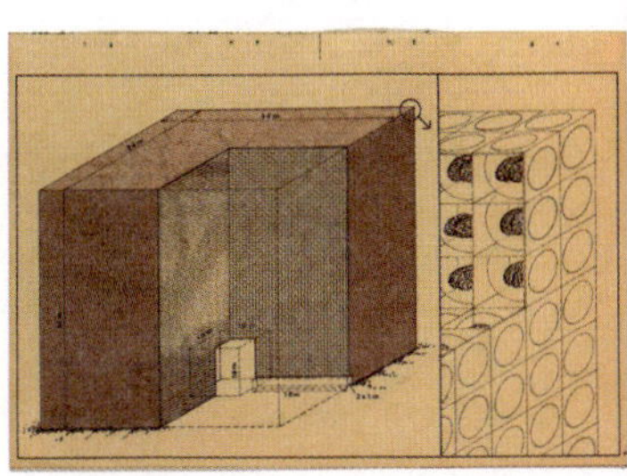

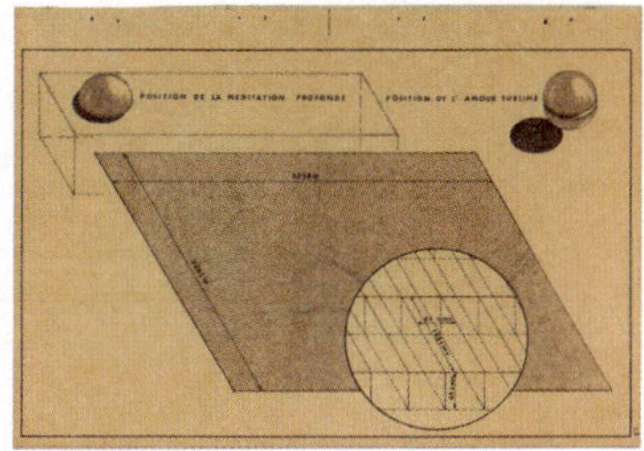
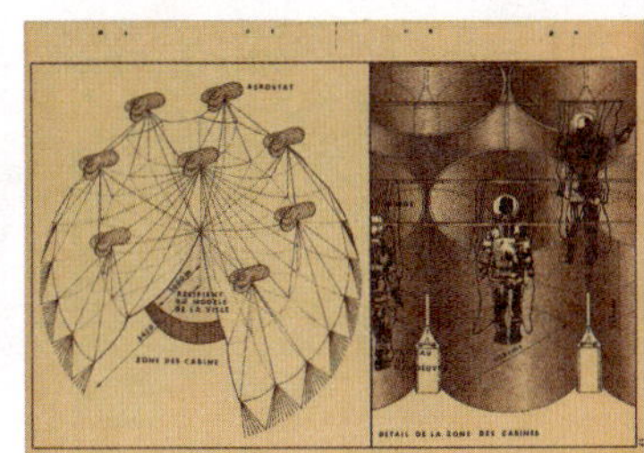

Fig. 5_ Superstudio, *The First City* and *The Twelve Ideal Cities*, 1971.

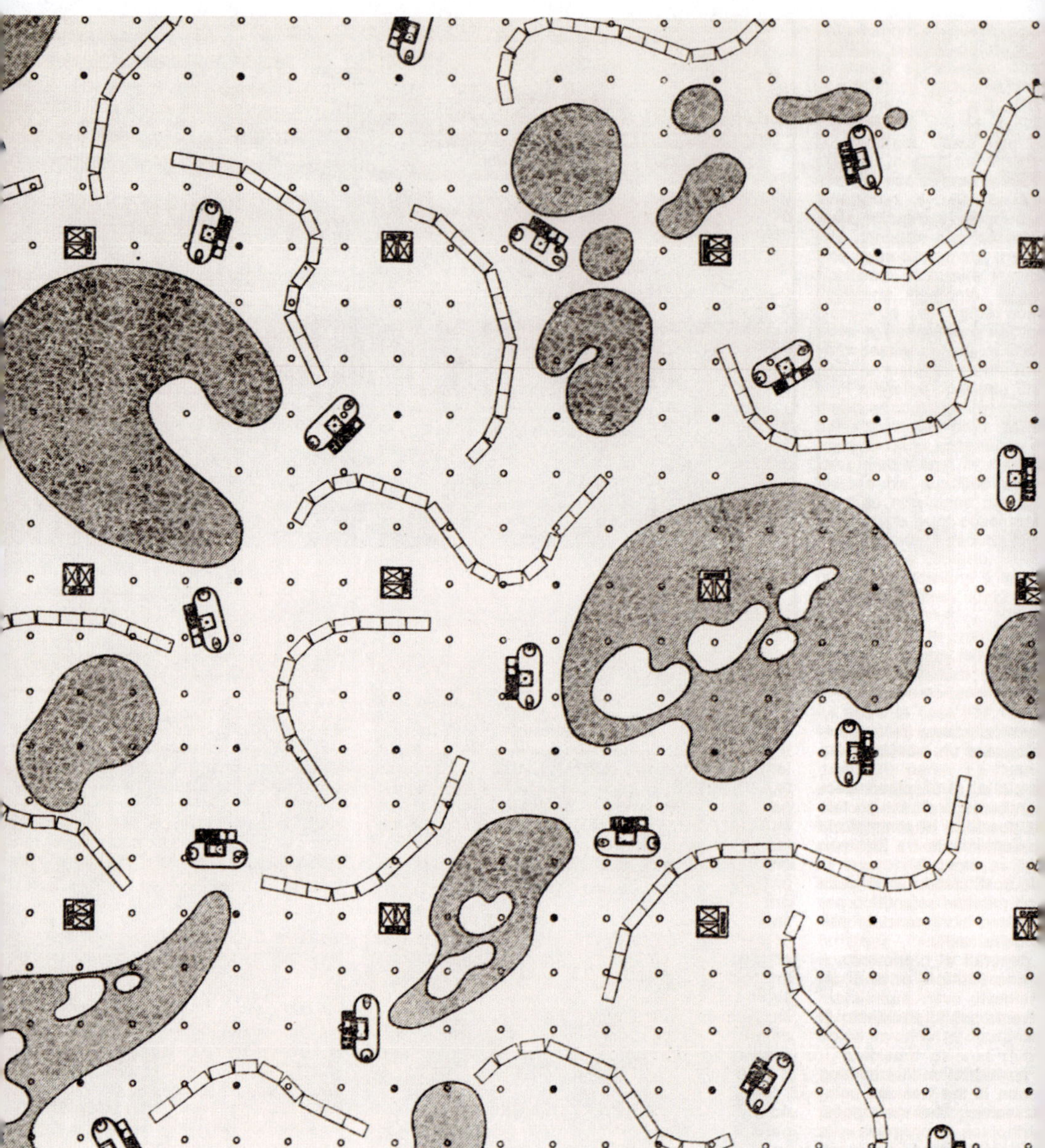

Fig. 6_ Archizoom, *Residential Park, No-Stop City*, 1969.

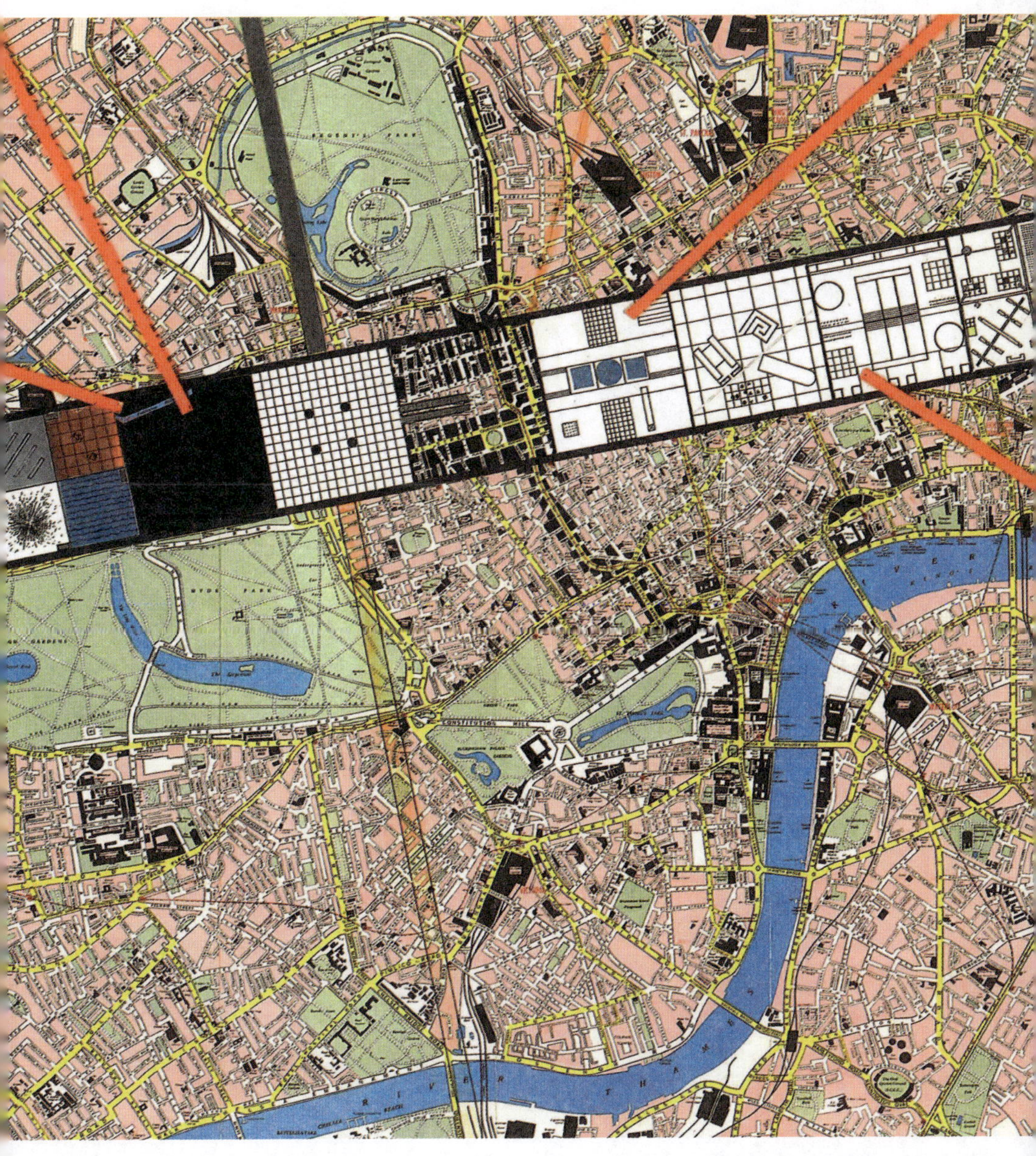

Fig. 7_ Rem Koolhaas, Elia Zenghelis, Madelon Vriesendorp, Zoe Zenghelis, *Exodus, or the Voluntary Prisoners of Architecture: The Strip*, 1972.

Fig. 8 (Following pages)_ Renzo Piano and Richard Rogers, Centre George Pompidou, Paris, 1971-1977.

Utopia Rediviva, 1960-1972

Anthony Vidler

Utopia and the idea of the city are inseparable
Colin Rowe, 1959

Utopia 1960

In January of 1959, the Cambridge University student journal *Granta* published what it called a "Utopia Supplement" **(fig. 1)**.[1] Under its new editor, André Schiffrin, five articles considered the state of play evoked by the concept of utopia. The "Supplement" itself was put together by the young James Cornford, who had just gained his First in History at Trinity. Cornford, son of the idealist John Cornford who had died in the fight against fascism in Spain, and grandson of the classicist Francis Cornford, translator and commentator of Plato's *Republic* and *Timaeus* was well schooled in the history and practice of utopian thought, Cornford and his fellow-contributors were adamant in their attempt to reclaim a form of utopian discourse, despite the fact that, as he admitted in his introduction, the word "Utopian" itself had become a pejorative: "It may be taken to mean 'pleasant but impossible,' 'unpleasant but impossible,' 'quite inconceivable,' and so on. It suggests that writing Utopias is dangerous, unprofitable of just plain silly," he wrote, in marked opposition to the prevailing sense that the very notion of "utopia" historically (and in the present) was closely associated with totalitarianism, an anathema following the rise of Fascism and National Socialism in the 1930s.

For, in the immediate aftermath of the traumas of World War II, utopia was decidedly out of favor, castigated from Theodor Adorno and Max Horkheimer's *Dialectic of Enlightenment* to

Karl Popper's *The Open Society and its Enemies*, and, on a more popular level, from Huxley's *Brave New World* (1932) to Orwell's *1984*. Berdiaeff had already summed this negative sense of utopia up in a passage cited as an epilog by Huxley in the second edition of his *Brave New World*: "Utopias appear to be much more realizable than we used to think. And we now find ourselves faced by a question that is much more disturbing: how to *avoid* their definitive realization? Utopias are realizable, life marches towards utopias. And perhaps a new century will begin, a century where the intellectuals and the cultivated class will dream of ways to avoid utopias and return to a "non utopian" society, less "perfect" and yet more free."[2]

Popper in particular was the voice most listened to. Written in New Zealand during the war, *The Open Society and its Enemies*—"his contribution to the war effort," he said—Popper's first volume was entirely taken up with an attack on Plato, seen as the forebear of Hitler. Plato: "the first great political ideologist who thought in classes and races and proposed concentration camps," wrote Popper of Plato's suggestions for the isolation of malcontent citizens in the *Laws*. "The lesson which we should thus learn from Plato is the exact opposite of what he tries to teach us." It is a lesson which must not be forgotten [...] his own development proves that the therapy he recommended is worse than the evil he tried to combat."[3]
The Platonic approach, concluded Popper, represented a kind of utopian engineering. Opposed to this, the engineer-scientist Popper proposed a more gradualist and fragmented form of what he called "piecemeal engineering."[4] And in the second volume, he followed with a critique of the entire neo-Platonic tradition and its historicization with Hegel. These themes had been taken up by Bertrand Russell—"[Popper's] attack on Plato, while unorthodox, is in my opinion, thoroughly justified"[5]—followed by Lewis Mumford—"Plato's *polis* might be described as a walled prison without room for the true activities of the city within its prison-yard," governed by "totalitarian controls insulated by secrecy."[6] Utopias in their perfection were in essence totalitarian, he asserted as he castigated an ideal that seemed thoroughly aristocratic, Spartan, and ultimately humdrum.

On the side of utopia, however, the most powerful authority on the question was the Hungarian sociologist Karl Mannheim, who had emigrated from Germany in 1933 to teach at the London School of Economics and later the Institute of Education. His book *Ideology and Utopia*, originally published in German in 1929, had appeared in 1936, but had been little noticed until the mid-1940s when it was translated with *Part I* added especially for an English readership. Mannheim argued strongly for the need for ideal thinking as a dynamic counter to the static, and, in the conditions under which he wrote in the years before the Second World War, dangerous acceptance of the status quo:

> The disappearance of utopia brings about a static state of affairs in which man himself becomes no more than a thing [...] with the relinquishment of

> utopias, man would lose his will to shape history, and therewith his ability to understand it.[7]

In this context, the contributors to *Granta*'s "Utopian Supplement," evinced varied, but cautiously optimistic, positions. Robin Marris, already a lecturer and Fellow of King's, writing on the theme "Utopia and Conviction," preferred a dynamic vision of utopia as "a state to which we are continually aspiring but never reach" to the traditional vision of "a society so perfect that no further change (improvement) is conceivable."[8] Richard Layard, also at King's, contributed a detailed account of the development of the kibbutz in Israel entitled "News from Somewhere,"[9] while André Schiffrin, fresh from a history degree at Yale and the first American to edit *Granta*, argued for "The Need for Utopia" as an idealistic and practical infusion into the "empty world" of work.[10] For André Schiffrin, Mannheim offered a definition of utopia that fitted his own advocacy of radical change, aided by utopian ideas which transcend reality and that "when they pass over into conduct, tend to shatter [...] the order of things prevailing at the time."[11] Indeed, for the British Left in general, Mannheim's sociological propositions were an acceptable counter to the refusal of Marx and Engels to recognize "utopian" socialism. As Taylor and Steele note, "Mannheim's pursuit of the goal of a broader notion of the social sciences, rather than simply a statistically based sociology, created an important new tone in academic circles."[12] Historians began to discover the utopian roots of the labor movement: Edward P. Thompson's *William Morris* (1955) was extremely influential on Michael Young and his circle of post-Fabians;[13] Raymond Williams explored notions of culture with respect to the working classes, giving a measured account of both Morris and Orwell in his influential *Culture and Society 1780-1950* (1958).[14]

Cornford, in turn, contested the negative reception of Morris's *News from Nowhere* and Bellamy's *Looking Backward*, emphasizing their positive contributions to the class struggle. His title was optimistic: "Just Around the Corner."[15] These authors all went on to develop careers in surprising continuity with their early views. Schiffrin (son of the émigré Jacques Schiffrin, founder of the publishing firm Pantheon) was to join the firm in New York in 1961, editing his first major success, Gunter Grass's *The Tin Drum*.[16] Marris, as an economist, having worked with the Gaitskell and Wilson governments advocating universal access to education, returned to the struggle, after a period of disillusion, with his 1996 book *How to Save the Underclass*.[17] Layard, also an economist, developed what he called "Happiness Research," investigating the relations between economic policy and mental life in an effort to lessen social inequality. Cornford, himself, true to his distinguished idealist heritage, was, according to his obituary in the *Guardian*, a "committed Robert Owen-type socialist all his life," finding his vocation as a social reformer in charitable foundations, think tanks, "participating in somewhat utopian enterprises," and as a government adviser on constitutional reform and freedom of information.[18]

Perhaps the most critical of the contributions was that provided by the newly appointed Emmanuel College tutor and lecturer at the School of Architecture, Colin Rowe, who, had arrived in Cambridge in 1959, after a few years teaching at the University of Texas, Austin, and Cornell. His essay, "The Architecture of Utopia," succinctly summarized the long and imbricated history of millennial dreams, utopian narratives, and the ideal city projects of architects from the Renaissance to the present. For Rowe, architecture's entrance into the utopian romance had contributed little more than sterile diagrams of urban form, from Renaissance star patterns to the geometrical uniformity of modernist urban plans. His article was neither an endorsement of utopianism, nor written from a Left-Labour position. Under the title "The Architecture of Utopia," he traced a succinct "descent" of the utopian idea in architecture, from its hybrid origins in "Jewish millennial thought" and Platonic forms, through its reification in the centralized star-patterns of Renaissance ideal cities, the less "convincing" geometries of the Enlightenment, the "somewhat provincial" plans for redeeming "the lower strata" in the nineteenth-century, to the divergent utopian impulses in modern architecture, split between the "mechanistic, vitalistic city of the Futurists" where life was premised on "an absolute orgy of flux," and Le Corbusier's Ville Radieuse, with its "boring" "schematic monotony."[19] While he admitted that there was inevitably an aspect of utopianism in every architectural project, it was the wholesale realization of the ideal in reality that disturbed him. Contesting Mannheim definition of utopias as "orientations transcending reality,"[20] he countered, with reference to the ubiquitous effects of Le Corbusier's Ville Radieuse: "if we ask with what ideas an 'orientation' which 'transcends reality' is constructed we are obliged to wonder whether contemporary society can really tolerate such an 'orientation.'" Buttressing Rowe's skepticism was his enthusiasm for Popper, whose work, as he noted in an addendum to "The Architecture of Utopia" in 1973, while openly available, had been ignored by the contributors to *Granta*.[21]

In writing on *architectural* utopia, Rowe was responding to an already growing literature on the subject, most immediately the recently published work by Helen Rosenau, *The Ideal City in its Architectural Evolution* (1959).[22] Rosenau, at the Warburg Institute where Rowe had studied, had long been a follower of the work of Emil Kaufmann, the Viennese art historian forced into immigration in the early 1940s. Kaufmann had spent the interwar period researching a group of little known French architects who had been inspired by the ideas of the Enlightenment philosophes—Etienne-Louis Boullée, Claude-Nicolas Ledoux, and Jean-Jacques Lequeu. Kaufmann's first book on the subject, *Von Ledoux bis Le Corbusier* (1933) had largely escaped notice before the war, but in exile in the United States he was to deliver a lecture on Ledoux, at the newly constituted Society of Architectural Historians in Philip Johnson's Miesian apartment at Harvard, and publish a major study of *Three Revolutionary Architects. Boullée, Ledoux, Lequeu* in 1952 by the Philadelphia Philosophical Society **(fig. 2)**.[23] Posthumously, his comprehensive review of neo-classical architecture in England, Italy and

France, *Architecture in the Age of Reason* (1957) was immediately adopted in England and the United States as the last word on the International Enlightenment in architecture **(fig. 3)**.[24] Helen Rosenau at the Warburg Institute where Rowe had studied with Rudolf Wittkower, had capitalized on Kaufmann's research, publishing on Ledoux (1946) and translating Boullée's manuscript text on *Architecture: Essai sur l'art* (1953).[25]

Internationally, Enlightenment utopia had equally become a renewed preoccupation: Aldo Rossi in Italy published on Milanese neoclassicism, and in 1958, a full review of Kaufmann's *Architecture in the Age of Reason* for *Casabella*;[26] a year earlier, and signifying the terms of the emerging debate as to the deleterious effects of Enlightened rationalism, he had reviewed Hans Sedlmayr's *Verlust der Mitte* (1955) **(fig. 4)**.[27] This book, deeply indebted to Kaufmann's research, but taking a diametrically opposite point of view, was published in English translation in 1957.[28]

Utopia 1970

Not the least unexpected thing about the 1960s
was its reinvention of the concept of Utopia
Fredric Jameson, 1977

Despite the omnipresent skepticism of Popper and his followers, by the late 1960s the intellectual climate had changed: in the euphoria surrounding the events of 1968 utopia in its many different forms was back on the agenda: from B.F. Skinner's *Walden Two*,[29] investigating the potential effects, for better or worse of social and psychological behaviorism, to the commune movements with their vague evocations of Fourier and the Shakers, to the Metabolists and Megastructuralists, utopia was seen as eminently realizable (Paolo Soleri), or as a critical tool (Superstudio). Systems theorists analyzed utopia as a primitive version of a cybernetic system; historians looked critically at the late eighteenth and early nineteenth-century utopias of France and the US; other historians, notably the late Robin Evans, uncovered modernity and functionalism in the shape of Bentham's Panopticon (and, it must be said much earlier, and more critically than Foucault's belated use of the analogy). Architectural interest in utopian thought continues to be stimulated by historical studies such as that of Leonardo Benevolo, whose study of the origins of modern urbanism included a long section on nineteenth-century utopias, with diagrams of Fourier's *Phalanstery* and by Françoise Choay's influential anthology of urbanist texts.[30] Academic interest in the utopianism of American groups—Shakers, Rappites, Hutterites—was joined to exploration of the fates of newer, nineteenth-century foundations from Europe—Fourierists, Owenites, Icarians; architects like Liselotte and Oswal Mathias Ungers made it a point to visit as many former community sites in the US and catalog as many surviving buildings as possible.[31]

Thus the neo-finalist philosopher Raymond Ruyer published his revisionist history of the genre, arguing for the study and practice of utopian thought as "a speculative exercise on the lateral possibilities of social reality;"[32] Ruyer was citing from the introduction to the posthumous collection of essays by the sociologist Georges Duveau, *Sociologie de l'utopie* who had argued for a revision of the opposition between communism and utopian socialism. [33] Roger Mucchielli, who would publish his own study, *Le mythe de la cité idéale* in 1960, saw utopia as the product of human nature's "exigence de plus de justice et de liberté, principe régulateur de toutes les réformes, de tous des progress politiques." For him, the aspiration to provide models that were "mieux que le réel" was less the vehicle of pure imagination than that of "le sur-réel, le méta-historique et le méta-empirique."[34]

Interest among the students of the mid to late 1960s in utopian thought was equally intense, and many courses were developed to satisfy the demand: Jean Servier, an ethnologist whose field work had been accomplished among the Berber tribes, researched and delivered an entire history of utopian thought for his students at Paris's École d'Architecture de Montpellier, published in 1967 as *Histoire de l'utopie;*[35] Hubert Tonka, assistant to Henri Lefebvre, with architects Antoine Stimco, Jean Aubert, and Jean-Paul Jungmann, together with Jean Baudrillard conceived the publication *Utopie: Sociologie de l'urbain* in late 1966 **(fig. 5)**; under the beneficent patronage of Lefebvre it ran for the next ten years. A year after '68, Louis Marin, in Montreal, subjected the texts of Thomas More, the cartography of city plans, and the mock utopia of Disneyworld to the rigors of structural and semiological analysis (*Utopiques: jeux d'espaces*,1973[36]) through the lens of structuralism: utopia as *structural model.* Claude Lévi-Strauss had provided the approach in his *Anthropologie structurale* (1950),[37] systematizing his earlier studies of the Bororo villages in Brazil with their tempting circular layouts, while Roland Barthes's explications of semiological analysis and Derrida's parsing of Platonic rhetoric forced greater attention on the textuality of utopian narratives. Add to this Michel Foucault's construction of the institutional/spatial discourse of the Enlightenment, his interrogation of counter-utopias, or *heterotopias*, directly fabricated in the real world, and "utopia" could now be subjected to a rigorous deconstruction, its aporias, disjunctions, and implicit structures revealed. These re-readings were developed in the context of a re-reading of Marx and Engels themselves, stimulated by Louis Althusser and his students—Etienne Balibar, Jacques Rancière, Pierre Machéry; gradually social utopian thought was disengaged from the blanket strictures of the *Communist Manifesto*. This, in turn was accompanied by the editing and renewed interest in the writings of Walter Benjamin and Ernst Bloch, among other critical theorists of the 1920s.

In the Cold War climate of the United States, however, interest in Utopia was more concerned with its potential *dystopian* effects. On the right, anti-communism provoked Leo Strauss to examine the Spenglerian pronouncement of the crisis of the West through the lens of Plato and Aristotle in his study *The City and Man*, where he undertook a nevertheless subtle and incisive reading of the *Republic* concluding that while "Socrates makes clear [...] of what character the city would have to be in order to satisfy the highest needs of man," he at the same time demonstrated that "the city constructed in accordance with this requirement is not possible," thus demonstrating the "essential limits, the nature, of the city."[38] His followers, and notably Allan Bloom, were to deepen the conservatism of Strauss's anti-totalitarian reading. Bloom himself was to contribute one of the most instructive, quasi-literal, translation of the *Republic* published in 1968 **(fig. 6)**.[39] In a different vein, the social scientist and systems engineer Robert Boguslaw raised serious questions to the systems theory models developed by those he called the "new utopians" and their political reach into power centers, as in the RAND corporation and the Department of Defense.[40] As against classic utopians who tried to imagine social systems populated with "perfect human beings, perfect social structures, perfect situations or perfect principles," the new utopians, modeling "reality" through computation, "are concerned with no-people and with people substitutes. Their planning is done with computer hardware, system procedures, functional analyses, and heuristics."[41] On the left, Tomás Maldonado, assayed a comprehensive critique of the systems effect, seeing Boguslaw's identification of new utopianism as a guide to the understanding of Robert McNamara's faith in the technocratic control of military strategy.[42] Maldonado proposed a synthetic form of "design praxis," founded in Ernst Bloch's idea of "utopia in action," and informed by the science of knowledge and signs.[43]

In this context, it was easy enough to dismiss, or at the very least categorize Archigram, Superstudio, Archizoom as dystopians, as they used the mechanisms of technological futuriam and pop to integrate and market their special critique of consumer technology as architecture. Indeed, Colin Rowe, after his early essay blasting utopia in *Granta* 1959 (before his discovery of Popper), saw Archigram simply as a kind of high-tech version of townscape, English to the core, and exploiting all the tricks of Gordon Cullen and the *Architectural Review* Townscape movement: "Archigram." He wrote, "would seem to be making *picturesque images of the future.*"[44] "For all of the unplanned randomness, the happy jerkiness, the obviously high-pitched tonality, the aggressive syncopation, all of the famous ingredients of Englishness in action are now given a space-age gloss. Anything might happen here: the death of architecture, non-building, Andy-Warhol bug-eyed monsters, immediacy of feeling for life, instant nomadism, the wished-for end of all repression. We are presented with townscape in a space-suit; but whereas the idiosyncrasies are supposedly attributable to the pressures of context, the Archigram images are generally presented in an ideal void which, for all intents and purposes, is the same void as that in which "the urban model of c.1930" is located." [45] In seeing Archigram as a return to a modernist past (and he might equally well have been referring to the Italian variants) Rowe was thus consigning it to the dust-heap of failed architectural ideals, or rather, of what he considered the failed architectural responses to the ideological pretensions of the 1930s, Marxist or otherwise; a consignment that was at least opportunistic with reference to his own program of the "return to classicism" and the assumedly palliative of a "mannerist" modernism and a "piecemeal" urban collage that was staged in *Collage City* as an over-literal illustration of Popper's "piecemeal engineering."[46]

For many (more often than not Marxist) critics, this seemed to doom the megastructures of *Living City* and the barren perspectives of Continuous Monument and *No Stop City* to a futile repetition of the same—images competing in the market place with all the positive programs of modern megastructures and concrete plans for urban redevelopment. Manfredo Tafuri, caustically dismissed the spate of utopian images produced by Archizoom and Superstudio after 1968 as a "destructive and cathartic orgy," the intention of which was "to haul a mythical proletariat onto the stage of psychedelic action," with the aid of dream material transcribed with an irony "that made nobody laugh." "In the vignettes that illustrated *No Stop City*," Tafuri concluded, "neoprimitives living in an absolutely barren environment use small air conditioners, expressing a monstrous marriage between populous anarchism and liberating events influenced by those of France in May 1968.""[47]

It was at this point that the image of utopia joined the program of total design imagined by those who, like Tomas Maldonado at Ulm, believed that an entirely new version of the traditional *Gesamtkunstwerk* was demanded by the complex environmental, social, and technological conditions of mass global society. Here it was that the "psychedelic" aspirations of the utopian left met, however uncomfortably, the systematic cybernetics of the rational center. As Tafuri noted, they were in fact soon to come together literally in public presentation: "Their designs conquered a market that had remained closed to the products of neoliberty; their desecrations, justified by appeals to Duchamp, finally gained international recognition at an exhibition organized by Emilio Ambasz at the Museum of Modern Art in 1972: 'Italy. The New Domestic Landscape'" **(fig. 7)**.[48]

This exhibition had been preceded some three years earlier by Ambasz's essay, with the overtly Benjaminian title, "Manhattan: Capital of the Twentieth Century."[49] Here he proposed a new site for the architecture of the information age; if Paris had established the metropolitan form for consumer culture, epitomized in the arcades, and had become, by the 1930s of Benjamin's research, the site of a pre-history of modernity, New York was already, by 1969, the consummate network city, exhibiting all the characteristics of an architecture of infrastructure. New York was, so to speak, only "delirious" in the sense that its nineteenth-century institutions—as Rem Koolhaas had already intimated—from Coney Island to the Racquet

Club—acted as cultural cover for what Ambasz discerned as the far more serious, and not at all delirious, "White Collar Culture." Each of these formulations, Benjamin's "Paris," Koolhaas's New York and Ambasz's "New York," were developed out of their own intellectual prehistories. Thus Benjamin's "Arcades Project" displays its "origins" in hundreds of citations and notes, but its principle epistemological source has to be seen as Surrealism: not the pure and single-issue Surrealism of a Dalí or even of a Breton, but the critical, almost scientific Surrealism of an Aragon. In his *Le paysan de Paris*, Aragon took on the environments of Paris—The Buttes Chaumont, the Passage de l'Opéra—as an exercise in modern urban pathology.[50] The "modern myth" he thus outlined, was a myth based on an arcade about to be demolished, which, through imaginary projection Aragon cast as living only in memory, and a park, constructed by Haussmann, that "resembled" nature only through the most extreme artifice. The "Paris" of Aragon's "peasant" was, in this sense, no more than a phantom, but a phantom that lived on in the traces of its materiality in order to obscure a present hidden from all but the future. Benjamin, taking up Aragon's wager to the extreme—"I am a limit, a line" Aragon wrote— worked in the Bibliothèque Nationale, itself a storehouse for the first consumer age, to identify and concretize the myth in material terms.

If there is a parallel prehistory for the "Fables" of Ambasz, it will not be found in the New York Public Library, however, but rather in those paradigmatic architectural visions of information and its networks drawn up by the so-called utopian visionaries of the mid-Twentieth Century—Archigram, Archizoom, Superstudio and the rest: those who responded in different ways to the call, initiated by the Situationists, to find, beneath the cobblestones of Paris, the sand of a new beach, a tabula rasa for a new urban future. Urban futures, as George Orwell indicated in the title of his dystopian novel *1984*, which of course stood for the year of its publication, reversed, 1948, are inevitably rooted in their urban present. In the same way the counter-architecture "utopias" of these 1960s groups, while ostensibly drawing their imagery from science fiction, were firmly based in a present that was, from the space program to IBM, always already there. And it was precisely in the MoMA exhibition of 1972, that included among the displays of contemporary Italian domestic design, that these "utopian" messages from the 1960s past found their domesticated present **(fig. 8)**.

Subtitled "Achievements and Problems of Italian Design," Ambasz's exhibition at MoMA might have seemed at first glance to be no more nor less than a trade show, a luxury shop-window for Italian imports.[51] But a closer look revealed that these "functionalist" and technologically savvy products, arrayed under the umbrella of a "new domesticity" and worthy of installation in the museum's modernist-oriented design collection were presented in environments and side by side with images that, produced by Superstudio and Archizoom were the very same images of utopia/dystopia that would in any other context have seemed antithetical or totally oppositional to any "Bauhaus" like tradition. Further inspection would reveal that this very utopianism—ironical, and witty in the extreme—was equally deeply embedded in the character of these "home designs," with their own apparently utopian visions of technologically progressive objects, themselves icons of the new domestic design. This invasion of functionalism by utopianism, and vice versa, simply confirmed the fundamental commonalty of the two: indeed the identity of both as "hyperfunctional."

The catalogue to the exhibition, introduced by Ambasz, was divided strategically into four major sections: "Objects," "Environments," "Historical Articles," and "Critical Articles." In this way the singular design objects displayed—selected according to their "formal and technical means," their "sociological implications," and their "implications of more flexible patterns of use"—were viewed as a preliminary to the more theoretically current theme of "environments," which signaled the expanded realm of design contexts into the kinds of questions then being opened up by theoreticians like Henri Lefebvre (to figure as a distinguished guest at Ambasz's symposium *The Universitas Project*, later in the year) around questions of "everyday life." In this way the work of Gae Aulenti, Ettore Sottsass, the recently deceased Joe Colombo, Alberto Rosselli, Mario Zanuso, Richard Sapper and Mario Bellini were "situated" in designed boxes, like Joseph Cornell's peepshows.

Thus naturalized, the new designs, clothed in the mantle of environmentalism, were, in Ambasz layout, "opposed" by a series of "counterdesigns" set up in similar black boxes, as "postulated" critiques. Thus, Ugo La Pietra, Archizoom, Superstudio, Gruppo Strum, and Enzo Mari (with Gaetano Pesce as an outlier "commentator") were entered into the orthodox canon of the Museum of Modern Art, as integral to the conversation that the exhibition proposed was the very essence and font of Italian design excellence. This sleight of hand, that absorbed radical critique as simply another version of good "design," seemingly passed unnoticed, save for the last entry in the "Critical Articles" section, Manfredo Tafuri's "Design and Technological Utopia."[52]

Here, in a trenchant history of design exhibitions, from the VI Triennale of 1936 to the XIII Triennale of 1964, and thence by implication to the MoMA exhibition, Tafuri analyzes the continuous complicity between design and capitalist development, and the relentless tendency for all "counter" design, however radical to be absorbed within and productively exploited by the technology of production. Hence his conclusion that

> Marcuse+Fourier+Dada: the designer absorbs all the ingredients for a systematic reconnoitering of techniques whereby the spectator can be reconciled with the future—since the present is condemned. Utopian space, often constructed without any irony whatsoever, leads directly back to the urban environment, sublimating its chaos, its multiplicity of dimensions, the constant

> mutability of its structures. These new *Merzbauten* offer the promise of a non-work continuum, guaranteed by the most advanced forms of technology and, consequently, by the world of development.[53]

A conclusion that extended the thesis of his earlier manifesto of 1969, "Per una critica dell'ideologia architettonica,"[54] where he had revealed the final exhaustion of the modernist urban utopia in Le Corbusier's project for Algiers, to include the new "utopians" of the 1960s:

> The nostalgic longing for magic, for the golden age of the bourgeois mystique, still continues to be cherished, even at the most highly developed levels of capitalistic integration, as a typical method of compensation. And this will be the case, as long as the magicians, already transformed into acrobats (as Le Corbusier himself finally realized), agree to the ultimate transformation of themselves into clowns, completely absorbed in their 'artful game' of tight-rope walking.[55]

In the *present* moment of utopian revivalism, one equally as unexpected as that signaled by Jameson in the 1970s, it is perhaps necessary to revisit, not only the extraordinary *Merzbauten* of "Superarchitettura," but also its critical reception, as we attempt to evaluate the instrumental relations of such counter-architectural images to the production neo-liberal global architecture today.

Fig. 1_ *Granta* LXIII, 1187, 1959 (journal cover).

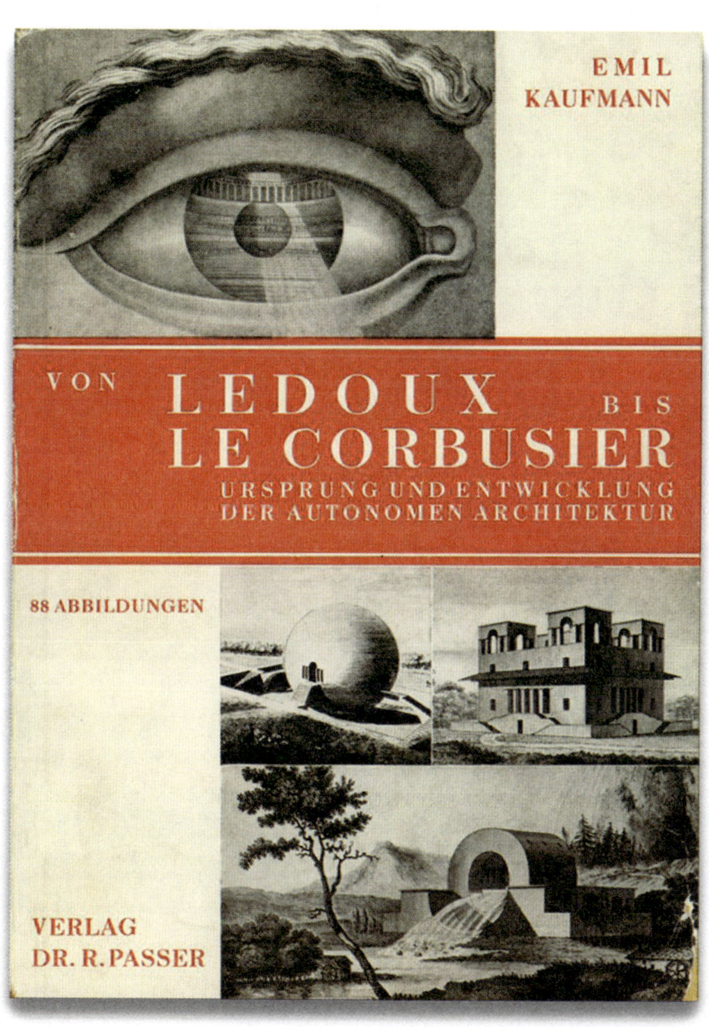

Fig. 2_ Emil Kaufmann, *Von Ledoux bis Le Corbusier: Ursprung und Entwicklung der autonomen Architektur*, Wien/Leipzig: Verlag Dr. Rolf Passer, 1933 (book cover).

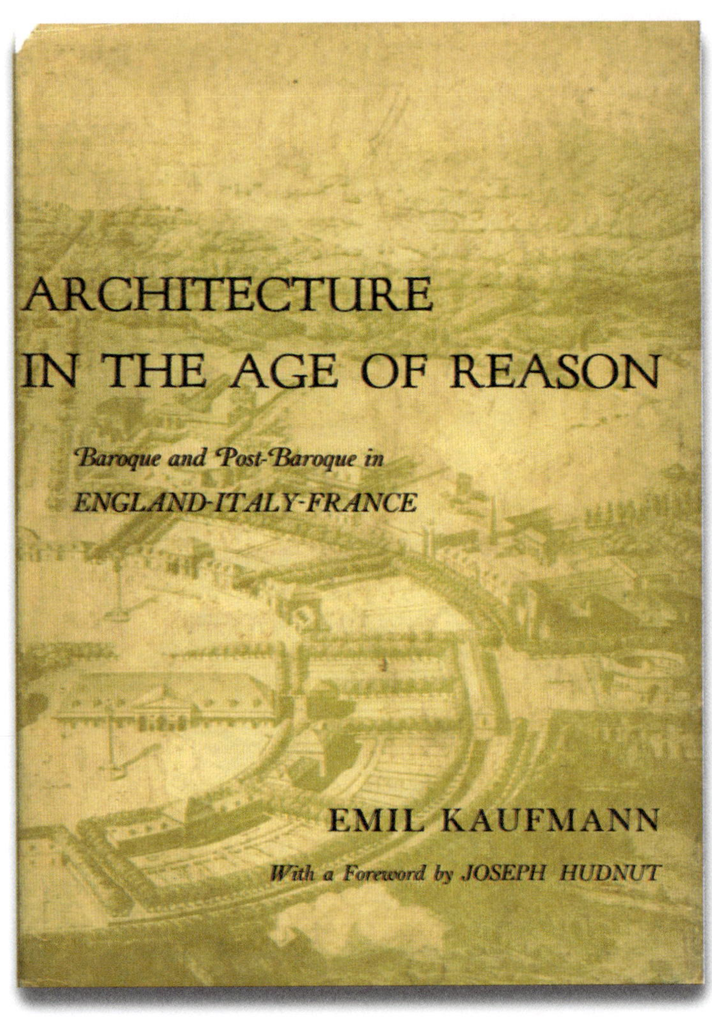

Fig. 3_ Emil Kaufmann, *Architecture in the Age of Reason: Baroque and Post-Baroque in England, Italy, and France*, Cambridge MA: Harvard University Press, 1955 (book cover).

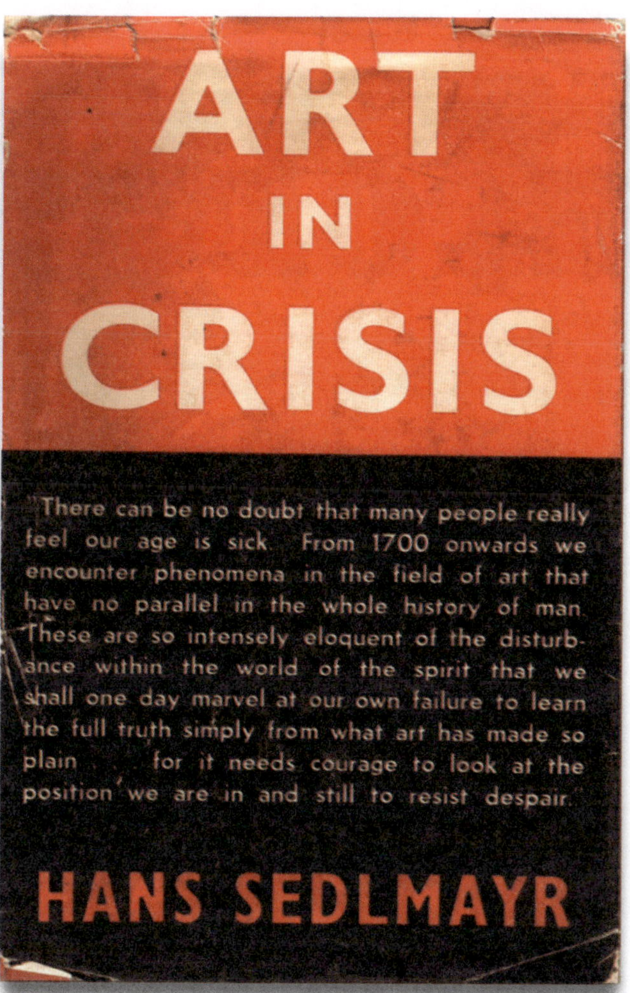

Fig. 4_ Hans Sedlmayr, *Verlust der Mitte*, Salzburg: Otto Müller Verlag, 1955 (book cover).

Fig. 5_ *Utopie: Sociologie de l'urbain*, no. 1, 1967 (journal cover).

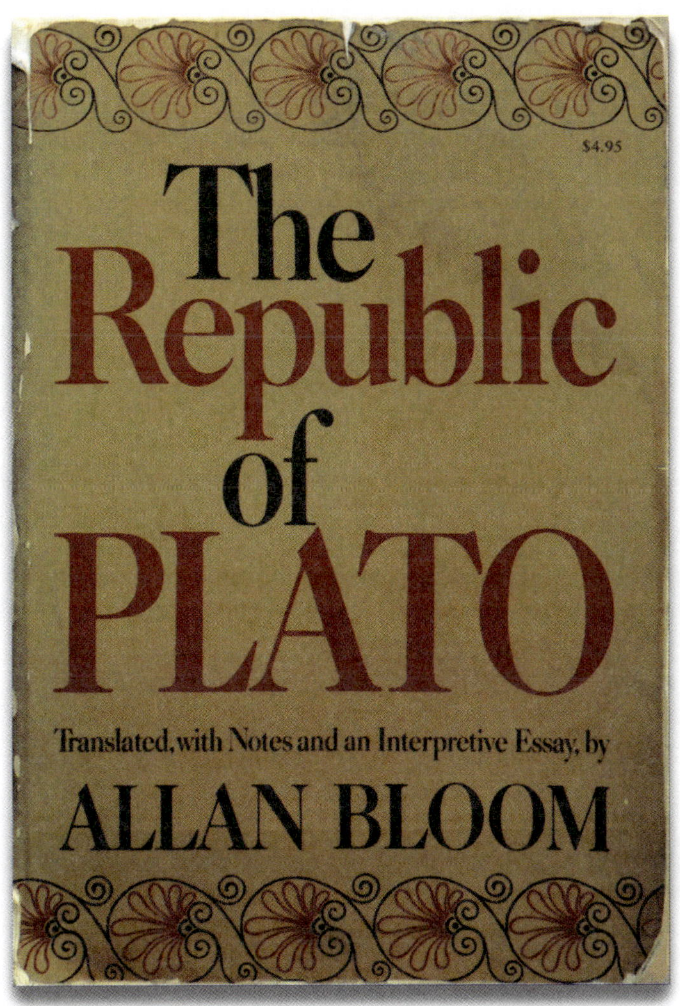

Fig. 6_ Plato, *The Republic*, translated by Allan Bloom, New York: Basic Books, 1968 (book cover).

Fig. 7_ *Italy: The New Domestic Landscape: Achievements and Problems of Italian Design*, edited by Emilio Ambasz, New York/Florence: Museum of Modern Art/Centro Di, 1972 (exhibition catalogue cover).

Fig. 8_*Italy: The New Domestic Landscape: Achievements and Problems of Italian Design*, New York, Museum of Modern Art, 1972.

Manfredo Tafuri and the Death of Architecture

Marco De Michelis

Manfredo Tafuri passed away more than twenty years ago, on February 23, 1994, at fifty-nine **(fig. 1)**.[1] In an unforgettable funeral oration, the Italian philosopher Massimo Cacciari described Tafuri as the master of "signs and conjectures" and not of "fixed assumptions and certitudes."[2] A year later—in January 1995—*Casabella* published a monumental memorial issue on Tafuri with articles by distinguished architects and scholars, such as Vittorio Gregotti, Rafael Moneo, Giorgio Ciucci, Howard Burns, Jean-Louis Cohen, Joan Ockman, and others **(fig. 2)**. Cohen's contribution emphasized the "epistemological break" in contemporary history effected by Tafuri's reflections on twentieth-century architecture: "a break whose consequences have yet to be fully assessed."[3] Ockman produced a brilliant portrait of American architecture during the seventies, divided between the neo-avant-garde of Peter Eisenman and the more pragmatic and nostalgic approach to history of postmodern architects—and how Tafuri broke into this context with a "culture shock" of unprecedented theoretical complexity, with seminal consequences for American architectural discourse during the last decades of the century.[4] In short, Tafuri's impact created a veritable disruption of the historical canon: new subjects; new actors; new contexts; new analytical tools; and new aims.

An essentially different point of view, however, prevailed at the time of his death. This was the reaction of the generation after Tafuri, who had not cultivated his personal friendship like the *Cantabella* contributors. Mark Wigley's obituary, published in *Archis* in the fourth issue of 1994, discloses the theoretical distance travelled between the years in which Tafuri had produced his most crucial works and the time of his death.[5] For Wigley, Tafuri already belonged to the past. "It is true that his extraordinary work was always flawed, riddled with gaps, leaps and contradictions. The texts had to be rejected, even called for their own rejection. But *some bond*, an unrepayable debt, was established in the very moment of rejection [...] It was the limits of the texts, the multiple points where Tafuri stretched his line of argument to breaking point, if not beyond it, that transformed the way we think about architectural discourse." For Wigley and his ilk, "There have been so many Tafuris... Each successive [theoretical] wake launched a particular trajectory of inquiry, making a new form of research possible." His texts started to be interrogated by his own methods. Followers become critics.

During these two decades not much has changed regarding Tafuri's body of work. Even in Italy it has become almost impossible to get his books reprinted. There have been few new translations. Here and there some younger scholars are producing new books and PhD dissertations on his work, but no complete critical edition of his immense oeuvre is forthcoming.[6]

It remains uncertain how to approach Tafuri's work now. Before everything else, we must ask ourselves what we seek in his texts. Are we problematizing the history of the European avant-garde? Are we (re)evaluating Sansovino and Palladio? Is our interest in the New York Five and late modernistic architecture **(fig. 3)**? Why do we need to reread Tafuri today? The answer is not so easy to find. Tafuri's books are written in a very enigmatic language. They have a labyrinthine structure. They are not the most suitable source of "facts." They put an enormous number of sources into play, but not in a systematic way. One compelling reason to continue reading Tafuri is that he transformed the history of subject itself. Let's consider why and how.

We should look back to one of his most celebrated works: *Architecture and Utopia*, published in Italy in 1973 and translated into English three years later.[7] The small book was an extended revision of a long 1969 article: "Towards a Critique of Architectural Ideology."[8] The cover of the American translation is Aldo Rossi's drawing *The Murder of Architecture*, which was originally dedicated to Tafuri. The book has been widely interpreted as the origin of the infamous "death of architecture" announced by Tafuri.

The late sixties and early seventies were characterized by several crucial publications, conferences, and exhibitions on architecture. Rossi's *L'architettura della città* in Italy, and of Robert Venturi's *Complexity and Contradiction in Architecture* in the United States, both appeared in 1966.[9] One year later, in New York, Peter Eisenman founded the Institute for Architecture and Urban Studies (IAUS), in whose magazine, *Oppositions*, Tafuri—alongside Moneo, Rossi, Rem Koolhaas, and many others—would publish some of his most important critical statements.

These had been years of extraordinary political upheaval, in America and in Europe, from student rebellions, Vietnam War protests, the explosion of terrorist activities on the continent, to the Soviet Union's violent repression of "the Prague Spring" in Czechoslovakia. This was the context in which a new generation of theorists raised crucial questions about the essential meaning of architecture and its praxis, and its relation to other manifestations of technical and scientific knowledge. Collectively, they argued that architecture represented an autonomous cognitive tool constituting an independent discipline.

Aldo Rossi's assertion of the existence of an autonomous body of architectural knowledge addressed the crucial questions of a critical practice of architecture; of the reconquest of analytical tools specific to the city; and of the forms of its production. Architecture laid claim not only to its capacity to interpret the urban structure but to give it a new form, in accordance with the distinctive tradition of modernity. The effects are clearly recognizable in Europe, for instance in the successful experiments in the critical reconstruction of European cities like Berlin or Barcelona. In the United States, as well, the activities of the IAUS revealed that the issue of autonomy in architecture—and the connected critical revision of modernistic tradition—had become actual outside Europe.

At this point Manfredo Tafuri's theoretical work appeared on the scene with a dramatic destabilizing effect. Tafuri's approach to modern architecture recognized the condition of doubt and anxiety marking architecture's destiny. Of course, these questions had already been raised by the end of the seventeenth century, in the debate between the "ancients and the moderns" in Perrault's France. The controversies about classic orders challenged the narrative of architecture's foundations. The naturalistic analogy between the architectural column and the human body, between its proportions and a recognizable system of rules in the natural universe—not to mention the mathematical rules of perspectival representation of bodies in space—represented, during the "long Renaissance," that rational base which guaranteed architecture (the non-mimetic art *par excellence*) a status consistent with painting and sculpture. Architecture was not a perfect imitation of nature itself, but it was possible to transfer the "rules" and proportions which shape nature to its synthetic three-dimensional representation.

The crisis of this system dramatically challenged traditional notions of architecture itself. The received belief was that it had taken form through the interpretation of Vitruvius, beginning with the treatises of Alberti and Francesco di Giorgio, and continued until those proposed by Palladio, Serlio, or Fischer von Erlach. The history of Western architecture from the eighteenth century onwards may also be read as a struggle for architecture's survival.

How else can we interpret, for example, one of the most influential books of the eighteenth century, Marc-Antoine Laugier's *Essai sur l'architecture*?[10] Decades prior to its composition, French architects had already attempted to substitute the "objective" rules of classic orders with "subjective" notions of "character," which necessarily involved the observer's experience. (For instance, eager to establish the analogical connection with painting and poetry, Germain Boffrand introduced the idea of "speaking architecture.") Laugier's "primitive hut" constituted, in turn, a "natural archetype," a "genetic beginning or principle," from which the idea of "order" itself originated as a structural, aesthetic, and constructional—but not decorative—basis for all buildings.[11] In this way, Laugier strove to re-establish a coherent sequence, that started from the rule and moved towards perfection, whose task it was to eliminate the risk of freedom becoming arbitrariness. "The taste which Laugier propagated was one that aimed at simplicity, formal purity and structural sincerity."[12] But it also required "a guide that would lead it, and brakes that would prevent it from overstepping limits."[13] Beyond these limits, architecture was doomed to irrelevance.

We know that Tafuri paid little attention to Laugier's treatise, citing it, I believe, only to emphasize the new role of the city with respect to architectural practice. However, that his reflection on modern architecture addressed as a main feature "the negative utopia" of Giovan Battista Piranesi demonstrates how Tafuri defined a chronology of the "crisis" of architecture, starting as early as the eighteenth century.[14] It is not by chance that he recalls, at the beginning of *Progetto e utopia*, the definition of architecture in Quatrèmere de Quincy's *Encyclopédie méthodique*: "[It] sees to the salubrity of cities, guards the health of men, protects their properties, and works only for safety, repose and orderliness of civic life."[15] The paradox is that the very establishment of science and technique, as independent bodies of knowledge, separated and isolated architecture from the process of conformation to modern society and condemned it to a labored and irresolvable course.

This, for Tafuri, is the origin of the ideological nature of any modern architectural work: no longer the protagonist of the real transformations that capitalistic development produces, it can only interpret them *a posteriori*. It could be said that architecture was no longer permitted to give form to reality but, at most, to re-form it. Re-form is a keyword of modernity, and it addresses the desire to reestablish the order and rationality which capitalistic development essentially lacks.

However, the problem did not only concern the unrelenting separation of architecture from technological progress, new scientific knowledge, and the revolution of forms of industrial production, consumption, and politics. It did not only concern the by then worn-out separation of engineering and architecture as disciplines. The appearance of the notion of *tectonics*—a neologism coined in the archaeological sciences but soon taken on by architects—clearly assumes a crisis. Tectonics, the art of connecting a building's various parts, of unifying that which is originally discontinuous or intermittent, seems an expression of the consciousness of the lost unity of architecture. It signals a dilemma. It claims the possibility of re-establishing a system of relationships among parts that has been lost.[16]

Confronted by Joseph Paxton's Chrystal Palace in London in 1851, Gottfried Semper, perhaps the century's most lucid thinker on architecture, immediately recognized an extraordinarily threatening contradiction. Paxton's building, a greenhouse-structure of iron and glass re-formed into an enormous exhibition complex, seemed to Semper an event which was inconsistent with the notion of tectonics itself. Its ideal was to be as light as possible, reaching to the limits of immateriality. The joints between the glass panes and the metallic structure are repeated with such an unaccented regularity that they no longer correspond to any "compositional syntax" of elements. To save the notion of "architecture," Semper was forced to organize it into two well-defined categories. To the "monumental" architecture, alone, he assigned the task of keeping alive the idea of a well-proportioned composition of elements; the other function, the "useful" one, was left to the fate destined to it by technological progress.

Tafuri did not dwell directly on these themes, but rather grasped with precision the parallel, and likewise threatening, transformation of the city into the metropolis. The metropolis "which swallowed up in its formless body every architectural object",[17] which was absorbed in a continuous space, endowed with an invisible rationality, essentially different from that which had characterized the historical city. At the turn of the twentieth century, Otto Wagner wrote about a shocking new development: that is, the suburb—its vastness; the unusual and regular size of its streets and squares; the unstoppable process of its growth—for which metropolitan architecture was called upon to elaborate an equally new character, distinguished by an anonymous regularity, to the point that its own name changed. It was no longer designated architecture—with all of its historical conditionings—but "Baukunst," or the "art of construction."

This is the struggle to which Tafuri dedicated his "historical project." Not to the historicist reconstruction of the "facts exactly as they occur," but to the construction of an ideological constitution of contemporary architecture, the only one that could mount, even if contradictorily, a resistance against the *mise en abyme.* It is true that Tafuri spoke of the "death of architecture" and the anxious search to save it, or at least fragments of it, through ideology, up until the disenchantment of the avant-garde and its attempts to mirror that crisis of values which was threatening it. However, this was neither an announcement nor a condemnation. Tafuri's historical project "was to reveal this disenchantment for what it was."[18]

He did not wish to tell the history of the relationship between architecture and reality, but rather the contradictory attempts of architecture to "exist" in the reality of the contemporary world; to recognize the whole of reality as a "ready made" and thus be capable of transforming it.[19]

His heroes, therefore, are those architects who fight this battle, who "dispel anxiety by understanding and internalizing its causes."[20] His heroes move among the ruins, trying to interpret the meanings lying there. They are certainly not the protagonists of a commercial "generic architecture," who believe they can astutely turn their gaze elsewhere and go beyond ideology. Nor is his hero the ingenuous optimist of the neo avant-garde of the 1950s and 1960s, who believed, or still believes, in the possibility of a purifying immersion in the pulsating plurality of the manifestations of contemporary society, of being able to go beyond "architecture" by simply accepting reality and its materials "as found."[21]

The "archaeology of the present" practiced by James Stirling and in a different way, by Carlo Scarpa was much more fascinating to Tafuri **(fig. 4)**. In Tafuri's opinion Stirling reduced architectural language—not the reality itself—to fragments "as found." He manipulated; rewrote; mounted and remounted; and "sentenced it to meditate and reflect on itself."[22] "Stirling's architecture does not open new paths, does not indicate targets to aim at, does not entrust others, but only itself, with its own destiny."[23]

Of course, there have been victims of the Tafurian historical project: not just the neo-avant-gardes of the 1960s and so-called radical architecture. Louis Kahn also suffered under this analysis, his extraordinary complexity reduced by Tafuri to a symbol of mystic opposition, unaware of the true nature of the problem **(fig. 5)**. A reckless chimera and, thus, anti-historical for his claiming to re-establish a fullness of the meaning of architectural form, incompatible with reality. Paradoxically, Robert Venturi was similarly victimized; he, too, was responsible for an attempt at "refounding architecture" that was only apparently dissimilar to Kahn's. Venturi's program was also based on reintroducing a "significant form," a re-found "density of the architectural image," which appeared to Tafuri even more destructive than the modest quality of his projects and buildings **(fig. 6)**.[24]

We know Tafuri's "new knights of purity" well.[25] They are those architects—the Five in New York and Aldo Rossi in Italy—who at the end of the 1960s introduced critical revision of the modern tradition, of its peculiar instruments, aware that the final outcome of this process risked a retreat into the solitary subjectivity of architectural practice. (The result that Aldo Rossi would also recognize a few years later in his *Autobiografia scientifica* when he confesses that in writing *L'architettura della città*, he had "perhaps simply wanted to get rid of the city and, in reality, he had discovered his architecture."[26])

There is a subtle, profound, and even ambiguous affinity between the idea that architecture can represent itself as an autonomous cognitive tool and as an independent discipline; between Rossi's assertion of an autonomous body of architectural knowledge and Tafuri's declaration of the autonomy of historical research against design practice.

This affinity was explicitly claimed by Massimo Scolari, in the published exhibition catalogue *Architettura razionale*, curated by Aldo Rossi in 1973. For Scolari the progressive character of the rediscovery of architecture's disciplinary autonomy lay in recognizing the historical basis of its very tools of analysis and intervention, as opposed to the utopian season of the avant-garde. Scolari tried to define a "critical" condition for architecture's "autonomization." "Architecture is a cognitive process that in and of itself, in the acknowledgment of its own autonomy, now necessitates a re-founding of the discipline: one that refuses interdisciplinary solutions to its own crisis; that does not pursue and immerse itself in political, economic, social, and technological events only to mask its own creative and formal sterility, but rather desires to understand them so as to be able to intervene in them with lucidity."[27]

Having gotten beyond the apocalyptic dilemma on the "death of architecture," Rossi and Scolari seemed ready to make Tafuri's interpretation of the drama characterizing architecture in those years their own: that of "seeing itself forced to turn back to 'pure architecture'; an instance of form devoid of utopia; a sublime uselessness in the best of cases." "Yet," Tafuri adds, "to the mystified attempts to dress architecture in ideological clothing, we shall always prefer the sincerity of those who have the courage to speak that silent, unrealizable purity."[28] For Tafuri the utopia of the form had by now taken on the physiognomy of the "mask."

The "sullen indifference" of Rossi's architecture evinced the awareness of the disillusionment of the Italian architects during the reforms of the seventies.[29] His project for Modena's new cemetery turned its back on the "noise of the world." According to Tafuri, "The thread of Ariadne with which Rossi weaves his typological research does not lead to the reestablishment of the discipline, but rather to its dissolution."[30] At the 1976 Venice Biennale, Aldo Rossi presented the image of "The Analogous City" **(fig. 7)**, theorizing "that it could be understood as a compositional procedure 'centered on some primary facts of urban reality around which other facts are constituted within the frame of an analogical system.'"[31]

Tafuri entitled his review: "Ceci n'est pas une ville," playing on René Magritte's famous *calligramme*: "Ceci n'est pas une pipe."[32] For Tafuri, Rossi's "collage" was completely within the negative tradition of modernity: his message was "at once the manifestation of a negation and an interweaving of subjective impulsions and reality." It confessed the definitive impossibility of giving a new order, of attributing a new meaning to the city, thereby unmasking the purely ideological character of Rossi's pretense of constructing a "theory of the city" capable of governing its transformations.

In Tafuri's "Architecture dans le boudoir," published in *Oppositions* in 1974, we read: "Today, he who wishes to make architecture speak is thus forced to resort to materials devoid of all meaning; he is forced to reduce to degree zero every ideology; every dream of social function, every utopian residue. In his hands, the elements of the modern architectural tradition are all at once reduced to enigmatic fragments—to mute signals of a language whose code has been lost."[33]

"The Historical Project" was first published by Tafuri in *Casabella* (1977), and then in *Oppositions* (1979), before it became the introduction and the theoretical manifesto of *La sfera e il labirinto*.[34] The essay can be used today as a crux for interpreting the nature of the Tafurian historical strategy: its tortuous, labyrinth-like paths and meanings. Tafuri starts with a question about the nature of the architectural message and its translatability into linguistic terms. Does there exist an architectural language, or is architecture finally divided and multiplied "into techniques incommunicable among one another"?

Tafuri refers here to the micro-historical work that has been described and implemented by the Italian scholar Carlo Ginzburg, research in which "only some pieces are available, and theoretically more than one figure can be made from them [...]. For this reason, the fact that everything falls into place is an ambiguous sign; either one is completely right or completely wrong."[35] This metaphor of the "jigsaw puzzle" construes historical inquiry in terms of detective investigation.

At the starting point of the historian's research, very little presumptive evidence is revealed, or only a few pieces of our jigsaw puzzle. Through archives, primary and secondary sources, cross-checked information, comparisons, and even some subjective intuitions, the historian is able to gather more and more indications, more and more pieces. But the puzzle will never be entire or unitary: "Only some of the pieces are available and, theoretically, more than one figure can be made from them."[36]

At the same time, we are compelled to use *all* the collected elements, not only those pieces that correspond most easily to our critical intention. No, we have to use everything knowable to produce an honest "historical representation. The multiplicity and diversity of the materials available to historians pose one more dilemma. While we can speak about architecture itself, or about language, techniques, institutions, and historical context—each with their own intricacies—are we truly able to relate them to "an underlying or hidden structure"? In which of these areas can we find a common meaning on which to rest? Can we *translate* these different epistemata into one coherent narration?

For Tafuri, the peculiar aim of history is not merely interpretive, the production of hermeneutics, but rather the production of "meanings," through "the constant struggle between the analysis and its objects [...], beginning with the signifying traces of events; an analytical construction that is never definitive and always provisional; an instrument of deconstruction of ascertainable realities."[37] Mark Wigley has pointed out this "monstrous legacy of Tafuri," which is not "his specific analyses of particular events, but the scandalous introduction of contradiction into the heart of historical analysis."[38]

Tafuri describes his historical project as a "project of crisis." What does this formulation mean? It asks to go beyond the traditional relation—completely rooted in nineteenth-century positivism—between an "origin" and the "final point of arrival: a destination point that explains everything [and] that causes a given *truth*."[39] The notion of *genealogy* proposed by Michel Foucault props up Tafuri here. Genealogy does not know any linear path of history; it "is made up of little, not obvious, truths, arrived at by a rigorous method."[40] Genealogy does not know any "unity of history;" there is nothing to be "recognized" in history; nothing that we already know. For Foucault, "knowledge is not made for understanding; it is made for cutting."[41]

The encounter between Tafuri and the French philosopher addresses one of the most controversial problems for the interpretation of Tafuri's philosophy of history. It is evident that the critical sources for Tafuri are found in the German post-idealistic and Marxist tradition (Marx, Nietzsche, Adorno, Benjamin, Heidegger), not in French post-structuralist philosophers like Foucault, Guattari, Deleuze, or Derrida. The very crucial difference between Tafuri and the theorists of a deconstructionist critical approach lies in his conception of deconstruction as a provisional tool that inevitably presupposes a form of "reconstruction." For him the danger—or the mortal risk—that threatens "the genealogies of Foucault [...], as well as the disseminations of Derrida, lies in the re-consecration of the microscopically analyzed fragments as new units, autonomous and significant in themselves."[42]

For Tafuri, the point is to conceive the theoretical language as something comprising a plurality within itself: "the plurality of the subject, of knowledge, of institutions."[43] History must consider the multiplicity of languages and subjects, and all the thresholds that continuously displace its single protagonists and elements. Into this historical campaign Tafuri enlists the German philosopher and sociologist, Georg Simmel: "The secret of form lies in the fact that it is a boundary; it is the thing itself and at the same time the cessation of the thing, the circumscribed territory in which the Being and the no-longer-being of the thing are one in the same."[44] The historical work finds its place inside this tenuous and unstable interval.

Tafuri did, of course, work inside a Marxist tradition. But his originality and autonomy lies in his refusal to recover a "center," a final dialectical synthesis: the historian's path does not lead toward the certainty of "truth," but to "the divorce between the signifier and the signified," to the "multiple meanings" of reality. In this sense, again, Tafuri's recognition of the *mise en abyme*, of the dissolution, of the classical unitarian notion of architecture at the end of eighteenth century—split into the divided fragments of form and construction; of technique and architecture; of science and art—is crucial for recognizing the ideological character of modern architecture already evoked in his *Architecture and Utopia*. That work truly implements the famous metaphor, proposed by Friedrich Nietzsche, that knowledge "has to stumble over words that are petrified and hard as stones."[45]

One more vital dilemma needs to be addressed: "How to construct a history which, after having upset and shattered the apparent compactness of the real, after having shifted the ideological barriers that hide the complexity of the strategies of domination, arrives at the heart of those strategies; that is, arrives at their mode of production?"[46] For Tafuri, architecture is an ideal territory for the historian, exactly because of its complexity and because of the multiplicity of its languages and techniques. And modern architecture is even more fragmentary and fractious. We recognize in it the very different voices of politics, economy, philosophy, technical innovation, and scientific discoveries; the voices of the new sciences of social health, psychology, sociology, and so forth; and the echoes that arise and resound from the different universes and media of artistic creation.

It is this pluriform panorama that explains why, according to Tafuri, a philological approach seemed superfluous in his investigations of modern architecture. Re-reading Tafuri's texts on modern architecture today reveals a very precarious—even doubtful—approach to primary sources. But sometimes the phenomenal outcomes of his approach are the result of his extraordinary capacity to expand his inquiries into unknown territories, to fill the historical stage with unexpected actors and properties, and to establish a critical network between and among the different voices and objects of scrutiny. The history, no, the idea of modern architecture was framed anew through Tafuri's seminal investigations. It is the task and the duty of ensuing generations to grapple with it and give it form.

At this point, the paths of contemporary architecture broke off, irreparably, from Tafuri's "historical project." His "total disenchantment" was testimony of his awareness that there was nothing more to be found in the "hypnotic solitude"[47] of that architecture which he loved calling "hypermodern." In his 1969 essay in *Contropiano*, he had already written, "There is no more salvation to be found within modern architecture: neither by wandering restlessly through labyrinths of images so polyvalent that they remain mute, nor by shutting oneself up in the sullen silence of geometries content with their own perfection."[48]

Thus was revealed the dilemma that still confronts whomever takes the time to travel Tafuri's route: the reasons for abandoning the passionate confrontation with contemporaneity and the apparent retreat into the more conventional territories of philology and the Renaissance.

For Tafuri the autonomy of the historiographic project had its foundation in a condition of conflict between analysis and its objects. The historical project was always a "project of crisis." One of these was the long unitary and progressive myth of modernity. What remained, in his eyes, were now only fragments. Tafuri had moved on and was busily engaged in studying the Italian Renaissance, an epoch when wisdom and power were still blended and the forms of architecture did not seem separable from those of thought.

Just one year before his death, Tafuri tried to explain that modern historiography was missing a "large narrative"—the "grand récits" of Lyotard.[49] Renaissance architecture offered him precisely these broad—even heroic—narrative structures, for which the analytical tools had to extend themselves into the most sophisticated philology. In Tafuri's eyes the masterpieces of the Italian Cinquecento appeared as Nietzschean "words hard as stone." The Renaissance asked the historian for more critical vigor—and much more historical skill and courage to dismantle its apparent solidity and unity.

Facing Antonio da Sangallo's articulated urbanistic strategies for the powerful Medici family and Pope Leo X, Tafuri was prompted to attempt a graphic reconstruction of the design process. He would interpret as a draftsman (or designer) Renaissance architectural effects in a dialogue with a Raphaelesque study for a new façade of San Lorenzo in Florence **(fig. 8)**.[50]

Fig. 1_ Manfredo Tafuri with Carlo Aymonino, c. 1967.

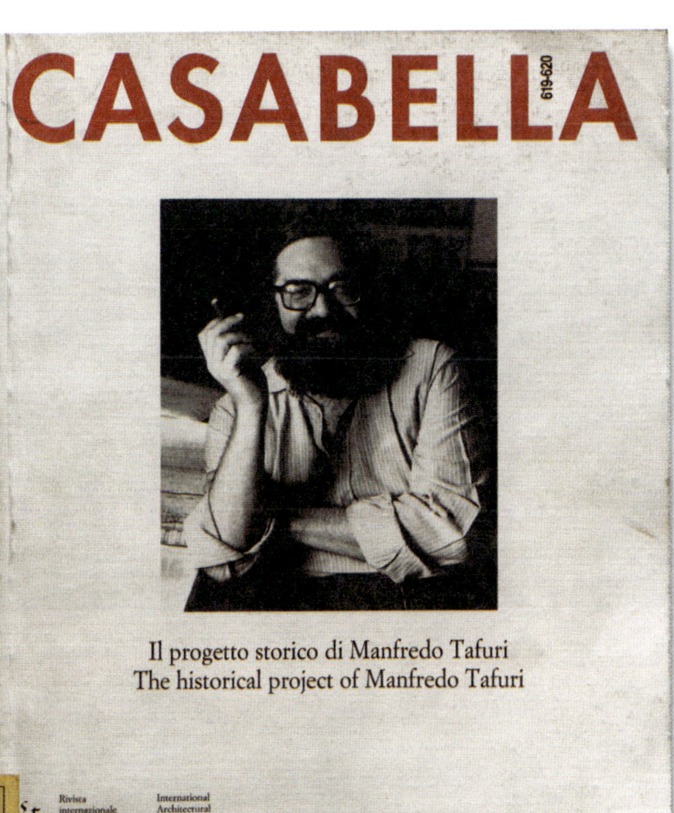

Fig. 2_ *Casabella*, 619-620, 1995 (journal cover).

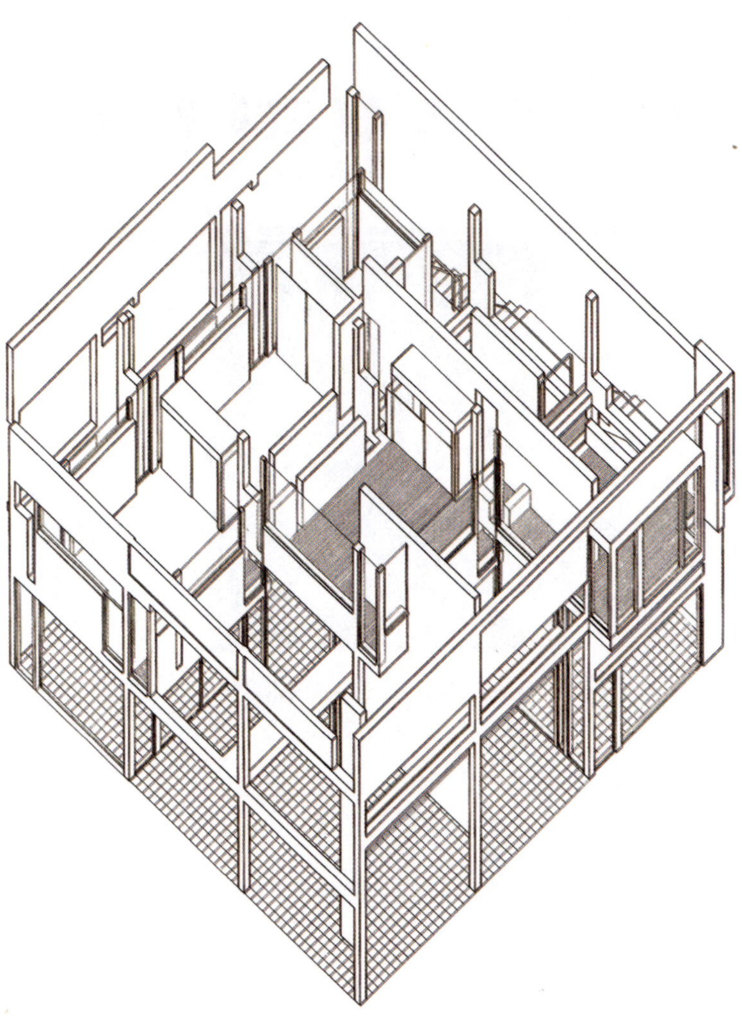

Fig. 3_ Peter Eisenman, *House II (House Falk)*, 1969–1970.

Fig. 4_ James Stirling, Staatsgalerie, Stuttgart, 1977–1984.

Fig. 5_ Louis Kahn, National Assembly Building in Dhaka, Bangladesh, 1962–1983.

Fig. 6_ Robert Venturi, Gordon Wu Hall, Princeton, 1980.

Fig. 7_ Aldo Rossi, *La città analoga*, 1973.

Fig. 8_ Manfredo Tafuri, *Reconstruction of Raphael's Proposal for San Lorenzo in Florence (1515–1516).*

Dystopia: A Positive Narrative for Architecture

Dominique Rouillard

Dystopia, as experienced during the radical trends of the 1960s, reveals the *narrative* nature of the architectural project. The dissonance created by the sharp contradiction between the terms "project" and "dystopic" sets counter-utopia as the locus of narration, holding no plausible content for the project, eliminating the fiction of utopia (or counter-utopia).[1] What remains, then, is just the narrative itself—the uncovered truth of the architectural project. This essay will trace the advent of the dystopic project, from the transient introduction of negative motifs to the point when mad fiction prevailed over reasonable function to became the project's true driver.

A rediscovery of the counter-utopic and dystopic nature of the architectural project emerged during the preparation stage of the exhibition *La Ville, Art et architecture en Europe 1870–1993,* which opened at Beaubourg in 1993.[2] The exhibition showed for the first time, and in a spectacular manner, what architects had been pondering for almost a century and a half: a means to control the development of the city and the urban future of humanity. Its mind-blowing iconography upset a few architects and critics, but at the same time ensured the event's massive success.[3]

Among the heroes who had lapsed into oblivion were Superstudio and Archizoom—along with their fiction-projects; their incomprehensible texts; and their iconoclastic vocabulary, concepts, and *formulae.* These were surprisingly akin to those associated with two architects who, nearly two decades later, were in the limelight of the architectural and intellectual scene: Bernard Tschumi and Rem Koolhaas (also the two frontrunners of the 1982 *Parc de la Villette* competition). Studying the movement in parallel with these two architects initiated my understanding of the period, forming the basis for my conclusion to *Superarchitecture.*[4]

In the 1970s, both Tschumi and Koolhaas had been students and then teachers at the London Architectural Association School (AAS) which, under the exceptionally inspirational direction of Alvin Boyarski, encouraged students' architectural experiences to develop around what they called project "units." References to literature and cinema were customary, as were acknowledgements of young architects devising pioneering new approaches intended, in Rem Koolhaas's words, "to open up imagination." (Archizoom and Superstudio were saying essentially the same thing with their "Discorsi per immagini.")[5] In 1969, shortly after the launch of Superstudio's flagship project *Il monumento continuo*, Koolhaas went to Florence to meet with architects capable of "projecting" such scenarios. His journalistic background made him particularly sensitive to the Florentine architects' project and its utterly unclassifiable status. My article on Koolhaas's Exodus, which was written simultaneously with the one on the Italian radicals in *La Ville* (1994), contextualized in a way his "homage to Superstudio," represented in one of the islands of the *City of the Captive Globe* (1972)—a reference that no one understood any longer at the beginning of the 1990s, when a massive interpretation of OMA's works began[6]

On his side, Tschumi—following the 1972 New York Museum of Modern Art's exhibition *Italy, The New Domestic Landscape,* and 1973's Milan Triennale on rational architecture—took his students to Turin to meet Archizoom's associates and invite them to London, together with Pietro Derossi and Germano Celant. The school's Urban Politics Unit introduced AAS students to the "photo-novel" project, like the Strum Group's *The Mediatory City, a Fotoromanzo* **(fig.1)**. The following year, the students were working on projects in the dystopic fashion of the Florentine architects, taking up figures and unlikely programs from Archizoom's *Impossible Theatre*, the checkered patterns of *The Continuous Monument,* and the scenographic form of Superstudio's *Fundamental Acts* **(figs. 2–3)**. The parallel between these movements in England and Italy in the 1970s was first hypothesized in 1992, during the seminar organized by the Fresnoy Art Center under the bilingual title ""'Radical' Architettura".[7] Tschumi, who had won the competition for le Fresnoy, confirmed those hypotheses, was perhaps the only one to understand what was at stake.

This detour has been taken to recall a more recent, almost contemporary story, which seems to have left traces only on the memories of those immediately involved. At once alive and dead, it resurrects a form of visual urbanism composed of scenes and situations. Although this iconic, narrative urbanism underlay architectural and urban thinking for nearly two decades, it was only then making its way into conscious mainstream urbanism. The dominant trait of these radical works, i.e., their counter-utopic and dystopic nature, had evolved from a theoretical concept into a useful tool.

The question turned to how some of that generation's most brilliant architects managed to produce such a level of innovation in a city as "provincial" as Florence, a fallen ancient capital—as Andrea Branzi would later describe it—whose devastating 1966 flood paradoxically handed it back to tourists and the world. Superstudio even made a project depicting the flood as a joyful, blessed catastrophe **(fig. 4)**. But the University of Florence was also at the forefront of the country's avant-garde literary production and criticism, embracing semiotic analysis with Gruppo 63, which included Umberto Eco. Its open-mindedness was encouraged by the distance separating it from the dominant and more dogmatic schools of Rome and Venice.

Hindsight permits us to rethink the "story" told by counter-utopia, and even to break free from tagging it as the generational and doctrinal adversary of the Modern Movement. This broader view allows for the emergence of project theory; its relevance and its inaugural character; the direction it took; and the times it stumbled and got back on its feet (again and again, even today). For the first time in the world of architecture, stories were giving place to cities, and not the other way around. This reversal was equally novel for its architecture as for the dystopic content itself.

What was the situation, then? What was the dense cluster of events and projects that animated and founded this inaugural moment?

What is Architecture?

The work of Archigram and the architect Hans Hollein in the 1950s and early 1960s is the link that allows us to understand the switch into another universe of reference and thought, in a discipline hitherto dominated by the Modern Movement's theory and its positivist avatar: the megastructure. They changed the discourse from a reflection on "the architecture of the future" to a reflection on "the future of architecture." "What is architecture?" asks Hollein in 1958.[8] Does architecture, as such, even have a future? During the 1960s, the invention of "a new architecture" or "new structures" progressively gave way to a new definition: an architecture that interrogates the existing world. London, Vienna, and Florence are the three poles where this new approach flourished during the 1960s.

Archigram started by bringing architecture as close as possible to the most impressive technical objects of the time and the American consumer goods that had reached the British market after World War II. Beginning with Archigram, architecture became indistinguishable from objects: a work of architecture could resemble a spaceship, an off-shore platform (*Montreal Tower*), or an astronaut's suit (*Suitaloon*). By comparison, despite the famous analogy, Le Corbusier's architecture never really looked like an actual ocean liner: porthole windows are not enough.

Hollein depicted this transformation using the *blow up*, by displacing objects: an aircraft carrier in the countryside, a Rolls Royce grille in Manhattan, or a railroad wagon as a monument to deportation. Architecture was thus transformed into an urban *ready-made*. Hollein understood that architecture could (unfortunately) become a sculptural object; many of his projects are indeed objects and clearly prefigure the contemporary situation.

This extreme closeness to the object underpins, then, the end of architecture's autonomy. Henceforth, the architectural world would be dominated by object production. This is the message that underlies his 1968 article "Everything is architecture."[9] Architectural modes now merged with those of other fields of creation: object and furniture design, fashion, art, cinema, the novel, literary fable, rock bands' sound shows, or virtual simulation techniques, among others. The extension of architecture to all objects and all forms of production set it on a path of doctrinal self-destruction and deprived it of a field of its own.

Another common trait between Hollein and Archigram was a vision of architecture as a trigger of emotion, and a gateway to a world of repressed or unprecedented sensations. Hollein imagined an *Architecture Pill* as "a sort of psycho-pharmacy that can induce satisfaction, happiness, freedom, etc," which thrills consumers well beyond the jollies brought about by the architectural space.[10] Hollein's pill derided the therapeutic mission of architecture and its statements on comfort and hygiene, implying that the modernist project might not have existed had the pace of progress in the field of medicine been faster. Architecture was potentially reduced to the production of chemical and medicinal effects.

The "Svobodair" architectural spray or the "Non-Physical Environment" pill, like *Suitaloon*'s inflatable clothing, pushed architecture toward the threshold of its own extinction. A final stage seemed to have been reached for any architectural project, including its own critique. These manifestos pushed architecture towards its negation, even evil, without claiming to do so (nor actually creating an explicit theory to justify it).

The Abasement of Utopia

Around 1968 political criticism of society pervaded the general mood. In this context, architects were left with two options: quit the drawing board and take to the streets—to combat the only infrastructure that counted, in a Marxist fight against the capitalist system—or develop projects that encompassed political criticism, The Parisian group Utopie did the former; Manfredo Tafuri chose the latter, having abandoned his work on the megastructures of the *Città territorio*. He began what he called "Critical projects." This approach, which Tafuri restricted to his writings (*Teoria e storia dell'architettura* was published in 1968), was picked up and carried further by Florence's young architects, to reflect on and accomplish the project. They also seized upon Tafuri's 1969 notion of *retroguardia*, criticizing the conservatism of American Pop Art that he saw as an offspring of the capitalist and consumerist system.[11] The Florentine radicals gave the concept an active dimension that turned the project into a means of experiencing a sort of reverse avant-garde. By bringing together the *retroguardia* with the "negative thinking" that Massimo Cacciari explores in Nietzsche and Schopenhauer, the Italians introduced negative utopia in architecture. It was following their first manifestos that Tafuri, using a language borrowed from the radical counter-culture, recruited Piranesi as the negative project's first retroactive hero and herald.[12] The declaration of the rejection of utopia by the affirmation of its opposite, the (clearly dystopic) negative utopia, was unprecedented in architecture, either in the eighteenth century or in the work of Ludwig Hilberseimer.

For the Italian radicals, rejecting utopia was not enough. Would it be for any architect? For them, utopias built on positive narratives had to be opposed by counter-utopias or even (why not?) negative narratives. Dystopia—utopia's hellish or evil side—established itself, from then on, as the actual place of the narration. Thus, the project slid into a universe never before visited by architects. Archigram had briefly introduced a negative vision in architecture (*Walking City*, 1964), and then a regressive vision by abandoning the *Living Pod* to Piranesi, in a famous collage of 1966 that reused that invention. Hollein evoked Kafka through the series of stressful corridors in his scenography for the Austriennale, but now, at the climax of the big consumerist party, humor prevailed. Against the malaise elicited by his early projects of compact or suspended cities, or turning the atomic cloud into a new reference icon, he created the playful Austria glasses **(fig. 5)**. Humor was also the reaction to the professed advantages of his spray and pill. At Milan's 1968 Triennale, Arata Isozaki presented *Electric Labyrinth*, a photomontage showing the ravaged structures of a future city in a devastated landscape: a re-ruined Hiroshima. It remains the most direct anti-futurist representation ever produced by architecture. A real personal trauma and an appropriated image of a past apocalypse allowed him to interpret the Florence flood as a cataclysm that would open the way for a regeneration of architecture. Isozaki was interested in the esthetics of disaster (*City in the Air*, 1962) but did not truly integrate it into his projects, instead just borrowing the anti-design grid pattern of Superstudio's *Histograms,* for a while (Gunma's modern art museum, Kita-Kyushu's City Hall's museum, Fukuoka Mutual Bank, 1972–73). It was not until 1991 that Isozaki introduced his 1972 project, *Computer Aided City,* as "a draft to describe a future dystopia."

The radical architects, particularly Superstudio and Archizoom, transformed these episodic excursions into mad architecture into a way to carry out their larger project. They developed a paradoxical form of criticism, stripped of the progress-oriented ambition of the megastructural utopias that they unavoidably evoked. They entertained a critical attitude toward projects of territorial scale and entirely air-conditioned environments. The apparent formal proximity between the megastructures and the radical projects masks their fundamental opposition, something that Tafuri—as many today—failed to see: both are subsumed into the same "Utopia International." In fact, the megastructure describes a "solutionist" project, for example a structure that would sweep above the Bois de Boulogne and bring an end to all the city's problems (Yona Friedman, *Spatial Paris*). On the opposite extreme, the radical anti-megastructure's narrative staged a scenario, for example the story of a fisherman who comes up to a glass wall that closes off the river, leaving us to imagine a forgotten, sealed-off city (Superstudio, *Il monumento continuo*, "O País do Sol").

The radicals accomplished a true debasement of utopia, which can be illustrated by the parallel between three projects situated in similar geographical configurations: the riverbed and its increasingly desolate banks. After the realist utopia of *Paris sous la Seine* (Paul Maymont, 1962), which frees the city and opens up bucolic river banks, and the dehumanized utopia of *Glacier City* (Raimund Abraham, 1964), where a city pushes on like a glacier and is reduced to its traffic circuits, came Superstudio's negative utopia: the architecture was flowing, this time, into a square shape, flooding the canyon to the point of choking it. The city bears no trace of humanity, as the glacial sheets have totally swallowed it; still, it is beautiful (*The Continuous Monument*, "Canyon," 1969) **(fig. 6)**.

The radical manifestos refused to make any pronouncements, presented projects which would never be carried out, ideas without models, criticism without solutions, an urbanism without architecture, an architecture without shape. Their goal was "to rise up against the search for the form of the future city. A future without form, without architecture."[13] Utopia is no longer to be realized. For the first time in the twentieth century, architecture no longer seeks to build for the good of humanity. Architecture will not improve the fate of the human species. Adjustment to a changing society, as had been advised by Team Ten in opposition to a Modernist Movement that strove to produce a new man—or the transformation of reality, reinventing the world through intercontinental megastructures—stopped being the point. The marching orders, now, dictate an acceleration of what exists.

The gap between the confident universe where Archigram was still evolving and the dystopic one of the Italian radicals becomes obvious if we compare *Architectural Design*'s cover of February 1967 with a caption-less picture published in *Casabella's* January 1971 issue. In the first an astronaut's faceless helmet suggests a vision of a future open to unimaginable perspectives; the second shows a woman trapped behind a gas mask, revealing only her heavily made-up, wide-open eyes, fixed on the reader.

To Conceive a Project is to Tell a Story

A parallel story can be written. At the start, the radical projects embraced the critique of the capitalist economy from a perspective that could be defined as terroristic or psychiatric, as when the members of Superstudio pretended to be clinicians or those of Archizoom impersonated terrorists.[14] But their projects soon turned into narratives, into ways of telling tales and describing ambiances, in other words, into architectural novels. Thus, *Il monumento continuo* spans the Alps, then reaches out across the Atlantic in the quest for New York, where it spreads like a sheet, remorselessly cutting through the city. In India, it dives into a swamp, and finally flattens into a bi-dimensional *Supersurface* in which life is being reinvented.

Unlike the megastructure architects, the radicals focused on the woes and flaws of contemporary society and the modern city and drew narrative projects out of them. Their projects did not work on the representation of apocalypse, committed though the radicals were to the task of annihilating design. Those narratives were never entirely negative, which accounts for the ambiguity of the collages and our difficulty interpreting them. They were, rather, visions of the hellish side of paradise or the paradisiacal side of hell. Whether outdoors, on Superstudio's *Supersurface,* or inside Archizoom's *No-Stop City*—where the saturated plan with windowless apartments coexists at others levels with the free, totally territorial plan—everybody was having a blast! Naked women did not seem to be suffering **(fig. 7)**. Biotechnology, the augmented body—very concretely augmented this time—allowed Alice to play jump-rope without sweating **(fig. 8)**, or hippies to live naked or in an architectureless community (*Atti fondamentali*, 1971–72). In this way, they transformed the nightmarish present or the immediate future into scenes of a joyful eventuality.

Manfredo Tafuri and two decades of critics after him failed to recognize what the new architects were bringing to the playing field. They attempted to judge the advantages of their projects for the future of man or the city by submitting them to a sort of truth probe without considering that, inasmuch as they were novels, they couldn't—in Tzvetan Todorov's words—be either true or false.

In other words, radical architecture introduced, or precipitated, reflection about how to generate the project. It revealed that engendering a project equals narrating. Ultimately, the story's negative character both from the point of view of its narration and of the "inhuman" project that it illustrates (Superstudio ultimate project in this direction was the one in *Le dodici città ideali*), comes second to its historical role within the theory of architecture. More precisely, what counts is not the content of the narrative itself or even its opposition to anything, to architecture's morale, or the values of modernity, but rather its very negativity, because this places architecture beyond the responsible and positive discourse that should underpin any architectural project.

The contradiction inherent to the negative project—and the exorbitance of its negativity—destined the project to be nothing but narration. The dystopic program of radical architecture's main projects could not be perceived except as fiction. No other meaning could be attributed to such a program, and the evidence spoke for itself: the project "told stories" that did not make sense, like straightening the Tower of Pisa by making all other buildings lean (*"Italia vostra, Salvataggi di centri storici italiani: Pisa,"* 1971). Thus, the narrative affirmed itself through a negative quality architecture could not embrace. Radical dystopia was a form of redundancy that aimed at annihilating the delusion of utopia's visionary breadth, but by doing so, pushed architecture into the realm of literary fiction.

These radical fictions could no longer be taken for architectural projects, despite their adherence to canonical representation (graphic nature, accuracy, realism, references, respect for conventional terminology, etc.), the professional status of their authors (duly certified architects, often among the best), or their dissemination channels (the specialized press). The ensuing confusion was deliberate: the project was not to be found where it usually would have been, but elsewhere. The goal became to divert the project towards issues other than the inescapable functions and use, and therapeutic and educational missions, of architects and architecture. Once pushed outside architecture, once "beyond architecture," freed from construction, society and even the plausible, the project could become a mode of investigation of the world through architecture and inventing life scenarios.

The Project Theory: The Narrative of Engendering

These radical stories, because of the implausibility of their scenarios, describe the reality of an architectural project no longer supported by *one* theory of architecture. Contemporary architecture is no longer engendered by of its own values—the values of architecture per se—but out of the narrative of its own generation, which is not necessarily the story that the actual project will tell. Architects no longer create by following *the* rules of conception, but create *their* own rules of conception. And these rules must be reinvented by each architect. This was the sense of the "postcards" published by Bernard Tschumi in 1976 (*Ropes and Rules*) **(fig. 9)** in the mode of radical architecture.

Increasingly, in the contemporary professional world, the architect must elaborate a strategy to engender a project that has become un-ruled. Overall communication, within and around architecture, demands the architect strengthen self-reflection, set himself at a distance, and elaborate an increasingly efficient "scenario." Thus, what is important in Superstudio's *Film Script* is not the story told but that architecture should define itself by the logic of the filmed narrative, above and beyond any other considerations. Tschumi's *Manhattan Transcripts* say this even more clearly, simply by using a cinematic vocabulary that was easier for the architect to acknowledge: words like "sequence," "editing," "framing" (all the forms of representation of the movement and the event absent from Superstudio's *Film Script*). This is why we must speak of a theory of the project and no longer about a theory of architecture.

The tragedy of contemporary architecture—that, too often, it produces nothing but more-or-less interesting advertising objects—carries on the transformational path that has been unfolding since the 1950s. Branzi had defined it: the Pirelli skyscraper in Milan of 1958, by Ponti, Fornaroli, and Rosselli, is the first example of design at an urban scale. In a society fully devoted to communication—the "world design" of late capitalism—design has become more important than architecture, and architecture stands no chance unless it resembles design. What the individual consumes is the narrative of the object of design.

The invention of dystopia, in architecture, amounts to the discovery of *fun* in architecture. Hollein and Archigram teach us to love architecture like we love objects, substituting entertainment, and the consumption of entertainment, for need, or even for pleasure in Alison Smithson's sense (*Small Pleasures of Life*, 1950). Today, those little pleasures of architecture are a thousand miles from the necessary life scenarios that, from this moment onwards, any project has been compelled to elaborate.

To conclude, consider the 1993 design competition for the *Seine Rive Gauche project*, particularly Ateliers Jean Nouvel's unsuccessful proposal. The buildings of the project—not represented in the drawing—are supposed to be surrounded by a park and visible through the trees of an age-old forest, amidst which Milan's extravagant Torre Velasca emerges. **(fig. 10)**.[15] Another 1958 monument of Milanese modernity moved to Paris, the building is shortened here, as if to bring it closer to the passerby. The Velasca Tower, at the time of its construction, was criticized profusely because its shape too closely resembled the city's medieval towers, and thus scandalously eschewed the critique of modernity elaborated by Team Ten. Nouvel's collage casts light upon the narrative power of that project, and also indirectly on his proposal: a castle-like building, instead of a banal apartment or office building (as it is described in the Parisian competition illustration). The Milanese skyscraper—like the project for Paris, almost 40 years later—was critical architecture en acte, a proto-postmodern architecture that already knew how to tell stories to ordinary people.

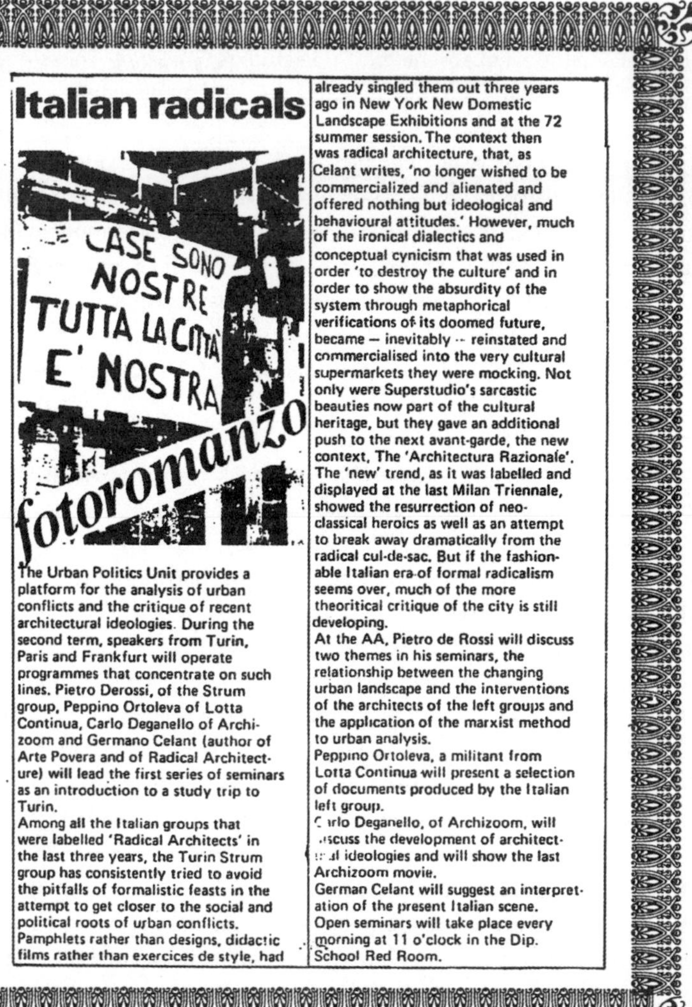

Italian radicals

The Urban Politics Unit provides a platform for the analysis of urban conflicts and the critique of recent architectural ideologies. During the second term, speakers from Turin, Paris and Frankfurt will operate programmes that concentrate on such lines. Pietro Derossi, of the Strum group, Peppino Ortoleva of Lotta Continua, Carlo Deganello of Archizoom and Germano Celant (author of Arte Povera and of Radical Architecture) will lead the first series of seminars as an introduction to a study trip to Turin.

Among all the Italian groups that were labelled 'Radical Architects' in the last three years, the Turin Strum group has consistently tried to avoid the pitfalls of formalistic feasts in the attempt to get closer to the social and political roots of urban conflicts. Pamphlets rather than designs, didactic films rather than exercices de style, had already singled them out three years ago in New York New Domestic Landscape Exhibitions and at the 72 summer session. The context then was radical architecture, that, as Celant writes, 'no longer wished to be commercialized and alienated and offered nothing but ideological and behavioural attitudes.' However, much of the ironical dialectics and conceptual cynicism that was used in order 'to destroy the culture' and in order to show the absurdity of the system through metaphorical verifications of its doomed future, became — inevitably -- reinstated and commercialised into the very cultural supermarkets they were mocking. Not only were Superstudio's sarcastic beauties now part of the cultural heritage, but they gave an additional push to the next avant-garde, the new context, The 'Architectura Razionale'. The 'new' trend, as it was labelled and displayed at the last Milan Triennale, showed the resurrection of neo-classical heroics as well as an attempt to break away dramatically from the radical cul-de-sac. But if the fashionable Italian era of formal radicalism seems over, much of the more theoritical critique of the city is still developing.

At the AA, Pietro de Rossi will discuss two themes in his seminars, the relationship between the changing urban landscape and the interventions of the architects of the left groups and the application of the marxist method to urban analysis.

Peppino Ortoleva, a militant from Lotta Continua will present a selection of documents produced by the Italian left group.

Carlo Deganello, of Archizoom, will discuss the development of architectural ideologies and will show the last Archizoom movie.

German Celant will suggest an interpretation of the present Italian scene.

Open seminars will take place every morning at 11 o'clock in the Dip. School Red Room.

Fig. 1_ Bernard Tschumi, *Fotoromanzo: The Urban Politics Unit*, Architectural Association School, London, January 18, 1974.

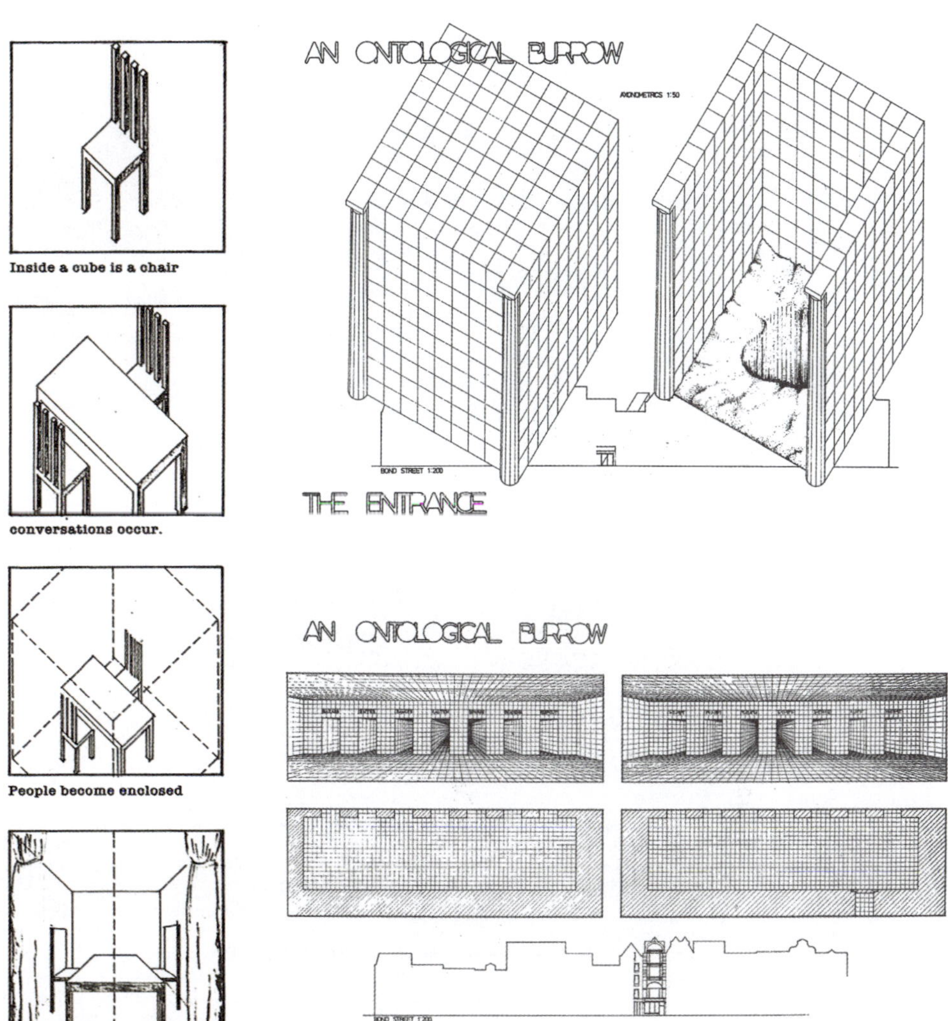

Figs. 2, 3_ Bernard Tschumi, Caroline Willoughby-Foster, Alan Sive, *Chronicle of Space, 1974–1975*, Unit Master, Architectural Association School, London, 1975.

Fig. 4_ *Itinerario di Firenze moderna, 1860–1975*, Firenze: Centro Di, 1976 (book cover).

Fig. 5_ Hans Hollein, *Austriennale*, 1968.

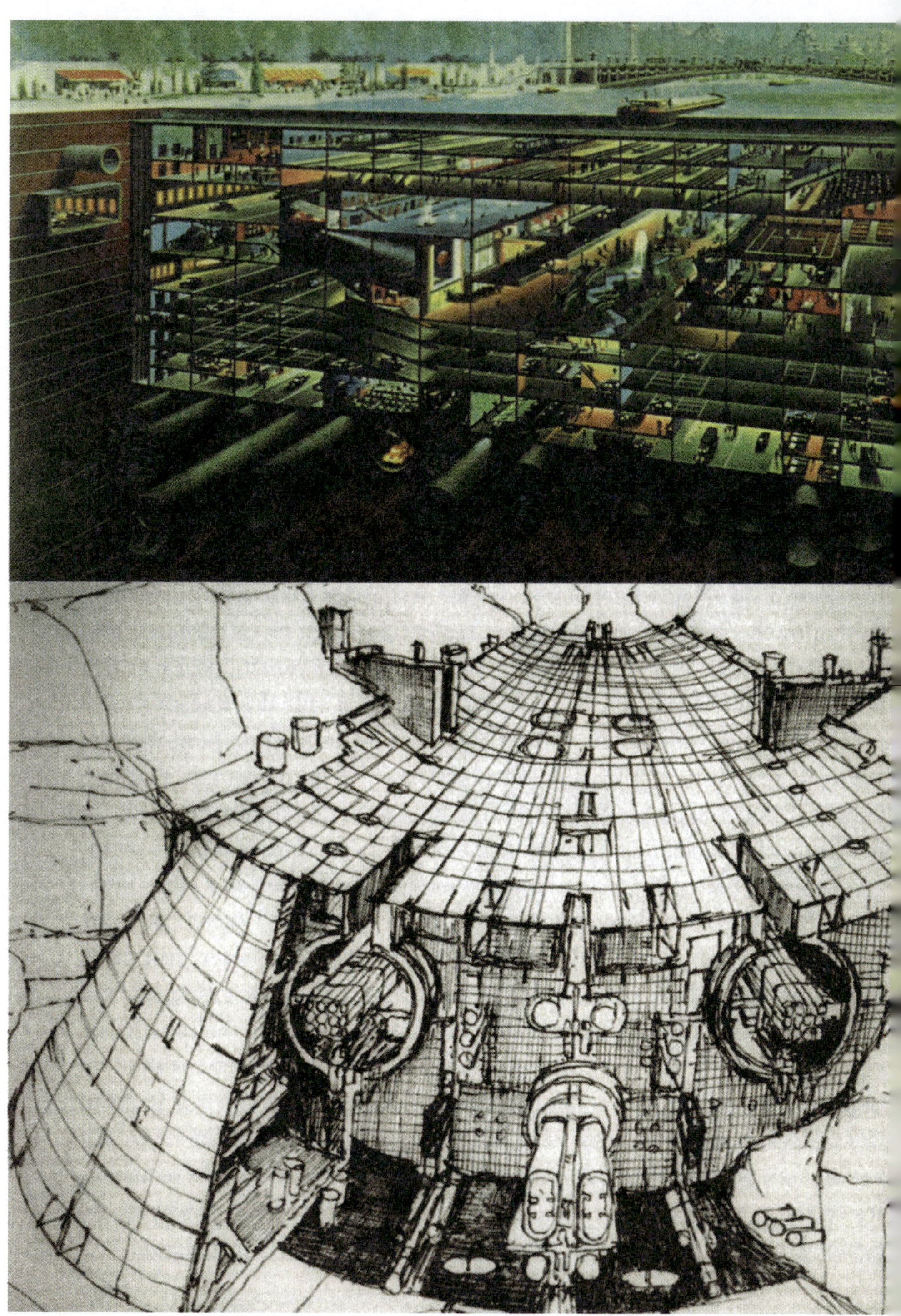

Fig. 6_ Paul Maymont, *Paris sous la Seine*, 1962 / Raymund Abraham, *Glacier City*, 1964 / Superstudio, *Continuous Monument*: *Canyon*, 1969.

Fig. 7_ Archizoom Associati, *No-Stop City: Internal Landscape*, 1970.

Fig. 8_ Superstudio, *Atti fondamentali. Vita. La montagna lontana*, 1971–1972.

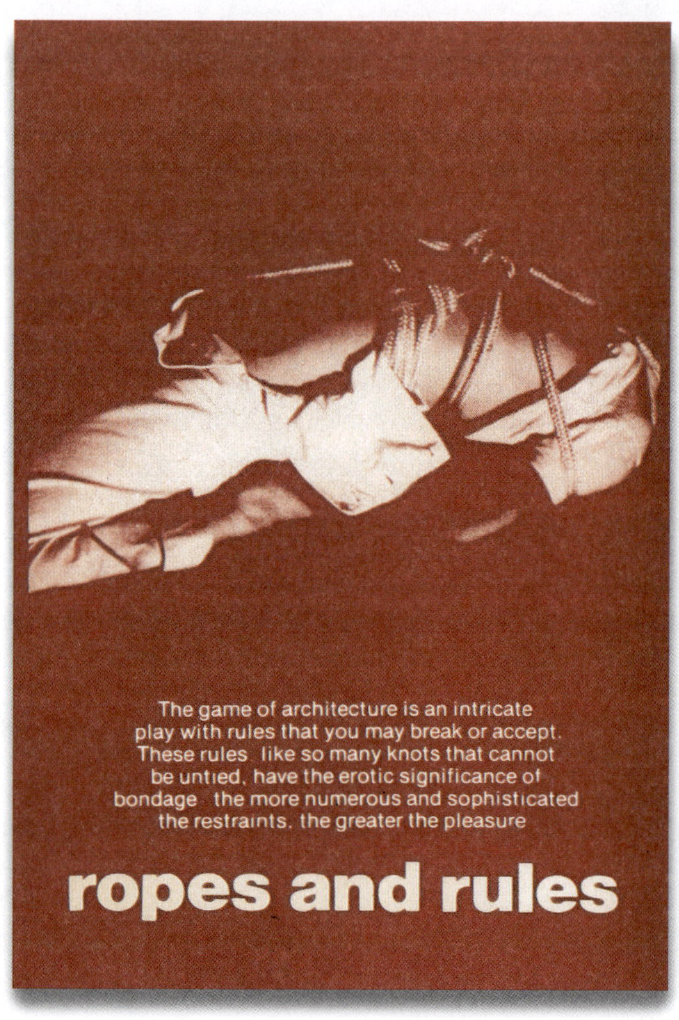

Fig. 9_ Bernard Tschumi, *Advertisements for Architecture: Ropes and Rules*, 1976.

Fig. 10 (Following page)_ Jean Nouvel, *Paris-Seine-Rive-Gauche: A Castle Seen from the Future Park*, 1993.

Architecture on Paper: Cedric Price and the Scientific Aesthetic of Diagrams

Maddalena Scimemi

The two decades of architecture following World War II can be illustrated through a sequence of projects that borrowed compositional laws and spatial arrangements from genetics and the natural sciences. Architecture was conceived and perceived through a lens colored by different scientific disciplines, establishing a tighter relationship with the world of nature to capture its aesthetic appeal. This may have represented yet another nostalgic impulse of the positivistic era, shared by a generation of designers who had survived the tragedy of the world wars. Alternatively, it could have reflected a more disenchanted call for intensifying the relations between disciplines (architecture and science, in this case), producing somewhat arbitrary outcomes.[1] Either way, the effect on post-atomic visual culture was a widespread enthusiasm for molecular images, in some cases as rhetoric as the formalist approach of the pre-war totalitarian regimes.

By 1945, the search for the formal compositions in pursuit of a new modernity in the nuclear age was already evident. The cover of that year's January issue of *Arts and Architecture* announced the "Case Study House Program,"[2] a new residential design research project dedicated to the needs of post-war living, with Swiss émigré Herbert Matter's "photo-graphic" image inspired by atomic structure **(fig. 1)**.[3] Molecules would later inspire the hypertrophic nodes and connectors of the *Atomium* pavilion, built for the Brussels World Exhibition (1958), and reimagined in the endless structure of Warren Chalk for Archigram's *Underwater*

City (1964).[4] Biology's impact was just beginning in a sequence of experiments in growth and flexibility, leading to I. M. Pei's proposal of a three-dimensional spiral for the *Helix Apartments* in New York (1948–49), later culminating in the *Helical City* by Kisho Kurokawa (1961). Even the new monumentality proposed by Louis I. Kahn and Anne Griswold Tyng employed the double helix of DNA to shape an organic skyscraper in the *City Hall Tower* for Philadelphia (1953–58).[5]

Two decades later, the phenomenon had to be acknowledged. In his 1965 book, *Changing Ideals in Modern Architecture, 1750–1950,* Peter Collins included a biological analogy among the possible paths toward modern architecture using a functionalist approach to design.[6] It was an illuminating idea, based on the recognition of the influential comparative approach theorised by Banister Fletcher in *A History of Architecture on the Comparative Method* (1896), enriched by the inclusion of the reign of biology.[7] Yet Collins's theoretical treatment of the topic, congruent with the title of his book, did not provide any discussion of formal solutions, nor did it give examples of built architecture inspired by this analogy. Instead, Collins concentrated on the concept of "form follows function" and on the opposition between architecture as "science of life" (biology) and as "science of form" (morphology).[8] A subsequent investigation of the biological analogy was conducted by Philip Steadman, whose book *The Evolution of Designs: Biological Analogy in Architecture and the Applied Arts* (1979)[9] stressed the importance of the evolutionist theories of the English philosopher Herbert Spencer in the United States at the end of nineteenth-century, clarifying the foundational principles of the organic approach of Sullivan and Wright.[10] Far from establishing a deterministic relation between science and architecture—and given that a comprehensive survey of both the architectural implications of the biological analogy and the newly emerging aesthetics of the post-World War II debate would be too ambitious to outline even in a more specific context—the focus here is on some proposals which revolved around architectural diagrams, intended as two-dimensional representations derived from scientific divulgation.[11]

During the 1950s such diagrams became ideal instruments for displaying and visualizing an interdisciplinary debate. Their recurrence appeared with increasing frequency in the British context during the 1930s and 1940s, when diagrams had jumped from the pages of pioneering books of the 1920s, to show up on the desks of urban planners, architects, and graphic designers. The figurative diagrams illustrating the books by Scottish biologists Patrick Geddes and D'Arcy Wentworth Thompson,[12] the dynamics of visual perception explored by Lazlo Moholy-Nagy,[13] the call for synthetic representations pursued by Le Corbusier[14] and amplified through the CIAM debate,[15] inspired the most interesting protagonists of the London scene between the wars. These included both British nationals and immigrant architects, urban planners, and engineers, collaborating in collective architectural and structural engineering practices, such as Tecton, the MARS Group, and Arup Associates, to mention only the most renowned **(fig. 2)**.[16] Their extensive use of diagrams was creating a new narrative of communication for the discipline of architecture.

In the early 1950s the so-called Independent Group, a neo-avant-garde group, which gravitated around the Institute of Contemporary Arts of London (ICA), played a crucial role in the emergence of this diagrammatic architecture.[17] Artists and curators, in search of a new scientifically-oriented aesthetic, shared a deeper interest in the phenomenology of organic forms, and in the shapes and patterns of associations borrowed from the natural world, to provide a new stimulating image of the post-atomic world. The universe of natural science was seen as a possible response to the material and spiritual issues of reconstruction after the horrors of the war, and diagrams were strategically used to display this parallel. Lancelot Law Whyte, a "frontiersman without the authority of Science,"[18] established direct links with the ideas of Geddes and Thompson (both reprinted in the 1940s) and pointed out the suggestions of organic structures at different scales. His approach, discussed in the book *Aspect of Forms* (1951), was influential on the *Growth and Forms Exhibition* held at the ICA the same year.[19] Basically a work by the artist Richard Hamilton, the exhibition demonstrated the interest in the structural logic and the formal patterns of living beings—their geometry and their evolution in response to the environment—by using objects, microscope-photographic enlargements, and three-dimensional models.[20]

Young architects, as well as artists, were inspired by the organic beauty of nature. Even less radical architects of the "third generation" of the Modern Movement were fascinated by the fluid possibilities of combining exposed structure, separated volumes, and functional identity in a single building, as shown in the design of the Hallfield Primary School in Paddington by Denys Lasdun (1951, completed in 1955).[21] Interestingly, among Lasdun's drawings for Hallfield one finds the concept represented like a page from a nineteenth-century herbarium: a sort of "ideogram" combining fruits, vegetables, and seeds, intended to explain the functions and the forms of the parts of the building through the arrangement of a series of labelled plants **(fig. 3)**. The lesson of biology, through the reading of Geddes in particular, appeared effective even in solving large-scale problems of urban design, such as the "clusters" proposed by Alison and Peter Smithson, which were elaborated in the 1950s from the *Golden Lane Project* (1952) to *Berlin's Hauptstadt Competition* (1957–58). In the Smithsons's vision, high-density residential settlements would be oriented with 120-degree carbon-bond angles, designing a platform net overlapping the territory and evoking the shape of giant coral reefs, reminiscent of Geddes's diagrams of madrepores.[22]

Art historians and theorists also exploited the potential of diagrammatic representations when studying the dynamics of visual perception. They were used by György Kepes in his research on interactions between signs, arts, and sciences;[23] and, with a different background but analogous means by Rudolf Wittkower, who turned to diagrams in his pivotal analysis of Italian Quattrocento and Cinquecento architecture.[24] Above all, the architectural critic and art historian Reyner Banham promoted diagrams and diagram-users from the pages of *The Architectural Review* **(fig. 4)**, supporting the new nature of the techno-scientific approach of architects and engineers, such as the geodesic methodology of R. Buckminster Fuller or the stress on technical infrastructure in Kahn's design process.[25]

Personally connected to Banham since 1959, and earlier to Ernö Goldfinger, Lasdun, and the creative engineers gravitating around the Architectural Association in London,[26] Cedric Price (1934–2003) was the most consistent and prolific supporter of the logic of diagram communication and diagrammatic design thinking in post-industrial Britain during the Sixties and Seventies. Recognised as one of the most brilliant thinkers of the London scene, friend of the Archigram Group, and closely related to Theo Crosby (technical editor of the *Architectural Design* and *Uppercase* magazines), Price was very popular in the anti-academic community of British architects, as shown by the first "CP supplement" featured in the *Architectural Design* issue of October 1970.[27] Celebrated in 2014 by Hans Ulrich Obrist in the Swiss Pavilion of the Architectural Biennale of Venice XIV, Price's architecture is mostly documented in his professional archive with its hundreds of diagrams.[28]

His most renowned project, the *Fun Palace*, was described publicly for the first time by Joan Littlewood on the BBC's Monitor arts program of April 28, 1963.[29] Price referred to the Fun Palace as "resembling a large shipyard in which enclosures such as theatres, cinemas, restaurants, workshops, rally areas, can be assembled, moved, rearranged and scrapped continuously".[30] Every element of the structure of the *Fun Palace*, as well as its technical equipment, its installations and settings, fillings, and appliances, was labeled and its estimated life span considered: after a certain number of years, the materials of the original work would naturally deteriorate, facilitating the clearing out of the site in favor of a new building. Illustrated by diagrammatic sections, plans, axonometrics, and perspectives, Price's *Fun Palace* was praised by Banham as among the best megastructures ever conceived. Banham praised the adaptability and the expandability of the building, finally capable of resolving the conflict between big and small, design and spontaneity, permanent and temporary.[31] The widespread use of diagrams, as abstract and conceptual as possible—no thickness in materials, no details in the equipment—as well as much narrative as possible, picturing arrows and labeling each drawing with notes, was intended to minimize the risk of technocracy intrinsic to the mechanization of the design. The metamorphic nature of the space, with its moving platforms, swinging screens, pneumatic volumes, and giant cranes on the roof prevailed over its mechanical features precisely because of its synthetic representation through diagrams **(fig. 5)**.

A second, lesser-known project by Cedric Price, elaborated in 1963 but never realised, shows the power of diagrams: the proposal for the new headquarters of the Institute of Contemporary Arts in London. Since 1946, the year of its foundation, the ICA had been located in a nineteenth-century building at 17–18 Dover Street, but already in the early 1950s the Institute felt the need for a larger space, to fulfill its growing role as a cultural platform, which had gained a remarkable audience in the London artistic scene. Among the activities scheduled at the ICA in the late 1950s had been exhibitions and lectures, video projections, informal and open discussions, all inaugurated by the Independent Group in 1952. From 1956, when Price moved from Cambridge to London, until 1962, when he joined the ICA Exhibitions Committee, John McHale and Lawrence Alloway were most influential in guiding the debate at the Institute, both in pursuit of an interdisciplinary, anti-conformist approach, and interested in enhancing relations with the contemporary American scene.[32]

Price's proposal for the new ICA building was a truly diagrammatic project, consistent with the needs of the neo-avant-garde community which would have used the institution. Represented in plan, section, and perspective, the ICA design foresaw an administrative building equipped with exhibition spaces and large conference rooms, free space at the street level, and three levels underneath for parking, service, and storage spaces. It was a free-standing tower characterized by a hexagonal plan, resulting from a rectangular and a trapezoidal surface joined, and marked in its vertices by six free-standing "structural columns", as described by Price **(fig. 6)**.[33] In the center, a service core with stairs and an elevator shaft connected the seven different levels above ground: two administrative floors (with rooms for members and a library), with exposed brick façades; a third higher floor with variations on open-air and enclosed auditorium spaces; two gallery levels above, on the fourth and fifth floor, with glazed curtain-walls all along the perimeter. The top deck at the sixth floor was conceived without a conventional roof, with a watchtower/control cabin in the center, and six structural pillars projecting into the sky; adjustable screens on the sides and temporary roofing on top; mechanical joints on the six angles, with floodlights to light up the transmitting antennas and cables at night. The communicational elements of the tower were carefully designed. The third floor, with its exposed screen and lecture halls with stepped seats, would catch the eyes of citizens walking in the South Kensington area. The glazed, double-height exhibition floor would have worked as a bright electric sign to attract the audience at night, when the entirely transparent walls of Miesian memory would float above the lights of the city. If realised, a peculiar urban appeal would have expressed its predominant public function.

Some of the ICA Building's architectural details, such as the rough concrete and exposed brickwork of the administration level, the sloping floors of the halls, and the elaborate glass panelling of the gallery, showed direct connections with the project by Stirling & Gowan recently completed at Leicester University **(fig. 7)**.[34] Price's appreciation for the architecture of James Stirling was to a certain degree given for the twenty-nine-year-old architect, who circulated in the orbit of the ICA and the Architectural Association. Banham himself, a major protagonist on these two stages, had praised Stirling and his Leicester work as the most interesting example of the New Brutalist architecture.[35] On one hand, therefore, the choice of a tower was probably stimulated by the spectacular set of vertical volumes differentiated in height, shape and function, erected at the engineering building in Leicester. But on the other, the ICA tower might have been conceived as a sort of alternative option for the *Fun Palace*, in case the mainly horizontal volume had not encountered enough success or available land. Adopting a tall building type for a socially useful structure, Price was leaving behind the British socialist tradition of the horizontal Mechanics' Institutes of the nineteenth century, and instead adopting the North American solution of skyscrapers.[36]

An extraordinary precedent for Price, in terms of similar program requirements, was Kahn's proposal for a *Laboratory of Education*, submitted for the Jefferson National Expansion Memorial Competition in St. Louis (1947). Kahn's Laboratory, if realized, would have displayed a multifunctional welfare complex, with television and radio sets, a public library, laboratories and offices, a publishing department and, at the ground floor, the Municipal Office for Urban Planning.[37] How much Price took advantage of Kahn's St. Louis brief when designing the ICA tower is difficult to say. Yet Kahn's distinction between "servant" and "served spaces" seems to have inspired the concept of Price's structure from the beginning. One aspect was genuinely Price's conception: the description of the top deck as suitable for a "future vertical expansion of the total building," which revealed the third dimension of the tower, its expandability and changeability. The absence of a fixed roof, with the structure's elevation on parietal pillars and a central core, would allow the building to grow higher according to the needs of the institution, establishing a conceptual parallelism between the growth of a building and the life of an organic being.

The ICA building proposal ended without any real outcome, and the years from 1963 to 1967 saw Price in his most immersive phase of work on the *Fun Palace* through diagrams and models, which were never realised. Price's clear, ordered archive reveals his most consistent visual diagrammatic approach at every step of the design process. His unconventional architectural narrative through diagrams is easily understood and propagated, and his proposals are still buildable, as demonstrated by European architecture over the last five decades.[38] It is precisely the dimension on paper which today seems worthiest of interest: his focus on the issue of vision as an active, dynamic process, logically determined and measurable. The analytic and synthetic quality of these diagrams, their capability of generating open visions and displaying diachronically a world of possibilities and variations, result from combined interdisciplinary approaches (ecological, material, sociological, economical, functional, structural, and technological). Price's diagrams echo Stirling's words: "a drawing must be planned (from a critical point of view). The information removal is crucial and achieved through a series of design decisions, often taken in fast sequence; sometimes made deliberately (and maybe giving birth to the less effective drawing). What is left in the image is the minimum amount needed to report the maximum of information with the best clearness."[39] They may be less effective as drawings, according to Stirling, nevertheless Price's diagrams achieve the greatest clarity, freeing the imagination of the observer and preventing him from falling into a technocratic *dérive*.[40]

How, therefore, can we define Price as an "anti-architect," a counter-voice already acknowledged by his contemporaries? His attempt to solve the seemingly irreducible contradiction between the structures and the metamorphoses of living beings, and consequently of human artefacts (to follow Collins's interpretation), led him to the field of utopian design. Utopian was his adoption of an analogic method to achieve artistic value through the authority of sciences, and to pursue universally valid models, indifferent to the context, and prefiguring a harmonious urban society. Utopian was his illusion of providing masses with enormous amounts of information, achieving social consensus and pretending to remain neutral with respect to the market economy. Utopian by definition are his diagrams, following the words of Anthony Vidler in considering diagrams as transgressive devices "capable of endless transformation and becoming," of producing a fluid and unstable new type of reality.[41]

If realised, the *Fun Palace* would have been almost two times longer than Le Corbusier's Unité d'habitation in Marseille. Its giant impact bursts out of the scale in a particular diagrammatic drawing, aimed at picturing the circulation around one of the "Service Towers," which here becomes worthy of special consideration. In it one can recognise all the characteristics of diagrams: the perspective has a vanishing point so far away as to appear an axonometric drawing; the arrows imply the direction of movement; the isolated vertical element outlines a fragment of a wider platform, whose section is suggested by a ramp running down into a lower level **(fig. 8)**.[42] Something uncanny is happening, though, and it is related to the scale of the human beings animating the diagram. The *Fun Palace* seems to acquire a suspended atmosphere, crossed by escalators cantilevered in the void, as in the urban dystopic scenography of the film *Metropolis* by Fritz Lang (1927), or in the vertiginous staircases of the *Carceri d'Invenzione* by Giambattista Piranesi (1745–50) **(fig. 9)**.[43] In the expanded field of architectural representation, nothing could seem more distant from one another than a capriccio and a diagram, yet in the clashing association of the *Carceri* with the *Fun Palace*, one might harness the challenging power of diagrams: a quintessential rational representation in its "first state" definition, capable of yielding a spectacular fantasy-architecture.

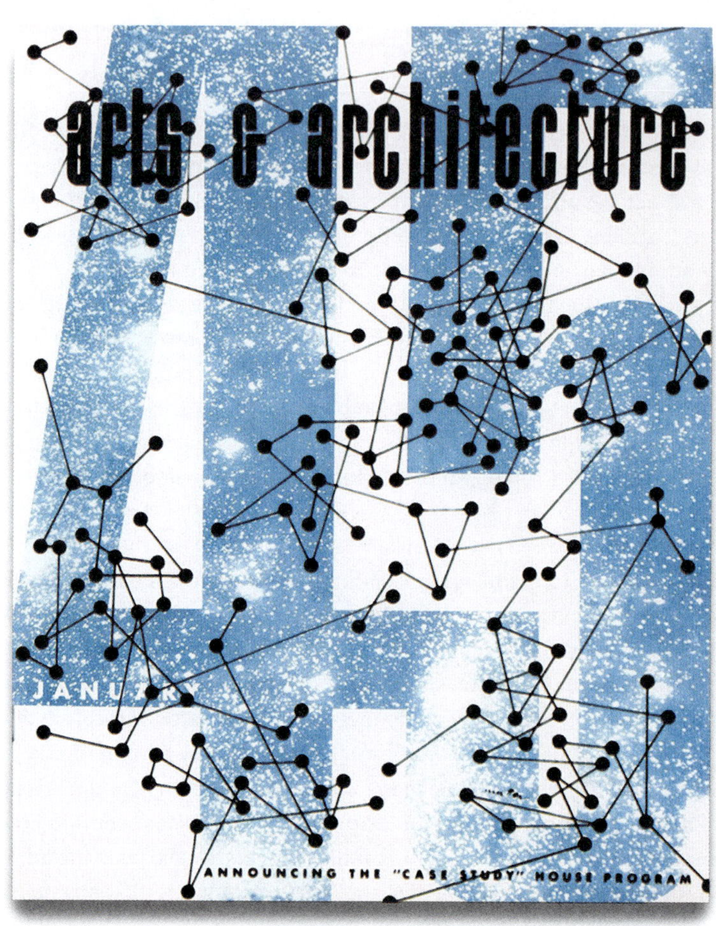

Fig. 1_ *Arts and Architecture,* 45,1945 (journal cover by Herbert Matter).

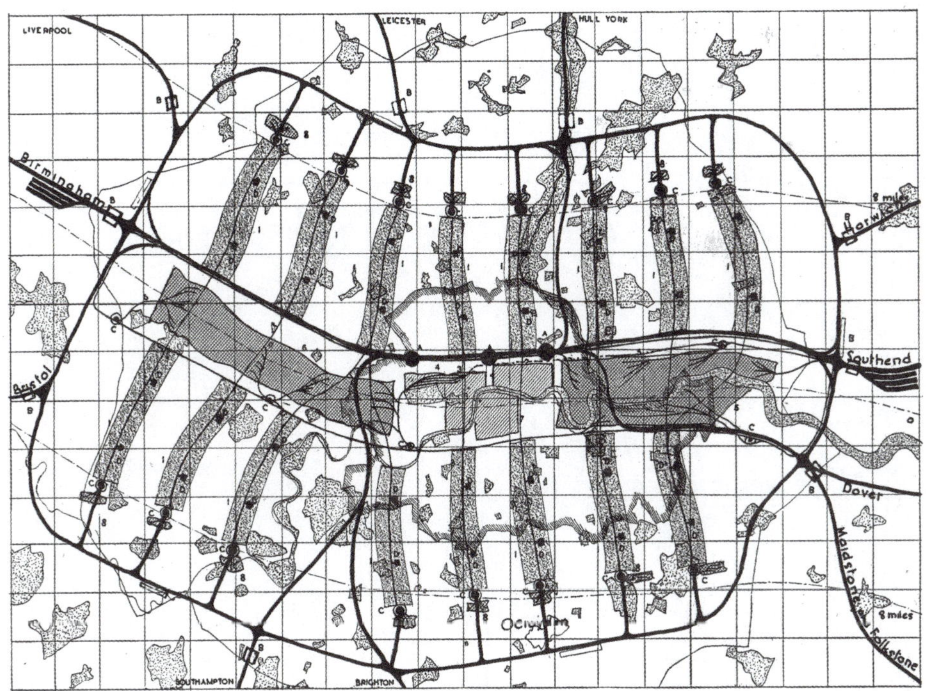

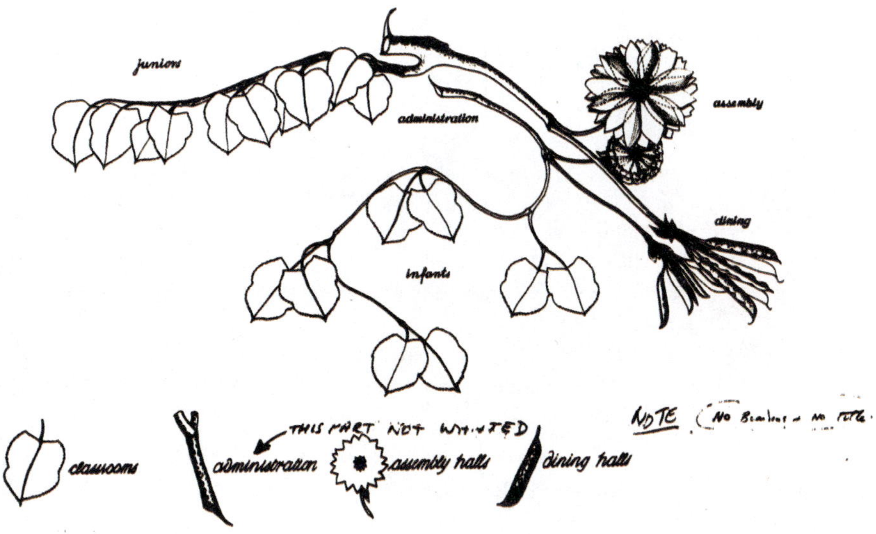

Fig. 2_ *The MARS plan for London (1937-42)*, from *The Architectural Review*, June 1942.
Fig. 3_ Denys Lasdun, *Hallfield Ideogram*, 1951.

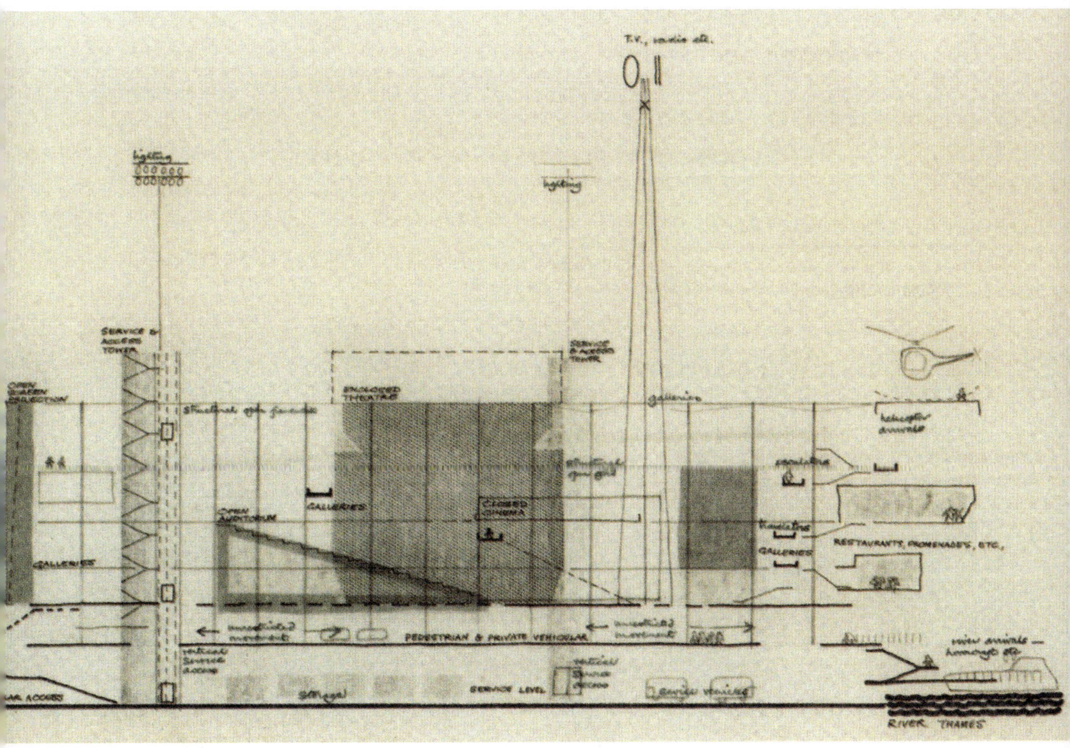

Fig. 4 (Previous page)_ Gordon Cullen, *Diagrammatic Capriccio*, from *The Architectural Review*, 707, 1955.

Fig. 5_ Cedric Price, Fun Palace, from *Art in America*, 54, 1966.

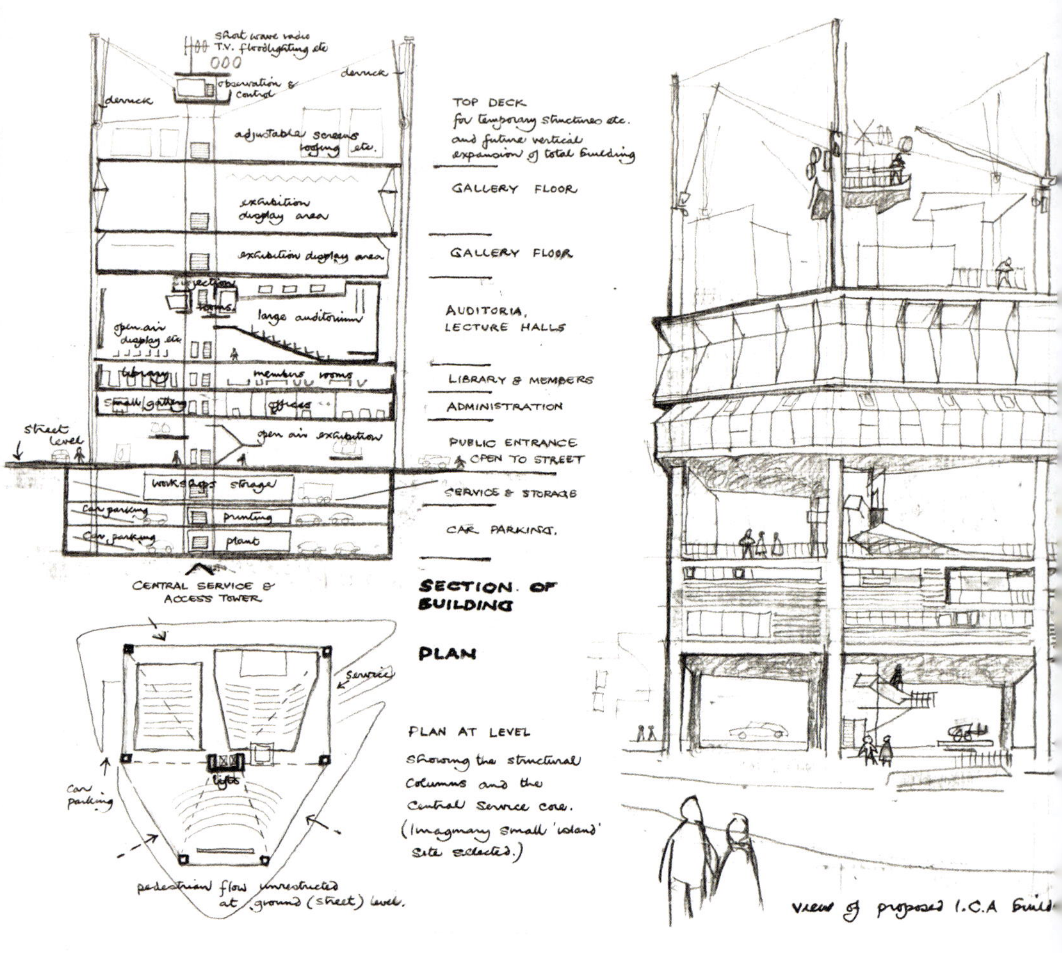

Fig. 6_ Cedric Price, *ICA Building*, 1963.

Fig. 7 (Following page)_ James Stirling, James Gowan, in collaboration with Frank Newby, Leicester University Building, Leicester UK, 1959-1963.

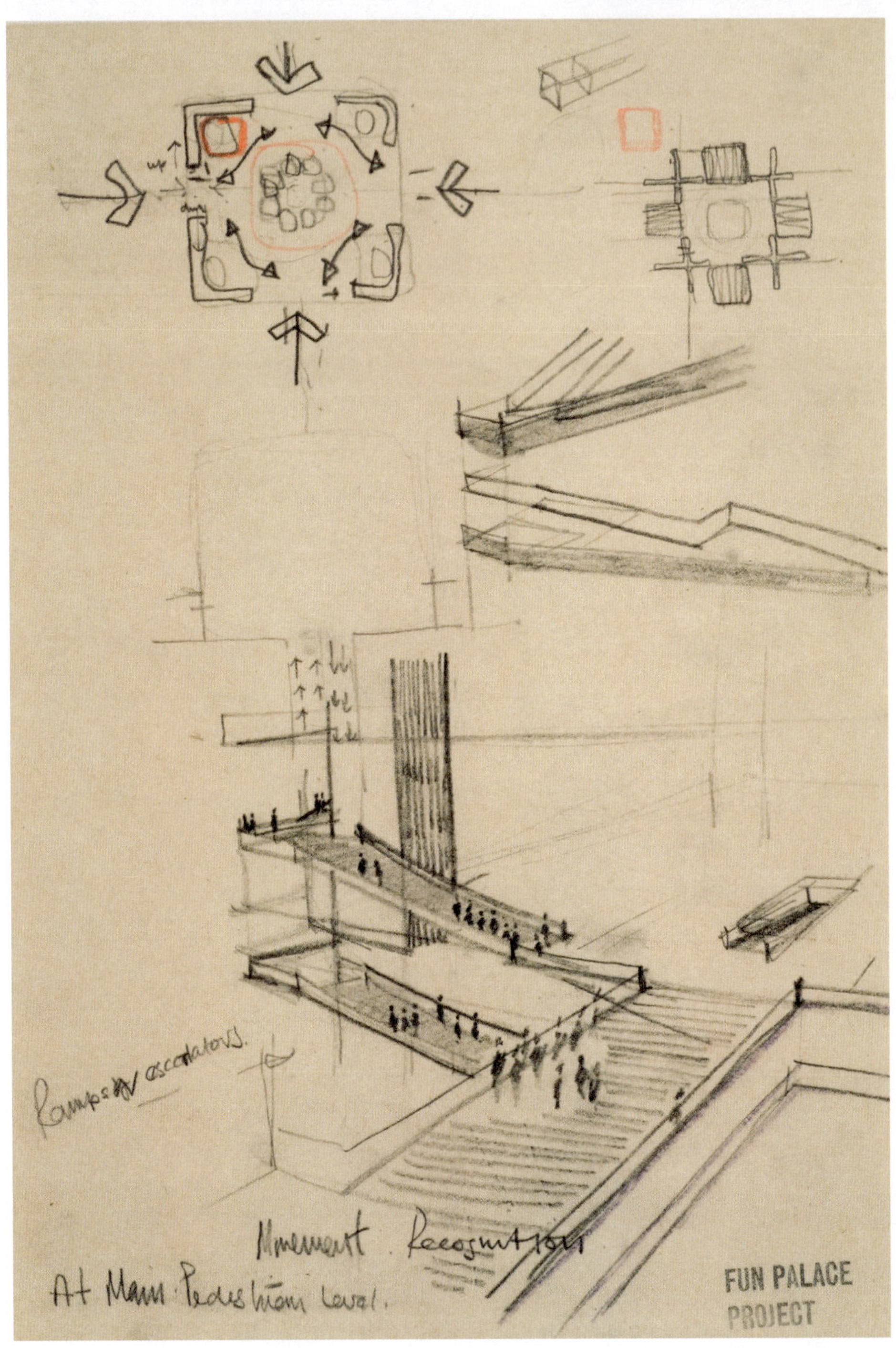

Fig. 8_ Cedric Price, *Fun Palace Project: Services Towers,* 1963.

Fig. 9_ Giovanni Battista Piranesi, *Carceri di Invenzione*, 1745-1750.

Learning from No-Stop City: Archizoom's Utopia Revisited

Marie Therese Stauffer

In December 1969 the Archizoom group of architects published a series of photomontages that can be described as utopian proposals for ways of positioning large-scale architectural volumes in the city or countryside.[1] The volumes appear enveloped in planer, unarticulated surfaces that mainly take the shape of geometrized bodies or frame structures. Several of the photomontages also feature more identifiable forms—for example, a series of rocky pinnacles, a rectangular rod with fleshy leaves, and a gigantic spoon. One image is in the shape of a lightning-flash, stamped into the urban texture of Bologna and representing Archizoom's logo **(figs. 1–3)**.[2]

By 1969 the Archizoom group consisted of the architects Andrea Branzi, Gilberto Corretti, Paolo Deganello, Massimo Morozzi, Dario Bartolini, and Luisa Bartolini-Morozzi. Founded in 1966, the Florence-based group had begun to gain recognition in the field of design.[3] In their urban photomontages, these architects were now turning toward the "architecture of the city."[4]

Shaped Volumes

As a starting-point for discussion, one photomontage from the series may be singled out. It shows an imaginary intervention in the historic city center of Florence and consists of an orthogonal structure surrounding the Cattedrale di Santa Maria del Fiore **(fig. 4)**. The cathedral, which interrupts the urban texture of Florence through its large volume, thus has a kind of modern frame of similar size added to it. The frame, articulated in elementary shapes, dominates and even superimposes itself on the church's nuanced volumes in a way that appears both radical and provocative.

Before questioning the theoretical position behind such a proposal, another remarkable aspect of the image should be considered: Archizoom's photomontage shows the city and the cathedral area from an atypical viewpoint. The great majority of photos of the city of Florence and its religious building are taken from the south, with the cathedral and its *campanile* located in the center. Sometimes, depending on the focus, additional elements such as the Palazzo della Signoria, the buildings along the River Arno, or the chain of the Apennine mountains that form the northern boundary of its valley are visible. For their intervention, however, the Archizoom architects have chosen an image taken from the northwest, nearly the opposite viewpoint. The historic center is therefore *not* in the foreground. The focus is not on buildings that date from the Middle Ages and the Renaissance—or those of the long 19th century, during which numerous street lines in the inner city were renovated to fit into an "improved" replica of the historic fabric.[5] In Archizoom's proposal, urban structures of the 20th century occupy the foreground of the image. Buildings dating from the very recent past are particularly visible. By using this angle, Archizoom was focused on the urban development that had taken place in the 1950s and 1960s both in Florence and elsewhere, development, which strongly affected the peripheries of these cities. Thus, one of the central topics of the photomontage is the 20th century urban phenomenon summed up by the term "suburbanization."

There were of course several prerequisites for suburbanization: economic expansion after 1945 (particularly strong in northern Italy), increasing affluence, the growing urban population, and the motorization of society. Indeed, the increasing availability of the automobile and public transport accelerated a factitious separation between home and workplace. Construction of new districts on the periphery of Italy's cities was carried out largely without any municipal or regional planning, resulting in an uncontrolled and disorganized sprawl on the outskirts of existing cities. With no official planning, the design and construction of the new districts were largely determined by commercial interests.[6]

Expansion and Reduction

For Archizoom, the relationship between the historic center and the periphery was a central topic. Branzi remarks that although many of our contemporaries now live in the modern and more recent estate areas on the periphery, they do not regard these zones as directly being "the city." For example, they may live in a district on the outskirts of Florence, but will say that they are going "into town" for shopping or work—meaning into the historic center.[7] It could therefore be said that their place of residence is neither the city nor the country, but rather a distinct, more or less undefined intermediate zone: an area that stands in relation to a historic urban core, but is distinct from it at a structural—and thus also at a symbolic—level. In contrast to the historic city center with its symbolic architectural fabric, new suburban buildings are almost invariably characterized by insignificant architecture. Such "poor" urban structure from the second half of the 20th century was to become a major issue for Archizoom towards the end of the 1960s.[8] By that time, the widespread lack of planning had already long since been raised in architectural debates in Italy.[9] But unlike many of their contemporaries, Archizoom directed their criticism towards the result of this unplanned development: urban sprawl. In 1970, such sprawl had not yet become an established topic in architectural discussions. Very early, Archizoom was addressing a phenomenon that would become crucial in the decades that followed.

From 1970 onward, the Archizoom group continued its reflections on the current state of the "architecture of the city" under the project title *No-Stop City*, which evolved in several stages.[10] Archizoom used photomontages and manifestos, but also drawings and installations, which were published in such journals as *Domus*, *Casabella*, and *Architectural Design*.[11] Once again, the message delivered by this theoretical project was the problematic "poverty" of design, made evident in an architectural form that was homogeneously expanding on all sides in accordance with the interests of capitalist enterprise. As a result, *No-Stop City* described an extremely reduced, completely uniform type of construction capable of infinite growth. Its lateral surfaces had no openings, so there appears to be no exit from *No-Stop City*; but roof terraces provided a view of the surrounding countryside **(fig. 5)**. Inside the construction, horizontally stacked levels stretched out on a regular, inconspicuous supporting structure, extending to infinite distances **(fig. 6)**.

The city's infinite spaces were thus (almost) empty, in the sense that they were minimally equipped and the facilities provided were formally extremely reduced. Artificial lighting and ventilation allowed a free arrangement for a wide variety of functions: residential and circulation areas, and locations for production and consumption, could be installed with the greatest flexibility, then altered or dismantled again **(fig. 7)**. The completely homogeneous infrastructure provided identical conditions in every location in the city for all users and for all possible uses. To the extent that everything was available to everyone, the various aspects of human coexistence would become a game of endless combinatory strategies, set against a neutral, infinite grid. In its published drawings, photomontages and models, Archizoom only presented a few of these possible variations.[12]

Fields of Reference

The radical quality of Archizoom's approach is clear from the various aspects of *No-Stop City* presented above, as well as its earlier 1969 urban collages. In their time, the group was decisively influenced by an informal network of young architects and designers that emerged in Florence in the late 1960s and attracted attention through experimental projects that combined architecture, design, the visual arts, and theory. In this context, retrospectively termed *architettura radicale* by the Italian art critic Germano Celant, numerous design projects, art-related campaigns and installations were developed, deliberately testing the boundaries of disciplines.[13]

By pushing the limits of taste and of what was capable of being thought and expressed, *architettura radicale* sought to counter a crisis in architecture well recognized in the profession all over the Western world, far beyond Italy. The Archizoom architects anchored their reflections on this crisis with detailed historical explanations. The project's theoretical starting-point was the premise that the "modern" city is in every respect a product of industrial capitalism. On this basis, Archizoom defined the "capitalist city" as an "extension of the model of the factory to society itself."[14] As a "projection of the logic of capitalist production," the city had increasingly taken on the form of a "functional system" during the nineteenth century, so that individual areas of the urban corpus were categorized into specific functions: residential sections, industrial districts, service zones, etc.[15] According to Archizoom, the development of capitalism during the 20th century had gone beyond this differentiated functional system, and promoted another completely artificial urban system, with an entirely homogeneous structure: the supermarket. For Archizoom, these two systems represented the fundamental urbanization models of their time, and they were therefore used as the basis for *No-Stop City*.[16] Archizoom's project also reflected an engagement with the history of modern architecture. With references to 18th–and 19th–century urban theories, the group's manifestos discuss the development of the "modern" city, in particular the development of urban functionalism. At the visual level, their reflection on the historical foundations of architectural modernism is expressed both through specific iconographical references and an allusive formal language. The so-called revolutionary architecture that developed around 1800 thus figures as the starting-point for a developmental process that culminated in the *razionalismo* of the 1920s. Accordingly, historical visual references include a heavily abstract version of the ground plan of Claude-Nicolas Ledoux's *Maison de plaisir*, incorporated into the plan of *No-Stop City* **(fig. 8)**.[17]

References to other projects by Ledoux, as well as by Claude-Etienne Boullée—utilizing geometrically based, expressive architectural bodies on a monumental scale—were used by Archizoom for both *No-Stop City* and their previous urban photomontages. Starting from these, the group established links to the architectural avant-gardes of the 1920s and 1930s. As a specific reference, one version of *No-Stop City* mentions a scheme by Le Corbusier in which he contrasted traditional perimeter block construction with *lotissements à redents,* to advocate the dissolution of the dense city into large forms set in the countryside **(fig. 9)**.[18] More general allusions to the modern architecture of the 1920s and 1930s can be found in the plain, abstract volumes of *No-Stop City*, the maximum rationalization of its standardized ground-plans, and the extreme flexibility of its spaces **(figs. 6, 7, 10)**. Other formal references to 20th-century modernism can be found in the use of grids and a ubiquitous serial quality that is both aesthetically and conceptually evocative of serial planning procedures and serial construction methods **(figs. 6, 9–11)**. All of these aspects arose in the discussions held at the Congrès Internationaux d'Architecture Moderne (CIAM) around 1930 and in connection with the "International Style" exhibition held at the Museum of Modern Art in New York in 1932.[19] By the end of the 1960s, architectural debate had progressed some distance from the visions and practices of the 1920s and 1930s. This distance allowed reconsidering the qualities of modern architecture, but also its problematic aspects. Indeed, attention had long since been drawn to the reductive aspects of the urbanism developed during the first five CIAM meetings; criticism came not least from within the CIAM circle itself: for example, from its members who joined together into Team X.[20] This was associated with critiques of the 1950s and 1960s projects in which CIAM's early urban visions had rigidified into a form of sterile functionalism. This criticism also applied to post-1945 buildings that had been superficially "modernized," although the threshold to purely commercial architecture had already been crossed.[21]

On one hand, Archizoom's *No-Stop City* reflected this critical rethinking of architectural modernism. On the other, the group also championed the so-called mega-structures of the 1960s. Here, modern functionalism combined with new or future technologies to convert entire cities into singular, expressive forms of monumental scale. During their studies at the University of Florence's faculty of architecture, in the first half of the 1960s, various members of Archizoom had themselves designed large-scale projects in *la nuova dimensione*, as the mega-structure was called in Italy.[22]

With regard to both the structure of the city, and the group's interest in developing expressive and significant architectural forms on a large scale, the writings and projects of the Italian architect Aldo Rossi were particularly important.[23] Rossi's point that monuments give structure to the city and withstand the passage of time was especially meaningful for Archizoom's approach to urbanism around 1970. Additionally, the shift in viewpoint undertaken in Rossi's book *L'architettura della città*—namely, perceiving the city as (an object of) architecture and thus analyzing different scales at the same time—led to intense debates among specialists during the 1960s.

Intonation and Intention

It should be noted that the references used by Archizoom, which have been discussed so far, were made in such a way as to radicalize their historical reference-points, exaggerating them, and even pushing them to absurdity. In my view, it is possible to identify an ironic rhetorical strategy here. This strategy is further revealed by the "rupture points" in the texts, where the architects themselves provide hints about how to understand their project correctly. In the manifesto "Città, catena di montaggio del sociale," the group described the project as a means to "drive the system's brain crazy."[24] The Florentine architects were insisted on this approach because they were well aware that they themselves were part of the (capitalist) system—a system that the group strongly criticized. It was for this reason that new suggestions, which could never be anything more than models merely perpetuating the system, were to be rejected. Thus, *No-Stop City* was not an "anticipation of a different model for the system." Instead, this utopia was "a critical hypothesis *about* the system itself," as Archizoom stated again in "Città, catena di montaggio del sociale."[25] In "Utopia della qualità, utopia della quanitità," the group writes that "an urban model of this type does not represent an alternative to current reality, but rather current reality at the level of a new critical awareness."[26] Archizoom was using irony as a means of criticism. With *No-Stop City*, the group did not propose solutions to problems, but expounded the problems themselves.

Since I have discussed the ironic aspects of *No-Stop City* in more detail elsewhere,[27] I will dedicate my attention here to the central function of Archizoom's rhetorical strategy: irony allows an ambiguous form of expression that creates a distance with the problematic aspects of the object discussed, without dismissing that object entirely, making it possible to preserve its more positive aspects.[28] An element of ambivalence is expressed through this ironic reconsideration of the modern city and its foundations in architecture, history, society, and the economy. This allows Archizoom to oscillate between rejection and affirmation, without ever becoming clearly tangible at either of these poles. The acuteness of the critique expressed in Archizoom's utopia is accordingly combined with a lighthearted playfulness: a gloomy reality brightened by the poetry of the irrational.

Regarding Art

By 1970, however, the group's reflections were no longer only directed at the history of their own discipline. At the levels of both form and content, Archizoom's urban photomontages and *No-Stop City* were fundamentally shaped by their interest in the contemporary visual arts. This was an interest the Florentine group shared with other architects. However, the incorporation of approaches drawn from the art world into Archizoom's working methods was particularly motivated by the ongoing crisis of architectural practice at the time. The Florentine group turned to art, as well as then-current theoretical discussions on topics such as Marxism and Italian semiology, to broaden the horizons of their own discipline. Actually, these interests preceded the group's practical work from 1966 onward. Branzi, Corretti, Deganello, and Morozzi had been enthusiastic about Pop Art since the start of their architectural studies in the early 1960s.[29] Such artists such as Roy Lichtenstein, Andy Warhol, Tom Wesselmann, James Rosenquist, and Claes Oldenburg fascinated them because they engaged with the production and consumption of consumer articles to make use of them in aesthetic processes. By employing banal mass-produced goods, commercial images, and second-hand everyday objects, the Pop artists were exploring ways of removing the individual signature and the broad gestures of Abstract Expressionism from their works. Besides Pop Art, the Florentine group were also concerned with Minimal and Conceptual Art. The common denominators were a formal language where concept took priority over execution, and an engagement with topics such as serialism and progression.[30]

Another point of reference for Archizoom were the artists associated with Land Art, such as Robert Smithson, Dennis Oppenheim, Walter de Maria, and Michael Heizer.[31] From the end of the 1960s onward, these artists had carried out projects in settings belonging to the urban periphery: on abandoned areas, on the outskirts of metropolises, and often on the boundaries of what was publicly accessible. These works, most executed in the open air and using local materials, were created on sites that were doubly marginalized, in that they also lay on the periphery of the "art system": far away from galleries and museums and not (directly) marketable within these circuits. Archizoom drew not only on the peripheral moments in Land Art but also, as the *No-Stop City* depictions show, on its large geometric forms and their juxtaposition with uncontrolled environments. The Archizoom group drew its own conclusions from this movement. In fact, their readings of Land Art contributed to transferring the uniform and banal structures of urban sprawl into compact volumes clearly juxtaposed with their surroundings **(figs. 1, 5)**. Artifact and natural landscapes even faced each other antagonistically as sharply distinct areas: "On the one hand, architecture ceases to be natural, while on the other nature ceases to be cultural," as they stated in 1971.[32]

"Auto Operation"

A scholarly study of Archizoom's numerous relations to art has not yet been undertaken and is outside the scope of this article. Therefore, I shall focus here on the connections with the work of two key artists, Ed Ruscha and Dan Graham, who were also addressing themes of the urban periphery and suburban architecture in the 1960s. In his *Thirty-Four Parking Lots* (1967) and *Twenty-Six Gasoline Stations* (1962), Ruscha cultivated a laconic, almost lapidary photographic style, which evokes the American documentary genre of Walker Evans, for example. Ruscha's photographs of gas stations and parking areas simultaneously highlight the bleakness of suburban landscapes and their *raison d'être*: the automobile. The sites documented in *Thirty-Four Parking Lots* **(fig. 12)** are totally empty, lifeless zones of automobile infrastructure, revealing in their repetitive regularity the same organizing principles as the assembly-lines of automobile plants, as well as those of prefabricated building material factories. For its part, Archizoom created a version of *No-Stop City* with two ground plans illustrating structures similar to Ruscha's parking lots **(fig. 13)**.[33] Another version of that project is subtitled "Residential Parkings."[34]

With *Twenty-Six Gasoline Stations*, Ruscha focuses on the serialization of the consumer, the increasing motorization of society, and the repetitive architectural typology of the service station. These topics again illustrate the moment of repetition—since a moving car always has to be refueled. Ruscha's 1965 work *Some Los Angeles Apartments* **(fig. 14)** focusses on another automobile related phenomenon, postwar tract housing developments. The pictures show impersonal modular buildings erected quickly and cheaply, which appear to have landed indiscriminately in the no-man's land of suburban Los Angeles. In these images we find the same dominant themes of anonymity and uniformity at the center of Archizoom's *No-Stop City*.

Virtually Unvarying

Dan Graham's 1966 "Homes for America" **(fig. 15)** also addresses the issue of tract housing. Originally conceived as a slide-show presentation, Graham's photographs document suburban architecture, showing a wide range of building types, all serially produced prefabricated constructions.[35] Superficial variations in the typologies, materials, and decorative details do not express distinctiveness and individuality; instead, they merely facilitate increased supply, leading to more of the same.

In a second stage of the project, Graham published the photos together with a text in the journal *Artforum*. The themes of mass production and serial construction methods in suburban housing development, as well as others evoked by Graham, would be taken up three years later by Archizoom. Philippe Vergne's note on Graham's use of the journal medium is revealing in this regard: "[*Homes for America*] was an artwork informed and distributed by the means of information itself, by the medium of the magazine as a public space. It was not art *about* the media (like Pop Art) but art *as* media, art as information." Graham used information as an aesthetic and the media as a vernacular form appropriate to the nature of his discourse.[36]

Likewise, Archizoom used the architectural project—plans, photomontages, and models—as information, as a medium *in and of itself*. The group's overt references to the work of artists living in the United States—as well as in Britain—, prompts the question of the information networks to which the Florentine architects had access. One important Italian forum for international art was the Venice Biennale, which became a "gateway" to Europe during the 1960s for major artistic trends in America and Britain. Archizoom was also able to study the latest contemporary art through such journals as the American *Art Forum,* which was already distributed in Italy. There was also the Italian *Flash Art* and, in particular, the architecture journals where the group published its own projects from 1966 onward: *Domus* and *Casabella.* In the columns of these journals, critics such as Germano Celant, Tommaso Trini, and Pierre Restany reported regularly on Italian and international artists, current debates, and exhibitions.

(Re)considering Utopia

No-Stop City and the previously published urban collages have been described here as representing a *utopian* project. Building on the major thematic aspects evoked above, and the key references behind *No-Stop City*, I shall now examine Archizoom's concept of utopia in greater detail.[37] The word and the concept are derived from Thomas More's *Utopia,* published in 1516.[38] Wolfgang Biesterfeld sums up the paradigm to which the influential, early modern book gave rise as follows: "Ever since More, who set the example by choosing an island as the location for his state and the city as a specific area within it, 'utopia' has been used to refer to the idea of a previously unachieved society, to a pattern of organization for human coexistence for which there are no precedents in history: a social fiction in which imperfect reality represents a challenge to work out a better way of doing things."[39]

Archizoom's projects correspond to this definition in two respects: first, they are offended by a reality that is regarded as defective. Second, they are motivated by the conviction that existing conditions are unacceptable. However, their urban utopias differ from More's in that the architects are *not* aiming to develop changes for the better. The projects are intentionally unrealistic and impossible to implement, serving only as a rhetorical strategy to criticize existing conditions.

According to Miriam Eliav-Feldon, the aspect of critique is a constituent element of utopia: "A Utopia is an invitation to perceive the distance between things as they are and things as they should be. It is a presentation of a positive and possible alternative to the social reality, intended as a model to be emulated or aspired to. Since it is an appeal to perfect the social environment, it expresses explicit and implicit criticism of the things as they are".[40] The decisive difference between Archizoom's projects and utopia as typically defined is that they are patently not proposing any alternatives.[41] Although they appear to be bona fide proposals, they do not actually posit projects that would transcend reality. The urban collages and *No-Stop City* thus neither represent an affirmative "anticipation of the future," as Hanno Walter Kruft defined it in his *Städte in Utopia* (1989), nor are they a manifesto for a "not-yet" state, for utopia as something actually possible and involving a change for the better, as Ernst Bloch presented it in his *Principle of Hope* (1959).[42]Archizoom's negative attitude is based on a refusal to become integrated into the production processes of the capitalist system. In an article published in *Notiziario Arte Contemporanea* in 1971, the architects discuss the specific connection between the function of utopia as a positive projection and capitalism: In fact, utopian work is increasingly starting to take on the role of a spurious hypothesis about the practicable future of capital, precisely because it is expected to help solve inequalities and contradictions in development (in other words, it is expected to overcome the 'anarchy of capital', and for this reason it is not focused as much on capitalist production as on the inefficiency of capitalist distribution).[43]

It is clear, therefore, that the concept of a positive utopia was no longer acceptable to Archizoom. Moreover, in the context of Italian *architettura radicale,* the conventional architectural utopia (and to some extent modern utopia as such) is regarded as a means of enabling the privileged classes to retain their power, ensuring that the underprivileged remain trapped in a situation of disadvantage: ideas with which Archizoom did not want to be associated.[44]

By extension, *architetti radicali* referred to debates on architecture and capitalism developed by Manfredo Tafuri as well as on workers and capital proposed by the philosophers Mario Tronti, Massimo Cacciari and others.[45] Tafuri in particular discounted the "possibility of [positive] utopia for the architecture of the era of late capitalism"[46] in such articles as "Per una critica dell'ideologia architettonica" (1969), and in his book *Progetto e utopia* (1973).[47] Similar to the approach of Tafuri, but also of Tronti and Cacciari, Archizoom's rejection of a positive utopia is clearly in line with Marxist thought. The basis for this rejection is provided by Karl Marx and Friedrich Engels themselves, for whom utopia is an out-of-touch "dream," as it represents "theory" divorced from practice and is merely "abstract thinking".[48] This negation of the utopian concept continues right down to Theodor W. Adorno and Max Horkheimer. The two Frankfurt School theorists recognize the critical function of utopia, to the extent to which it expresses a rejection of existing conditions. However, in their *Dialectic of Enlightenment*—a text that can be regarded as being of central importance for the Italian *architetti radicali*—they nevertheless distance themselves from the use of utopian concepts.[49]

Although the Florentine architects continued a tradition of mistrust for positive utopias, they nevertheless did not refrain from using the concept of utopia. However, just as they appropriated the language of postwar suburban architecture to better criticize it, the concept of utopia was exploited for its own subversion. In "Città, catena di montaggio del sociale," for example, the Archizoom architects described their concept of utopia as "optimal communication", with the aim of formulating a "critical hypothesis about the system itself." In "Utopia della qualità, utopia della quantità", the group reiterates what the potential function of the utopian element represents for them, in the following words: "The utopia we use is thus only a more general form of critical discourse that allows more direct and more effective communication".[50]

Archizoom's definitions suggest therefore, that the 1969 photomontages and *No-Stop City* presented aspects of a negative utopia: what is depicted in the projects is intended to become the subject of a critical discussion; the rhetoric of apparent agreement thus serves to encode negative content. In addition to the authors' definitions, another negative aspect lies in the fact that Archizoom's utopias have a temporal quality that not present in positive utopias. The projects are intentionally eclectic constructs that related their contemporary context to historical phenomena. Ultimately, the Florentine group uses utopia as a conceptual form for their critical discussion which actually rejects utopia as a modern instrument for architectural progress.

Now, these last aspects also make clear that the concept of utopia used by the Florentine architects goes beyond a simple negation to become a reflexive model, in a dual sense. On one hand, the reflection on utopia in *No-Stop City* reflects it *as an instrument*. On the other, *No-Stop City* becomes an instrument for reflection *in and of itself*, for a continuous and progressive process of critical thought. Archizoom writes, for example: "Our UTOPIA does not have any definitive and ideological value, but only a strategic one, and for this reason it can be continually and indefinitely updated."[51] Indeed, there is a positive dimension identifiable in this conception of utopia as an instrument for continual critical reflection: it represents a graspable potential that makes further insights possible.

There are other aspects for which the adjective "negative" falls short. For example, the discussion of Archizoom's ironic writing style—in particular the element of protectiveness that emerges from it—has made two things clear: first, the ambivalence between negative critique and affirmative enthusiasm. It is an ambivalence that expresses a clear awareness of the limitations of reality and the inaccessibility of the ideal. Second, there is a strong poetic and playful quality in Archizoom's *work*, which is linked to reflection. In these aspects, the creative work of the Florentine architects develops a specific, unconventional aesthetic **(fig. 16)**. In view of this aesthetic dimension of the Archizoom project, the concept of a negative utopia, or dystopia, appears to me not entirely adequate: the urban photomontages of 1969 and *No-Stop City* should therefore be described as *reflective* utopias.

Fig. 1_ Archizoom, *Belvedere (Urban Photomontage)*, 1969.

Fig. 2_ Archizoom, *Utopia della qualità: grattacielo con foglie di ficus*, 1969.

Fig. 3_ Archizoom, *Sventramento a Bologna*, 1969.

Following pages:
Fig. 4 (Above)_ Archizoom, *Edificio residenziale*, 1969.
Fig. 5 (Below)_ Archizoom, *No-Stop City, struttura urbana monomorfa*, 1970.

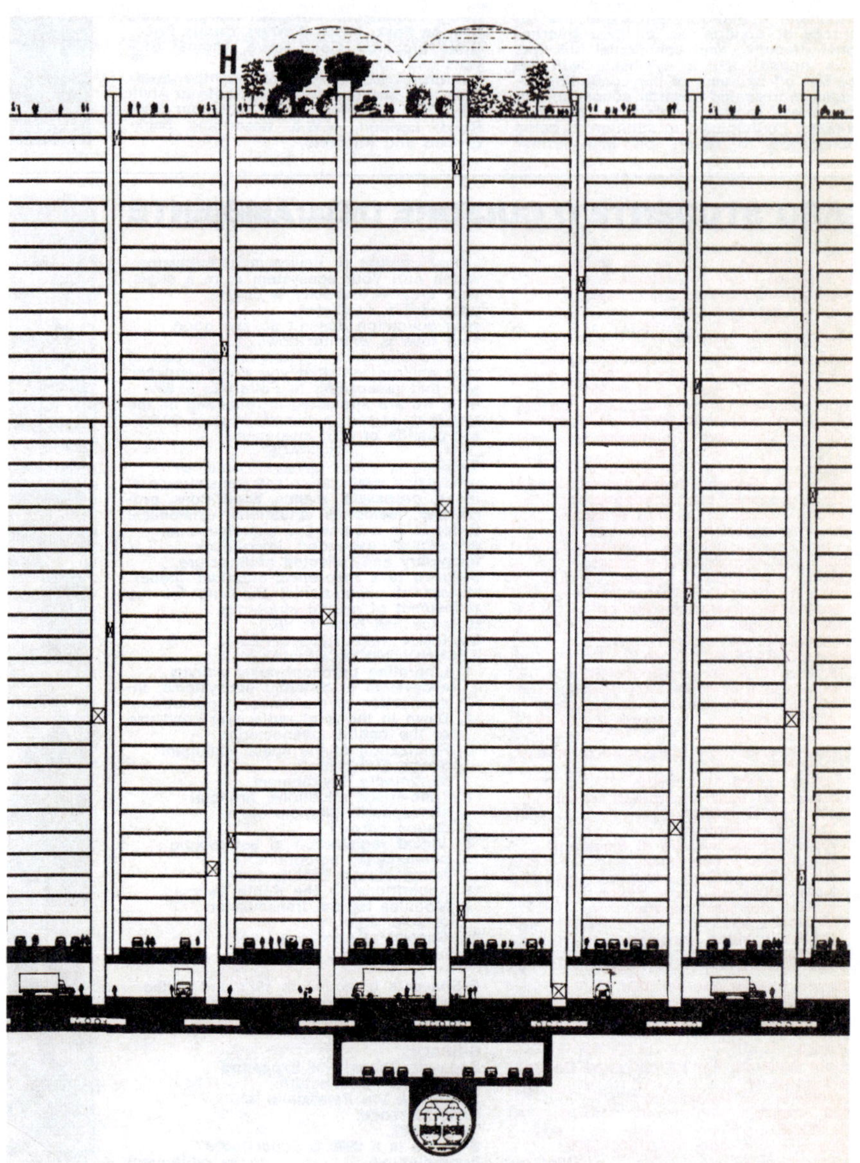

Fig. 6_ Archizoom, *No-Stop City* (section), 1970.

Fig. 7 (Following page)_ Archizoom, *No-Stop City* (interiors), 1970.

CHIPS
RITZ

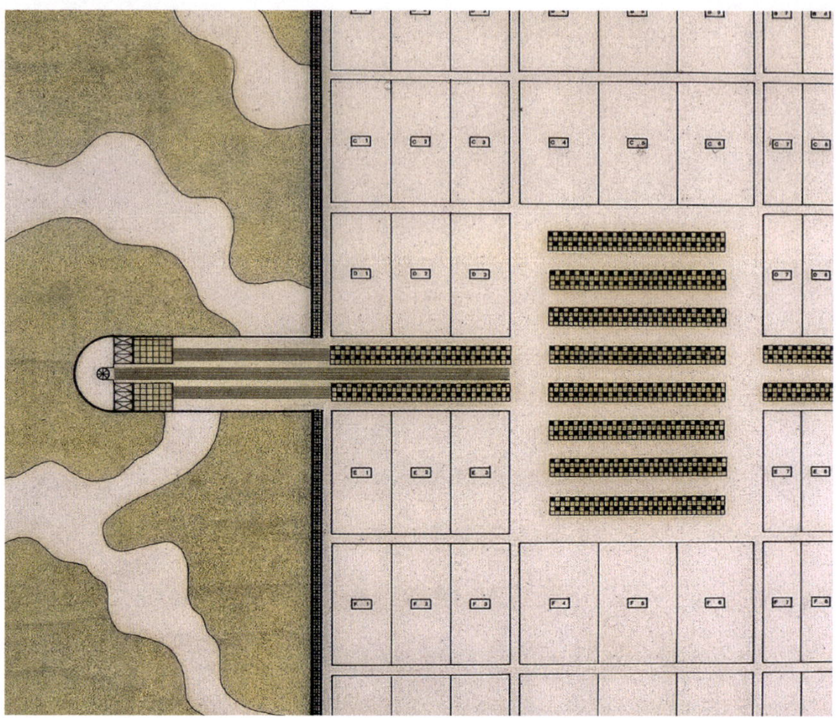

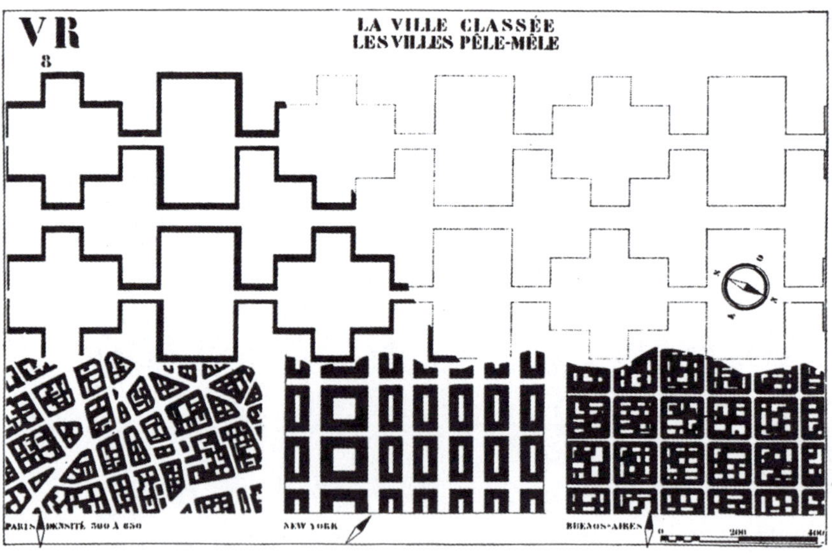

Fig. 8_ Archizoom, *No-Stop City* (plan), 1970.
Fig. 9_ Archizoom, *Project for the University of Florence*, 1971-1972.

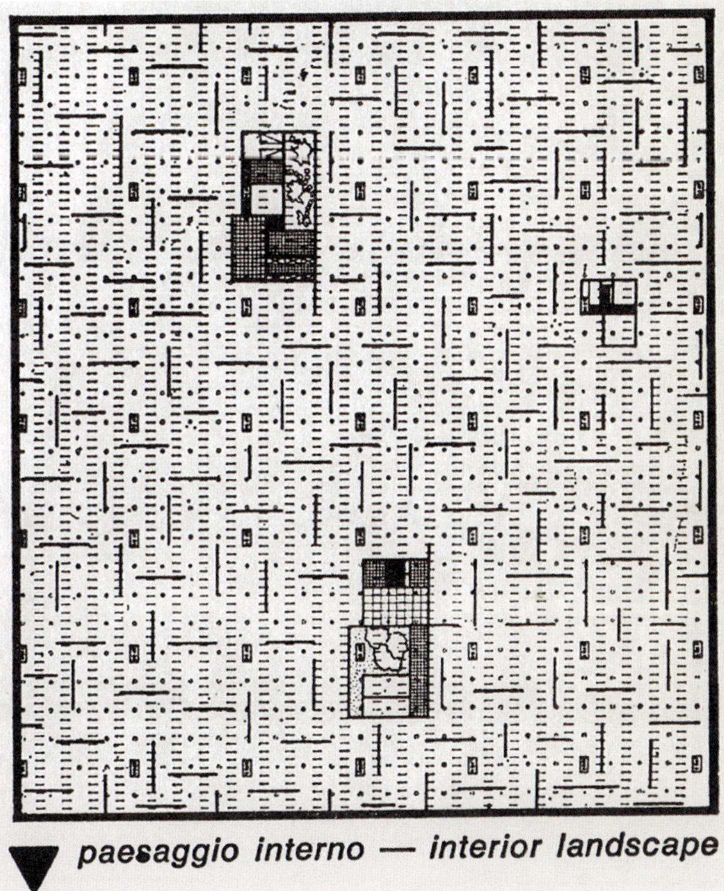

Fig. 10_ Archizoom, *No-Stop City* (bird's eye view), 1970.
Fig. 11_ Archizoom, *No-Stop City* (plan), 1970.

Fig. 12_ Ed Ruscha, *Parking Lot in Los Angeles* (from the series *Thirty-Four Parking Lots*), 1967.

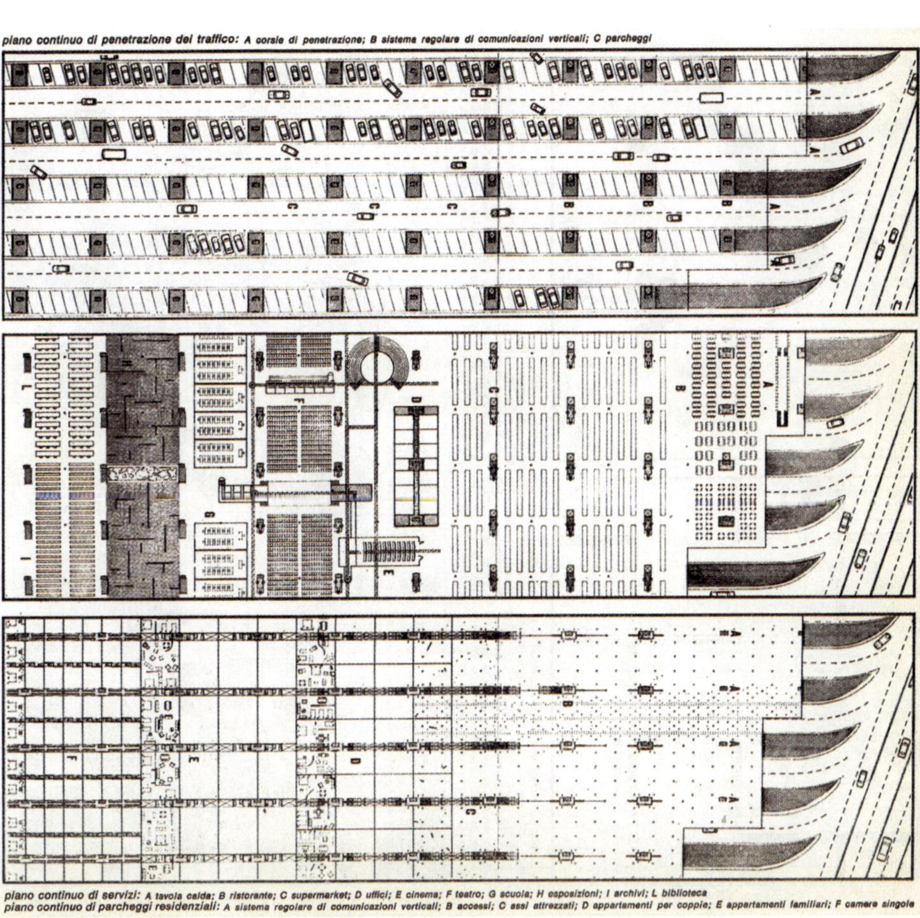

Fig. 13_ Archizoom, *No-Stop City* (plan with parking area), 1970.

Fig. 14_ Ed Ruscha, *Apartment* (from the series *Some Los Angeles Apartments*), 1967.

Homes for America

Early 20th-Century Possessable House to the Quasi-Discrete Cell of '66

D. GRAHAM

"Contingencies such as mass production technology and land use economics make the final decisions, denying the architect his former 'unique' role." Above: Wooden Houses, Boston, 1930, from American Photographs by Walker Evans, published by The Museum of Modern Art. Below: house plan courtesy Cape Coral Homes.

Fig. 15_ Dan Graham, *Homes for America,* from *Arts Magazine*, 41, 3, 1966-1967.

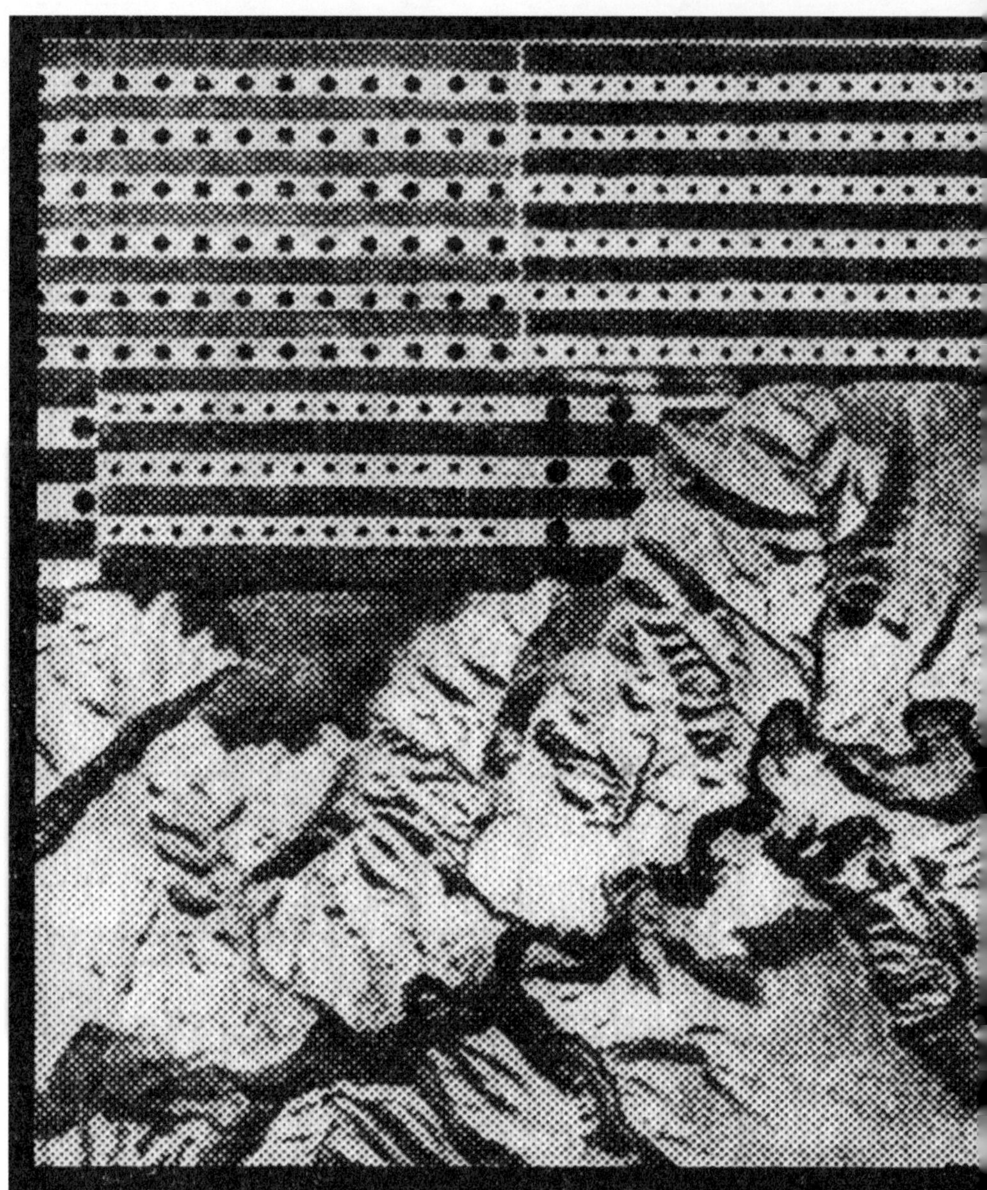

Fig. 16_ Archizoom, *No-Stop City* (view from above), 1971.

Leisure in a Time of Utopia[1]

Massimiliano Savorra

Il est probable que l'avenir est à une civilisation de casaniers, périodiquement en proie à des migrations saisonnières nommées vacances.[2]

Michel Ragon

Où vivrons-nous demain?

While writing *Où vivrons-nous demain?* a book on *l'architecture de l'avenir*—in 1963, even before he had started the Groupe International d'Architecture Prospective (GIAP)—Ragon was wondering about the forms of the city of the future: forms marked by nightmarishly large numbers, by huge mutations, by the rise in urban concentrations, by the problem of traffic, by secondary residences **(figs. 1-2)**. After the Second World War, with prosperity reaching large sections of the population and under the constant threat of the atomic bomb, utopian or dystopian visions of the future spread among numerous observers, including writers and artists as well as architects. The latter, Ragon remarked in his essay, were suggesting an infinite number of possible solutions in extraordinary drawings and proposals, ranging from the industrialization of homes to the creation of "sculpto-architecture."[3] Almost all of them laid claim to a new concept of leisure as well as, of course, everyday lifestyles.

Such a theme was so characteristic of a Zeitgeist dominated by the radical critique of society and of advanced capitalism, that it had been widely touched upon by a number of leading practitioners from a variety of disciplines under the influence of the Frankfurt School.[4] It was not an accident that the ***Société du Spectacle*** prophesied by Guy Debord was coming to light thanks to the growing "civilisation des loisirs," to quote the title of a study by Georges Hourdin,[5] a civilization which had made possible the evolution of the concept of work and of non-work, as well as a new perception of art, while also—in the analysis of other scholars[6]—enabling the post-war crisis to be overcome.

Leisure and holidays for all, now within everyone's reach, were no longer an illusion, and the future would hold the possibility of turning into reality the dream of living in fantastic cities where work, thanks to technological innovation, would be seen as liberation. On a number of occasions, from public debates to exhibitions, this new idea of leisure was seen as a political issue as well as an aesthetic one. The myth of play and young people, considered a new socioeconomic subject, went hand in hand with the myth of creativity on a daily basis. Building on the leading sociological work of Henri Lefebvre, the "critique de la vie quotidienne," the demand for a new reality joined the need for play and recreation to the practice of revolutionary fight.[7]

Alienation in society was dealt with by denouncing the conditions for the very existence of capitalism, first of all the illusion of plentiful consumption, the idea of turning life into spectacle, and the dominant, repressive urbanism. The newly envisaged life was instead to be based on the total liberation of human desires, in opposition to the conditioning of induced needs. In France and in Italy, the Situationists' movement was among the most active in denouncing the culture of advanced industrial civilization, which led to functionalism in architecture and the consumerist mass manipulation of leisure.

A Theoretical Contribution to the "Democracy of Leisure"

Three words, joined by equal signs, take pride of place in the middle of the page: "Leisure = Liberty = Choice."[8] They are preceded by a warning—"An a priori definition of leisure is dangerous and inopportune"—and followed by a clarification of the need to understand the complex meaning of leisure with a long dissertation on the urgent need to analyze its role of in people's lives, as well as on the opportunity to suggest plausible design models. Thus, the book *Planning and Design for Leisure* deals, perhaps for the first time in a systematic way, with the issue of architectures of mass tourism **(fig. 3)**. It was 1972, and the author was Georges Candilis (1913–1995), the well-known architect of Team 10,[9] summing up the results of his studies and achievements from previous years, suggesting, in his own words, an actual handbook of "genuine architecture of mass-leisure."[10]

Candilis starts from the assumption that coasts were undergoing change, and that pre-war hotels, casinos, summer residences and all other architecture for tourism—which in the past had been intended for the privileged class—were now practically "outdated." His introduction observes that holiday spots and *loisir* locations (yesterday's "privilege for one class," today's "right for the masses") were becoming, in the post-war years, prevalent everywhere and accessible to everyone, so much so that "large numbers" of holidaymakers had transformed and, sometimes, deformed, whole territories.

As well as being the architect—with Alexis Josic (1911–2011) and Shadrach Woods (1923–1973)—of numerous structures for holidays in France,[11] Candilis was an active protagonist in the theoretical debate on experimental projects for mass tourism; a proponent, in particular, of modular cells and mega-structures for leisure activities and especially about how leisure was taken into account in the construction of numerous tourist complexes and villages. The latter, according to some, had risen along the lines of communitarian-inspired seaside clubs; whereas, according to others, they had come about as camping sites later transformed into centers for "social tourism," thanks to a number of diverse corporate-sponsored clubs.[12]

Cellular Groupings for Tourism

The topic of leisure for the masses had already been dealt with in the early CIAMs, though "the sun, sea and sand industry" had played a fundamental role only from the 1950s onwards, not only in terms of national economies and cultural debate, but also in the theoretical reflections of architects and as a business opportunity for a large number of professionals. In particular, Candilis's research, made known in its fully-fledged form in his 1972 book, made a self-sufficient housing cell for tourist resorts the starting point for wider-ranging reflections. By means of a system of "predominance" (technological, functional, economic and esthetic), such cells—as shown in studies by other leading members of CIAMs—could be assembled horizontally or vertically (or a combination of the two), to give rise, when multiplied without limits, to a large homogeneous urban structure with a full complement of services.[13]

The leading idea underlying Candilis's projects for "democratic" tourism was the search for a human scale concerning four elements: a "family unit;" a "neighborhood unit" consisting of 20–30 bungalows; a "village autonomy unit" of 200 bungalows; and general facilities for the whole structure amounting to 1000 bungalows. Moreover, designing a large tourist complex could not happen without identifying and adopting simple technology. This meant that, in addition to defining blueprints and distribution of public spaces for the community—such as a small plaza with a theater, food distribution areas, boutiques, or sports facilities—it was of fundamental importance to study the organization of the cells and their aggregation patterns, down to the last detail.

Both the use of a grid and the rationalization of construction made for continuity in the distribution of collective functions corollary to housing functions. Moreover, by its very nature, the "context" of the construction, as well as the inspiration from surrounding smaller villages, offered a lesson on the distribution of the blueprints and on the design of architectural profiles. To this end, in his book Candilis set the images of a few tourism cells he had designed, with a 45°-degree orientation and arranged in the shape of a terrace, side by side with photographs of houses from an ancient nucleus in Cappadocia.

Among different types of cells, the architect also envisaged the "maison patio," an open-ended house on the Pompeii model designed by his partner Alexis Josic,[14] which, as well as meeting the requirements of the Mediterranean climate, allowed a large number of grouping patterns. (Candilis cited as examples his designs for Canet Plage and the Grau Village tourist complex at le Grau du Roi in the Gard, built by a group of architects led by Pierre Raoux.)[15] Such arrangements gave rise to a continuous and rational organization of volumes dovetailing into each other to form village units, called "maisons puzzle," which could develop in all directions.

In opposition to horizontal development, vertical development was determined by the necessity of a punctual "densification" which, in some cases, could be dictated by the need for a preferential view (in this way the garden-patio was replaced by a terrace-veranda). The concept of a modular cell also led to the "maisons dés," or "dice houses," which could be set up on their own or assembled in a number of combinations, up to building complexes on a territorial scale.[16] Such a concept harked back to the theory of the "cubical modular design" sketched in the 1930's by Albert Farwell Bemis (1870–1936). This theory of the industrialized housing cell developed, as is well known, from research on the *Mobile Home* by R. Buckminster Fuller (1895–1983), *Tomorrow's House* by George Nelson (1908–1986), and *Maisons à portiques* by Jean Prouvé (1901–1984). It continued well into the 1960s with the cells for *Maisons de vacances volantes* by Guy Rottier (1922–2013), the modules for the Finnish house *Futuro* by Matti Suuronen (1933–2013), and the *Bulles* by Pascal Häusermann (1936–2011)[17].

Mega-Structures for New Holiday Habitats

Apart from Candilis's theoretical reflections, it was precisely in the years between 1960 and 1967 that a definition of a multicellular mega-structure as an architecture for *loisir* started to gain ground. In particular, throughout "Megayear 1964," the year which saw, (as recollected by Fulvio Irace citing Reyner Banham), "the crystallization and offer as a product ready for consumption of an enormous corpus of drawings and ideas which had been in circulation for a long time."[18] However, it must also be remembered that 1964 was the year when the well-known Triennale in Milan adopted as a theme "Leisure Time."[19] The introductory part of the exhibition, with an international character, and set up by Umberto Eco and Vittorio Gregotti, raised questions on the very concept of "leisure," as conventionally intended, to offer visitors models far removed from the stereotypes to which they were accustomed: "rather than explain what leisure is, they clarify what 'it is not.'"[20]

In other words, during the Cold War years when the topic of the minimal cell was fleshed out in different ways (the United States saw the launch of government campaigns to persuade people to install prefabricated units as anti-atomic refuges),[21] nearly all visions and fragments of utopian cities suggested new habitats for holidays, based on the concept of a single-cell nucleus and "play" or "amusement" cities. It did not matter that such habitats would take on the look of a spaceships, of a micro-capsule refuge in a continuous mega-complex for post-atomic climates, or simply as a housing pod or a "cell as a uterus cavity."

From Candilis's theories and from experiments on cities as a macro-organism and on joinable capsules—one may think of such well-known examples as those by Archigram, the Metabolists or Italy's Archizoom and Superstudio,[22] but also those by Yona Friedman (1923–) and Justus Dahinden (1925–)[23]—two approaches had evolved by the end of the decade to deal with "large numbers."[24] On one hand, the idea of the holiday village as a small self-sufficient town or "miniature town," to use a term then fashionable; on the other, the concept of a mega-structure as the most suitable system for the creation of leisure-time settlements in any type of seaside or mountain landscape.[25] Among macro-complexes built in the mountains, for example, may be cited those by Dahinden in Rigi-Kaltbad, Switzerland and those built in 1966 by Michel Bezançon (1932–) on the Grande Plagne in Savoy **(fig. 4)**. While for the seaside, mention may be made of Guidel on the Gulf of Morbihan designed by André Gomis (1926–1971); the holiday village at Anglet near Biarritz designed by Aquitaine Architectes Associés (Jean Raphaël Hebrard, André Gresy, and Jean Percillier) **(fig. 5)**; and the complex built in 1968 by Kisho Kurokawa (1934–2007) for Yamagata Hawaii Dreamland near Tokyo.[26] (This last was a simplified transposition of the Sea City and Marine City projects designed years earlier by Kiyonoru Kikutake (1928–2011),[27] presented by Kenzo Tange (1913–2005) at the 1959 Ciam/Team 10 Meeting in Otterlo, and reworked in 1962, as the Ocean City model.[28]) It is interesting to remember that the utopian project for Tokyo by Tange in 1960 was presented in *Bauen + Wohnen* magazine together with "Ecumenopolis," a text by Constantinos Apostolou Doxiadis (1914–1975) on the city of the future, consisting of cells formed in already existing cities and by new centers created in remote areas.[29] After all, set-ups in remote natural areas were also characteristic of a few projects of mega-structures with a strong environmental impact, designed with the aim of exploiting to the fullest an area's potential for tourism, such as the 1967 proposal by Julio Lafuente (1921–2013) for a hotel built into the cliffs in Gozo, Malta **(fig. 6)**.[30]

Nevertheless, during the years straddling the 1960s and 1970s the poetics of mega-structural imagination—following the definition given at the 1978 Venice Biennale—dissolved, showing the full extent of its theoretical limits, in the search for new technological resources capable of meeting the growing demand for relaxation coming from mass society. That ethical imperative, even more than an esthetic one, moved the theoretical reflections of architects on the redefinition of the global touristic *polis*. The conviction that the attribution of a new meaning to the concept of such a *polis* also entailed the reconfiguration of a shared *ethos* resting on a vision of beauty capable of educating the masses. The most "militant" architectural culture came to terms with its failure to single out a *topos* that was alternative to reality and addressed its creative efforts toward "counter-design,"[31] denouncing the "anti-nature" condition in which humankind found itself. Yet the idea of a holiday village as a place *different from all other places*, built in accordance with new systems, remained for a few observers like Candilis the only guiding light which could modify, at least for a while, human behavior and define—in the general climate of the world's energy crisis—a new model of a habitat as refuge from the reigning middle-class consumerism (in this sense the "Polynesian dream" of Club Méditerrannée from twenty years earlier can be seen as pioneering work).

Innovations for *Loisir*: Prefabrication

In its various incarnations, the idea of an extensible cell still carried with it the concept of "cybernetic city" as imagined by the sculptor Nicolas Schöffer (1912–1992), and of domotics to fulfill the wishes of the new *Homo Ludens* (to quote the title of Johan Huizinga's book so beloved by the mega-structuralists).[32] In most cases, cities for holidays and leisure were based on the adoption of prefabricated serial elements that could be multiplied to create whole urban complexes in which the industrialization of building, installation, and setting processes became the main element of expression.[33] Whether integrated or not with residential and working cities, tourism citadels conceived between the end of the 1960s and the early 1970s were made up, at least in designers' intentions, by highly technological, easily transportable and (above all), functional, sectional dwelling units: thanks to the materials that were used.

Starting during post-war reconstruction, prefabricated homes for leisure—made out of the most innovative products from industry—had been the object of theoretical speculation and had already found space in journals and in exhibition sites for the general public.[34] During the following decade, characterized by the optimistic climate of the economic boom, the range of new materials available had further increased, making it possible to produce mobile and extensible units serially, which were also suitable for the needs of modern leisure.[35] As updated variants of trailers (such as the *Caravane Fleur* by Jean-Louis Lotiron and Pernette Perriand-Barsac), became extremely popular precisely in those years, such mobile units were conceived as bodyworks in resin, aluminum or steel, produced by companies investing in a constantly growing sector, especially in the United States, where nomadism was an established practice.[36]

Technical innovation was the starting point for holiday villages imagined in 1963 by Paul Maymont (1926–2007), made up of prefabricated cells and perched on remote coasts on steel cables, or floating on complicated systems of air mattresses as in his Thalassa project

(fig. 7): a man-made atoll off Monaco, inspired by the architect's 1959 experiments in Kyoto when he was a scholarship student.[37] Moreover, starting from the vision of the Metabolists, the "earthformation" of vast marine areas set aside for reception activities as well as for tourism had been prefigured in numerous other projects. One should think of the well-known visions of Manfredi Nicoletti (1930–) for Monaco's satellite city from 1966 **(fig. 8)**,[38] or the project by Paul Rudolph (1918–1997) for the Graphic Art Center imagined in 1968 for the Hudson River in New York as a vertical system from which prefabricated cells would "hang."[39]

In the wake of research by Alfred Neumann (1900–1968) and, independently, by Alfred Mansfeld (1912–2004), in many cases capsules were also devised in the shape of standardized stackable "boxes," as for example in the celebrated Habitat model by Moshe Safdie (1938–) at the 1967 Montréal Expo (resubmitted the following year in a project for Puerto Rico). Its residential units in prefabricated reinforced steel made for variegated combinations of geometry and typology, and showed how those cells—intended for dwellers infused with a new communitarian spirit,[40]—could be serially produced, raised for installation, and set up with extreme ease, so much so that the prototype as a whole was received by the press and by the critics as "an idea whose time had come."[41] By the end of the 1960s those prefabricated box-like elements, both sectional and single block, and intended for touristic use, started to make a name for themselves in countless articles in magazines as well as in composition exercises in schools of architecture.[42] Just like construction methods, patented systems, and modularity studies, theoretical suggestions of prefabrication were at the center of research on housing, and not just for holidays, giving rise to that "license for utopia,"[43] in Manfredo Tafuri's words, necessary for the creation of a new language.

Plastic Dreams

In the manifestos of "dreaming" architects (those who imagined cities with "retro-futurist" forms in *googie* style[44] and those who showed *ante litteram* "cyberpunk" dystopian settings), synthetic materials gave a new formal connotation to architecture, at least until the energy crisis of the early 1970s.[45] Starting from the prototypes by Ionel Schein (1927–2004) for *Maison tout en plastique* and *Cabine hôtelière mobile* presented at the Salon des Arts Ménagers in Paris halfway through the 1950s,[46] which were a throwback to the ideas of evolutionary habitat he devised together with Claude Parent (1923–)[47]—prefabricated single-block cells to be made of epoxy resins in the desired shapes and sizes—came to represent the most reassuring outcome of modern technological developments, applied to never-before-thought-of esthetic requirements.[48] Such plastic capsules could later be hooked, as had been envisioned in cluster cities, to vertical structures or set side by side until they formed complex housing units, as seen in *House of the Future* by Alison (1928–1993) and Peter Smithson

(1923–2003), the *Bakelite House* and *Corn on the Cob* by Arthur Quarmby (1934–), the plastic home by Renzo Piano (1937–), or the world-famous *Plug-in Capsule Homes* by Archigram's Warren Chalk (1927–1987).[49]

Variously interpreted as a model of association and free but systematized grouping,[50] the "cluster" concept was adapted by the Smithsons, in antithesis to Le Corbusier's idea of a city, to the needs of "flows," more than of "measurements," made possible by cells made of new materials such as epoxy resins, "a sort of derma-skeleton consisting of different parts with flexible joints to allow for temperature variations and structural discontinuity."[51] The "cluster" or "hive" could also be constituted of capsules made out of rubber, plastic, nylon, or asbestos, as hypothesized by David Georges Emmerich (1925–1996) in his elaborations of domes consisting of joined-up units, as well as in his projects for housing units called *Logemobile*.

Prefiguring an achievable dream, the plastic home made with a polyester bodywork would also become the distinctive cipher of hexagonal "multipurpose cells" and of "proliferating or parasite cells" devised in the early 1960s by Jean-Louis Chanéac (1931–1993), in collaboration with engineer Jean Nicoulaud. Longing for a recovered "biological memory" influenced the French architect's research, when he experimented with a cell prototype suitable for seaside and mountain settings, in isolated forms or assembled in "crater cities."[52] Research on plastics also interested Jacques Beufé (1926–2000), who in 1970—though the prototype is from 1972—devised the *Habitat de Loisirs modulable et flottant* suitable for wet sites and marshlands; Maurice-Claude Vidili (1937–), with experiments on the *Sphère d'isolement* from 1971; and Candilis himself who, in 1973, finalized the *Hexacube* cell **(figs. 9-11)** in collaboration with Anja Blomstedt (1937–).[53]

The circulation of ideas and images produced a number of comparable hypotheses similar in purpose and building technique. Among the many hypotheses that can be highlighted were the *Domobiles* by Häusermann and Patrick Le Merdy, in collaboration with Bruno Camoletti and Eric Hoechel;[54] the *Rondo* house devised by Angelo S. Casoni and Dante M. Casoni; the *Zip-Up House* by Richard Rogers; the *Tétrodon* by Atelier d'Urbanisme et d'Architecture; the *Maison de vacances DO-System* by Jean-Claude Ventalon and Ana Sklemar; the *12E Unit* by group Atelier 4 in Toulouse; or the *BANGA Cell* by Carlo Zappa.[55] All were designed, patented, and built between the early 1960s and 1970s.[56] Among these cell models the *Bulle six coque* outshone all others **(fig. 12)**: made in fiber-reinforced plastic and polyurethane by Jean Benjamin Maneval (1923–1986), it was used in 1968 for a holiday complex at Gripp in the Pyrenees by the ELF Oil Company (Société Nouvelle des Pétroles d'Aquitaine).[57] Twenty of these cells—designed in 1963,[58] but produced only from 1968 onward by the Bâti-plastique company (set up by Maneval with the Comité d'Entreprise des Pétroles d'Aquitaine)—were built, and consisted of a star-shaped structure made up of six polyester shells grouped around a core drop. Presented at Salon Batimat in Paris in 1967 and at Milan's Triennale in 1968, the *Bulle* met with astounding success, as it did when it was presented in 1971 at the IKA International Plastic Fair in Lüdenscheid, together with the *Rondo* house and the Finnish *Futuro* house.[59]

These polyester and fiberglass prototypes were used as seaside homes or mountain chalets, set on impassable terrains and in extreme climate conditions, and within a short time they were in great demand from countless companies eager to secure production rights. Suuronen succeeded in setting in motion the production of about a thousand *Futuro* houses, and the same number of the *Finlandia* and *Venturo* models, made of polyester, reinforced plastic, and fiberglass, and marketed through leaflets showing happy families on holiday **(fig. 13)**.[60] In 1967, along similar experimentally innovative lines, Roberto Menghi (1920–2006) also designed—for the Italian Touring Club holiday villages—some Shell units made of reinforced polyester similar to tents, characterized by virtually unlimited sectionality (they were produced by Industrie Composizioni Stampati and by Xilographia Milanese).[61]

Experimentation and Building Processes

The assumption that the birth of a new architecture would be made possible thanks to chemistry was the original utopian idea of William Katavolos (1924–), who had engaged since the early 1960s and well into the ww decade in research on different housing styles.[62] Under the effect of "activating agents," some chemical substances were able, in Katavolos's mind, to move from the initial state of dust or liquid to the solid state, thanks to a catalytic process. In this way the volumes deriving from it, intended for a variety of functions, could rise directly on the sea, thereby giving rise to whole cities. In any case, reinforced polyester (types, quality, calculation, molding) became the hot topic of the day, discussed in articles in specialized journals,[63] and presented in the complex structures of great expo sites, as for example at Osaka in 1970,[64] or in very controversial exhibitions, such as the celebrated Italy: The New Domestic Landscape curated by Emilio Ambasz at MoMA in New York in 1972.[65]

It should be remembered that, to control future developments in architecture and the high-density problems of "mammoth organisms," Rudolf Doernach (1929–) envisaged revolutionary changes: through the application of discoveries in biology and chemistry "today's scientists will be tomorrow's biochemical architects."[66] Plastic materials, in his opinion, would offer physical properties and ratios between weight and stability much more favorable than those of steel and reinforced concrete. This explains the use of expressions like "space age" and "mobile architecture," based on new building principles carried out by biochemical architects who would create "Biotecture."

To be sure, prefabricated cells made of heavy materials such as steel and aluminum (produced by building enterprises that had actually turned into industries) were penalized by high transport costs. Research therefore went toward light plastic elements, easy to move and set up, which could be produced at competitive prices compared to those of traditional components. Derived from methane or oil, thermosetting and thermoplastic materials in production (resins such as perspex, polyvinyl chloride, polypropylene, nylon) met designers' requirements for models suitable for actual or imagined lifestyles. On the other hand, the renowned "Monsanto House of the Future," devised by a team at MIT (Marvin Goody, Richard Hamilton, Robert Whittier, and Frank Heger) for Monsanto Chemical Company and built at Disneyland in 1956, had been made entirely of plastic materials.

At the end of the 1960s, attempts to create prefabricated modular housing on a semi-artisanal basis were set aside in favor of experimentation with reinforced polyester resins, which allowed for ease of transport and installation. Thus Architects engaged with designing tourist villages, not just with unit blocks, but also with elements such as "panel-walls" and "panel-coverings," sometimes also adopting mixed systems. A few examples of the use of "curved panels" and "pipes" in reinforced resin were presented in the early 1970s by Luigi Pellegrin (1925–2001) as the most suitable for tourist and hotel complexes.[67]

Moreover, controlling building processes was taken into consideration down to the last detail; insofar as it concerned single units, even as self-building and social participation were theorized as an alternative to industrial prefabrication. In the same way, "traditional" mixed building methods continued to be used, in particular when they were fast and cheap, as for example the *Siemcrete* building system (concrete, clay, and wood), used in 1968 by Fabrizio Carola (1931–) to build a tourist center in the shortest possible time for the French Touring Club in Taormina, near Al Kantara, consisting of microcell prefabricated elements.[68]

The same could be said of the process developed between 1969 and 1971 by Kristian Gullichsen (1932–) and Juhani Pallasmaa (1936–), who had devised a system called *Module*, useful for quick setting and dismantling of holiday villages, such as the complex at Savonranta—and for an invention in 1970 by Dante Bini (1932–), who created pneumatically-built semispherical cells made of reinforced concrete and designed in collaboration with Frei Otto (1925–2015) for a tourist settlement on the Isola dei Cappuccini at La Maddalena (Sardinia).

The ability to build housing with a "monocoque" structure cast on pneumatic formworks moved the scope of the discussion from the industrialization of the building process to relatively simple mechanized processes used as an alternative to heavy prefabrication.[69] With such a view, in 1967 Jean-Paul Jungmann (1935–) created the *Dyodon*, a pneumatic modular housing system; and, at the 1968 UIA congress, the Austrian Coop Himmelb(l)au presented its research on the *Villa Rosa* prototype, a project for "ballons palpitants"—as they were called by the architects— inflatable elements in PVC designed with the aim of stimulating the "imagination of bodies," since they theorized the disappearance of architecture in favor of modern technological devices and of seductive psycho-sensorial areas.[70]

Holiday Villages, "Genius Loci," and the Society of Spectacle

Aside from more or less utopian visions,[71] the idea of cells aggregated in mega-complexes for tourist purposes manifested itself tangibly in 1965 through the open competition for the San Sebastian Kursaal **(fig. 14)**, requiring "a luxury product, a container for the enormous summer fluxes, an opulent symbol suitable for enjoyment by a society capable of achieving through it the myth of its own wellbeing."[72] The search for a "typologically new form"—one that could fit into the environment and dialog with landscape morphology, climate conditions, and the urban fabric of the 19th-century city—was the organizers' aim. They further appreciated, not without misgivings, the winning project by visionary Polish architect Jan Lubicz-Nycz (1925–), precisely on the strength of its utopian force, divided as it was between "the surreal, expressionism, and science-fiction."[73] Such characteristics were also noticed by the jury members in the case of the multi-cellular mega-complex submitted by André Gomis's group; whereas submissions by Luigi Carlo Daneri (1900–1972) and by Sergio Jontof Hutter (1926–1999) offered a variation on the Smithsons's "cluster" concept, devised as a multi-center cluster, in which the "centers" were clearly visible both in plan and elevation.[74]

In Italy, an interesting case of large-scale application of Candilis's principles on modular cells could be found in the realizations from the early 1970s by OTE (Organizzazione Tecnico Edile Spa), a company assisting with the government-backed intervention program by EFIM Group to encourage the development of the tourist industry in the southern regions of the country (the *Mezzogiorno*). In particular, the holiday complex at Nicotera, built on behalf of the "Gioia del Tirreno" tourist company owned by the Insud holding on the area of a former military airport, consisted entirely of a set of typological elements made up of housing cells ranging over eight courtyards and linked to each other by paths designed like a "spatial model of urban behavior," to paraphrase the language used in those years by designers **(fig. 15)**.

The design team led by Pierfilippo Cidonio also included Pietro Porcinai (1910–1986), who devised a tree-planting program aimed at favoring each single cell while at the same time protecting them from sea salt deposits and winds. Similar complexes were built by OTE at Sibari, Isola di Capo Rizzuto, Simeri, and Crichi. Because of national economic plans which considered the expansion of tourist settlements as a fundamental instrument for the welfare of Italy's south, much work was carried out thanks to investment of public funds by the Cassa del Mezzogiorno, the "bank for the south." As a result, from the second half of the 1960s onward, a number of financial operations were started to create large holiday complexes, often without any regard for the landscape. Nevertheless, the idea of a village conceived as a set of multi-cellular structures inserted into the environmental context with respect for the *genius loci*, in accordance with Candilis's thought, is well represented by the *Gusmay* at Manacore, in the Gargano area between Peschici and Vieste,[75] by the settlements built for the ENI oil company at Pugnochiuso in the same area[76] as well as those designed on behalf of the Valtur tourist company by a team including Luisa Anversa Ferretti (1926–), Lucio Valerio Barbera (1937–), Gabriele Belardelli, and others.[77] Regarding formal repertoires devised to represent the "dignity of indigence," Claudia Conforti wrote—with reference to the experiments with social building by Ludovico Quaroni and Luigi Piccinato—that such efforts were "progressively intellectualized, until they made up a kind of vernacular esperanto, perfectly adaptable, in its manifold variations, to the tourist villages and holiday homes" that were mushrooming along the coasts of booming Italy.[78] Not only did the "most spectacular semantic reconversion take place through the tourist initiatives of the Costa Smeralda Consortium, coordinated by Michele Busiri Vici on Sardinia's east coast (1961–65)," but also through the "elegant formulations, diversified in relation to their environmental setting" in the Valtur villages at Ostuni (1967–69), Isola di Capo Rizzuto (1967–69), Brucoli (1969–72), and Pollina (1973–75).[79]

With reference to the villages built by Valtur—a company whose shareholders included, among others, Fiat, IMI, Esso, Alitalia, as well as Finmare and a few banks[80]—Carlo Aymonino wrote that the relationship between holiday village and setting is widened, to include "more fleeting references, though still present, such as natural elements—the coast, the trees, the terraces—or historical elements of the 'environment'—towns, isolated settlements, road networks—which may provide ideas for the settlement to be built from scratch."[81] At Ostuni, the existing farmhouse, the rocky valley, the country roads, and the skyline of houses were taken as leading motifs for the modular compositions of the village **(fig. 16)**; whereas at Capo Rizzuto, the coast, the brush vegetation, the terraced ground, and the olive tree plantations became inseparable from the multi-cellular warp-and-weft composition.

To be sure, aside from the idea of creating a set that would univocally hark back to its hotel function, "albeit in its complex and articulated form"—as Vieri Quilici wrote—it was necessary to identify an aggregation and an organization of cells that could meet the need for an "inspirational-recreational" order, that is to say forms that could engage the tourist psychologically.[82] That is why typological research as taught by Candilis became unavoidable, just as much as the search for a measured relationship between settlement and landscape, until it entered a homologous relationship with the landscape itself, "with its vocation, with its natural and cultural expressions."[83] For reasons to do with geology and anti-seismic measures, Valtur's village in Calabria took shape as a rigidly geometrical complex, whose brisk rhythm, as far removed from the picturesque as could be, recalled the "fastnesses looking over the sea, fortified villages, castles."[84] **In Puglia an extensive village of "farmhouses" was built by assembling modular elements, in different ways, around the hotel spaces.** Regarding the village at Brucoli in Sicily, critics noticed its "anthropo-geographical" aspect, highlighting its "compact" pattern, marked by the prevailing directionality of spaces arranged along an internal path with a perspective view, on which hinged the housing cells facing the seaside or Mount Etna **(figs. 17-18)**.

An Illusory "All-inclusive"

The backdrop sequences in villages flowed and ranged around small *piazze*, mostly opening toward harbors and other communal installations, which in some cases were the real engine behind realty activity as a whole, as at Port Grimaud in France by François Spoerry (1912–1999); Port El Kantoui in Tunisia by **Olivier-Clément Cacoub** (1920–2008); Porto Cervo in Sardinia by Luigi Vietti (1903–1998); and the island of Albarella—the site for the construction, starting from 1962 by Alideco, of two thousand units intended for a business clientele.

Unlike the above, devised from the start as exclusive locations, the Valtur complexes—modeled on Club Méditerranée, as for example the complex of Santo Stefano alla Maddalena (Sardinia) designed by Andrea Nonis (1929–) in 1965—contributed to the democratization of tourism consumption, in accordance with Candilis's ideas, through the illusory suggestion of a return to nature, wellbeing, and open-air life.[85] Such a suggestion was strongly characterized by a communitarian element, as Cesare de Seta remarked in an essay of 1977 with reference to studies by Hans Magnus Enzensberger and by Henri Raymond.[86] In other words, such an illusory suggestion came to be part, together with tourist villages, of the mythology of mass culture aspiring to the freedom of the "all-inclusive" package. This criticism was common among the intelligentsia of the time, which labelled the "villagers in the villages" conscious consumers of an "on-parole freedom" to be bought serially.

Holidaying masses from the early 1970's onward thus felt the need for communitarian living and new human relationships, which only tourist villages consisting of joined-up cells seemed able to offer. The playful activities imagined by Constant Nieuwenhuys (1920–2005) in his "New Babylon" and by all "situationists" in a transitory micro-world could take place in areas where theoretical momentary aggregations such as singing happenings, "aperitif games," or dancing shows found the appropriate location to manifest themselves, within the variable flexibility of the built environment.[87] In such a way, in the meeting of *imageability* and *expendability*, the renowned "Fun Palace," conceived by Cedric Price (1934–2003), as a scenic venue for multifarious drama experimentations,[88] was shattered into so many locations scattered along the coasts of the Mediterranean, a real "Toyland" suitable for receiving the masses longing to "participate," just as they did in many theater performances of the time, instead of being a purely passive public.

The axiom *par excellence* of pop culture—the equivalence of material and symbolic consumption—manifested itself in the idea of the "tourist village" in the shape of a tangible need. Many architects interpreted such a need by suggesting models of communitarian sharing and—applying Candilis's research—on new forms of housing in villages that also aimed, thanks to the combination of autonomous yet interdependent organisms, at a generic, as well as perceivable *genius loci*. A few of these models even became the expression of the everyday feeling of discontent experienced in the cities, long since deprived of a leisure component.

As in other artistic disciplines,[89] the reception of pop culture, for which everything could be seen in terms of consumption,[90] became manifest in a few showcase suggestions: specifically, in this case, in holiday centers which were impermanent, flexible, and appropriate to the ever-more mutable tastes of the *ordinary man*. It was fitting that in 1968 Guy Rottier should propose a touristic village consisting of housing cells made of cardboard to be burnt after use **(figs. 19-20)**. The architect's opinion was that the holiday town, in the service of "sheer leisure" was an illusion: "Amusement shall have to be in the cities where humankind may express itself. A town for holidays alone generates boredom. Amusement shall have to be one element of the city, a basic and complementary element. This is why holiday cities must disappear, leaving only a good or bad experience, everywhere. And nature shall remain untouched."[91]

Fig. 1_ Michel Ragon, *Où vivrons-nous demain?*, Paris: Robert Laffont, 1963 (book cover).

Fig. 2_ Jean Balladur, Yona Friedman, Walter Jonas, Paul Maymont, Michel Ragon, Nicolas Schöffer, *Les visionnaires de l'architecture*, Paris: Robert Laffont éditeur, 1965 (book cover).

Fig. 3_ Georges Candilis, *Planen und Bauen für die Freizeit/Recherches sur l'architecture des loisirs/Planning and Design for Leisure*, Stuttgart: Karl Krämer Verlag, 1972 (book cover).

Previous pages:
Fig. 4 (Above)_ Michel Bezançon, Tourist Complex on the Grande Plagne, Savoy, 1966-1980.
Fig. 5 (Below)_ Aquitaine Architectes Associés (Jean Raphaël Hebrard, André Gresy e Jean Percillier), Tourist Village, Anglet, 1969.

Fig. 6_ Julio Lafuente, Hotel, Gozo, 1967.

Fig. 7_ Paul Maymont, *Holiday Village*, 1963-1964.

Fig. 8_ Manfredi Nicoletti, *Satellite Town of Principality of Monaco*, 1966-1973 (maquette).

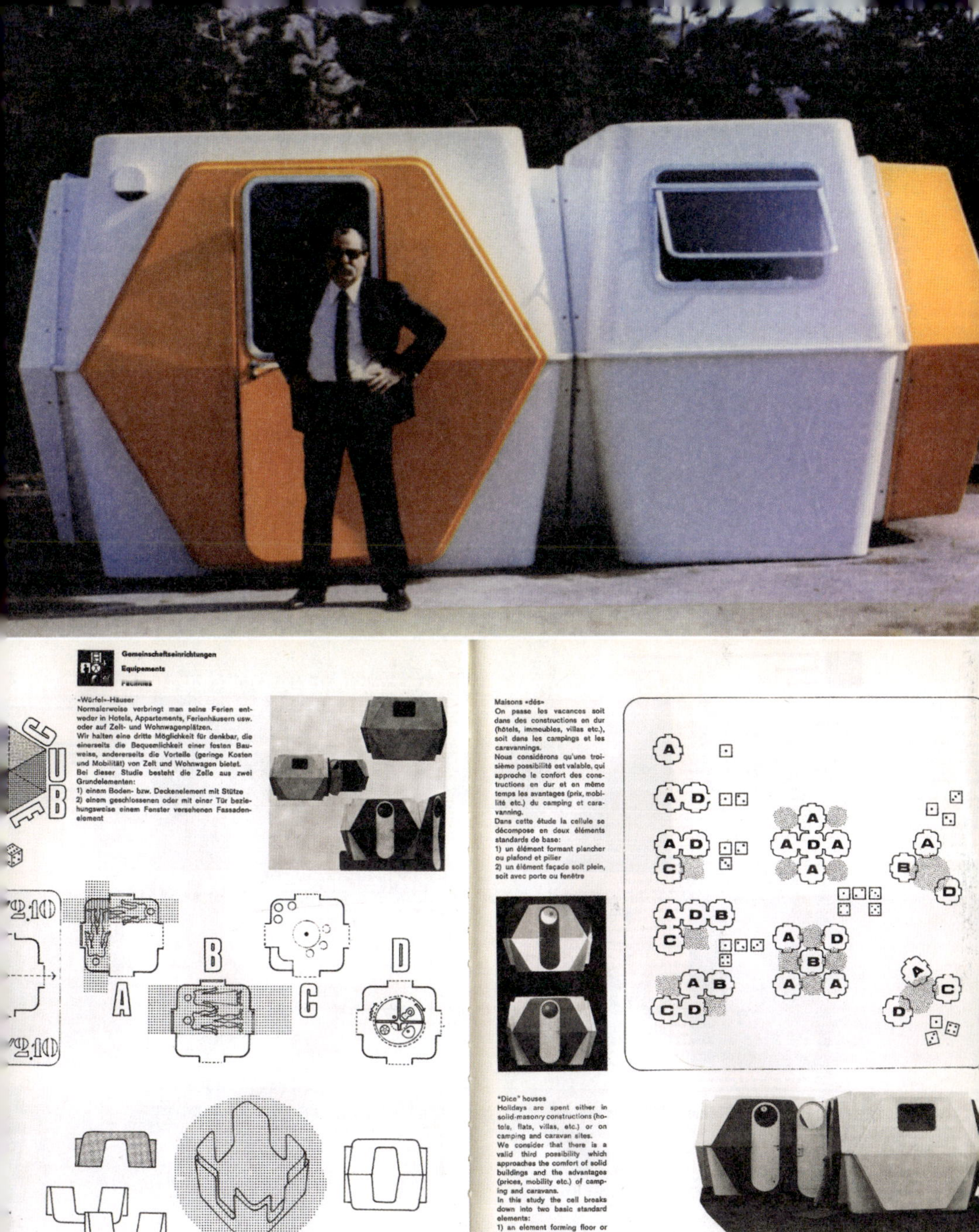

Gemeinschaftseinrichtungen

Equipements

Facilities

«Würfel»-Häuser

Normalerweise verbringt man seine Ferien entweder in Hotels, Appartements, Ferienhäusern usw. oder auf Zelt- und Wohnwagenplätzen.

Wir halten eine dritte Möglichkeit für denkbar, die einerseits die Bequemlichkeit einer festen Bauweise, andererseits die Vorteile (geringe Kosten und Mobilität) von Zelt und Wohnwagen bietet.

Bei dieser Studie besteht die Zelle aus zwei Grundelementen:

1) einem Boden- bzw. Deckenelement mit Stütze

2) einem geschlossenen oder mit einer Tür beziehungsweise einem Fenster versehenen Fassadenelement

126

Maisons «dés»

On passe les vacances soit dans des constructions en dur (hôtels, immeubles, villas etc.), soit dans les campings et les caravannings.

Nous considérons qu'une troisième possibilité est valable, qui approche le confort des constructions en dur et en même temps les avantages (prix, mobilité etc.) du camping et caravanning.

Dans cette étude la cellule se décompose en deux éléments standards de base:

1) un élément formant plancher ou plafond et pilier

2) un élément façade soit plein, soit avec porte ou fenêtre

"Dice" houses

Holidays are spent either in solid-masonry constructions (hotels, flats, villas, etc.) or on camping and caravan sites.

We consider that there is a valid third possibility which approaches the comfort of solid buildings and the advantages (prices, mobility etc.) of camping and caravans.

In this study the cell breaks down into two basic standard elements:

1) an element forming floor or ceiling and support

2) a facing element, which may be blind or have a door or window

127

Fig. 9_ Georges Candilis in front of the Hexacube Cell, 1970-73.

Fig. 10_ *"Dice" houses*, from Shadrach Woods, *Candilis-Josic-Woods: A Decade of Architecture and Urban Design*, Stuttgart : Krämer, 1978.

une nouvelle manière de vivre ...

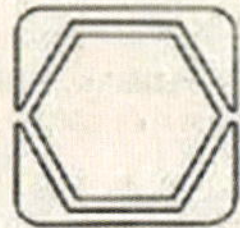

LE CUBING

avec l'HEXACUBE de Georges Candilis et Anja Blomstedt.

CIFAM s.a. **Compagnie Internationale des Fabrications Modernes**
2, chemin Ramelet-Moundi - 31300 Toulouse

TEL. : (61) 42.70.13 R.C. TOULOUSE 73 B 15 INSEE 735 31 555 0100 C.C.P. TOULOUSE 3132 58 M

Fig. 11_ Georges Candilis, advertisement for the *Hexacube Cell for Touristic Resorts*, 1970-73.

Fig. 12_ Jean Maneval, Bulle Six Coques, 1968.
Fig. 13_ Futuro House by Matti Suuronen on the left, the Bulle Six Coques by Jean Maneval in the middle, and Rondo House by Casoni & Casoni on the right, International Fair of Plastics, Lüdenscheid, 1971.

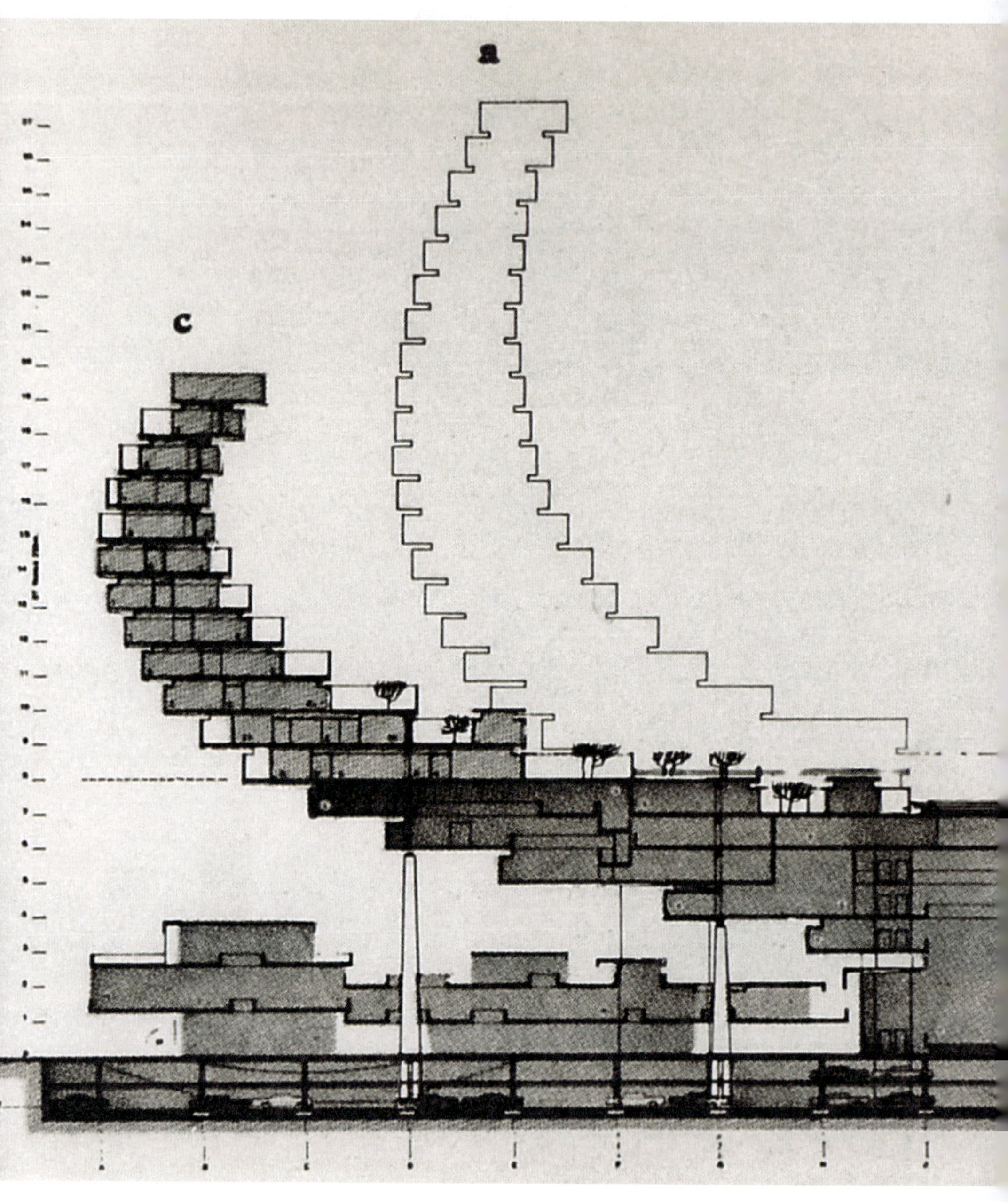

Fig. 14_ Jan Lubicz-Nycz, with Carlo Pelliccia and William Zuk, *Project of Euro-Kursaal*, San Sebastian, 1965.

d
b

Previous pages:
Fig. 15 (Above)_ OTE, Tourist Complex, Nicotera 1972.
Fig. 16 (Below)_ Luisa Anversa Ferretti, Gabriele Belardelli, Lucio Barbera, Claudio Maroni, Vieri Quilici, with Ufficio Tecnico Valtur, Holiday Village, Marina di Ostuni, 1967-1969.

Fig. 17_ Luisa Anversa, Lucio Barbera, Gabriele Belardelli, with Jean Weiler and Ufficio Tecnico Valtur, Holiday Village, Brucoli, 1969-1972.

Fig. 18 (Following page)_ Luisa Anversa, Lucio Barbera, Gabriele Belardelli, with Jean Weiler and Ufficio Tecnico Valtur, *Holiday Village in Brucoli* (plan), 1969.

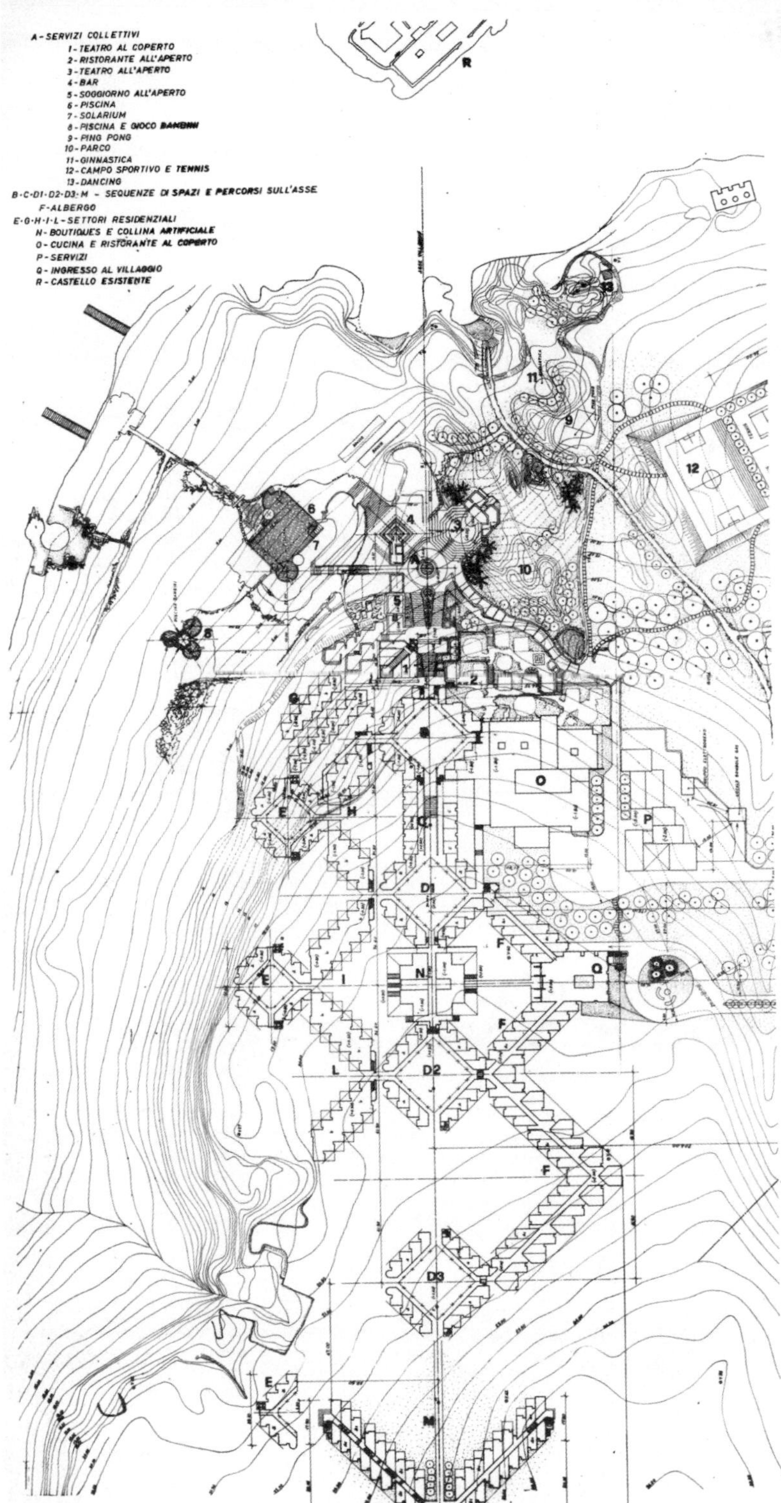
A - SERVIZI COLLETTIVI
1 - TEATRO AL COPERTO
2 - RISTORANTE ALL'APERTO
3 - TEATRO ALL'APERTO
4 - BAR
5 - SOGGIORNO ALL'APERTO
6 - PISCINA
7 - SOLARIUM
8 - PISCINA E GIOCO BAMBINI
9 - PING PONG
10 - PARCO
11 - GINNASTICA
12 - CAMPO SPORTIVO E TENNIS
13 - DANCING
B·C·D1·D2·D3·M - SEQUENZE DI SPAZI E PERCORSI SULL'ASSE
F - ALBERGO
E·G·H·I·L - SETTORI RESIDENZIALI
N - BOUTIQUES E COLLINA ARTIFICIALE
O - CUCINA E RISTORANTE AL COPERTO
P - SERVIZI
Q - INGRESSO AL VILLAGGIO
R - CASTELLO ESISTENTE
R
A
B
C
D1
D2
D3
E
F
G
H
I
L
M
N
O
P
Q

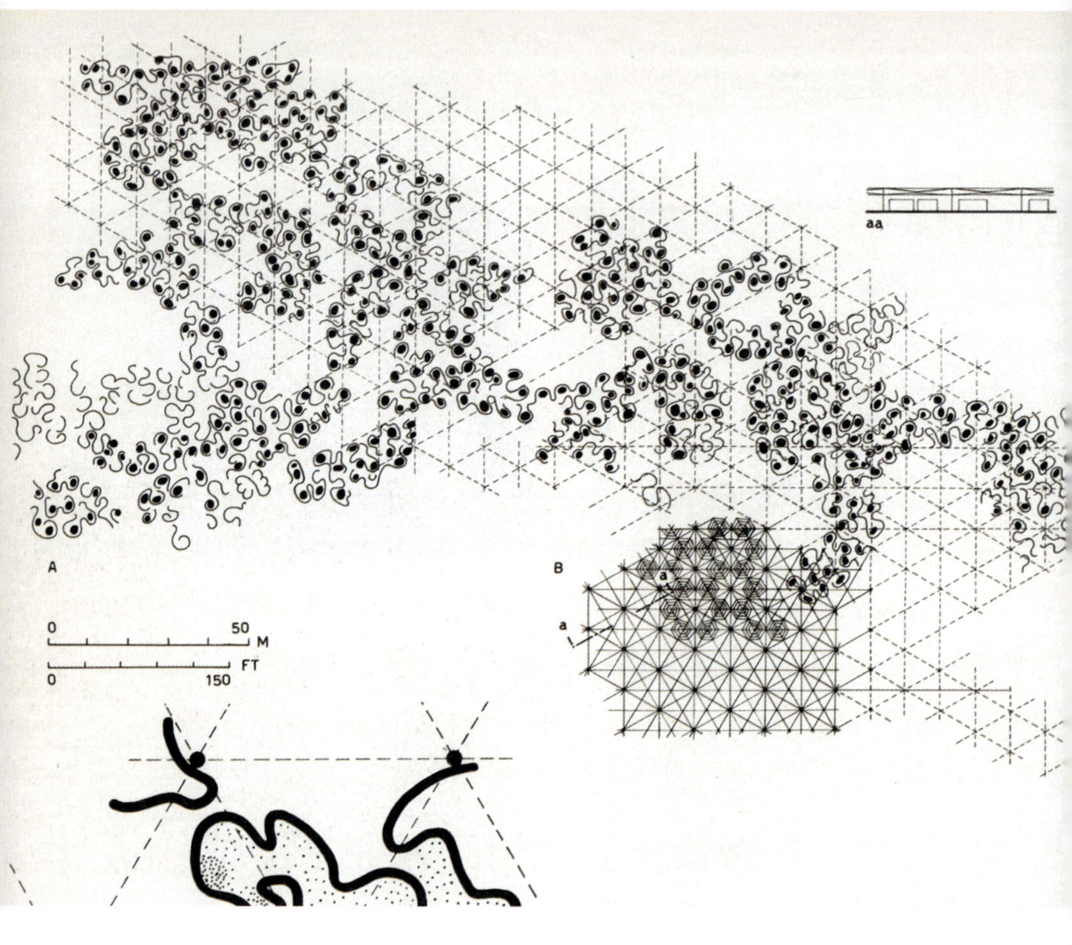

Fig. 19_ Guy Rottier, *The Relaxation Town, to Be Burnt after Use* (A: "Possible Assembly of Shelter Dwellings;" B: "The Spider's Web Mesh Completed by a Plastic film or Similar Cover;" a-a: "Section through the Typical Structure"), 1968.

Fig. 20_ Guy Rottier, *The Relaxation Town, to Be Burnt after Use*, 1968 (maquette).

Games without Frontiers[1]

Simon Sadler

Utopia has all but disappeared as a figment of the popular imaginary, whereas dystopian imagery can be readily brought to mind. *The Hunger Games*, to take the 2008 blockbuster book and movie series as an example, hits most of the key features of dystopia: domination, scarcity and inequality by the dictate of the state. The movie also makes games its central theme, and this essay will very briefly trace games from their keynote role in the early 20th century avant-garde's art-into-life program through to their establishment as a trope in architecture and design. This entailed a sublimation of utopianism into gaming, correlating with a waning of belief in the state and its planning apparatus as the preferred organizer of the future. In its stead games offered a strategic path to the future, and a prefiguration of it. Games became increasingly instrumental, to the point that the state itself could assume the guise of master of ceremonies, from the real 1965 pan-Eurovision television show *Jeux Sans Frontières* to the fictional *Hunger Games*.

Utopian Play from Pleasure to Organization

The realization of the self and the social through play was a point of departure for the modernization of culture from the Enlightenment on, since it promised to reconcile freedom and constraint. In *Émile, or On Education* (1762), Jean-Jacques Rousseau saw in children the "natural" source of the ideal citizen, and Friedrich Schiller, in *On the Aesthetic Education of Man* (1794), identified in humans a "play drive" able to reconcile such contradictions of experience as life and form, the pre-rational and the rational.[2] This foundational insight into play's valuable combination of rules and urges (glimpsed again, in different ways, in Friedrich Nietzsche [*The Birth of Tragedy*, 1872], Sigmund Freud [*Civilization and Its Discontents*, 1930] and Herbert Marcuse [*Eros and Civilization*, 1955]) remains important to an interpretation of the 20th-century avant-garde, for whom toys, games, play and pleasure were recurring tropes.[3] Among the puns included in cubist collages in the years just prior to the First World War, as the collages traced a formal, semantic and perceptual game invented by their artists, were plays on the French word for play itself, *jouer*; and at the end of a day in the studio, Pablo Picasso and Georges Braque would retire to an evening at the circus. Dadaists played games of chance; Surrealists generated spontaneous meaning through pursuits like Exquisite Corpse. So too was spontaneity central to vanguard politics: Picasso and Braque were typical of the artists and designers drawn in the late-19th- and early-20th-centuries to anarchism.[4] "One of our greatest architects, Walter Gropius," wrote the anarchist Colin Ward in 1966, "proclaims what he calls the technique of 'collaboration among men,' which would release the creative instincts of the individual instead of smothering them. The essence of such technique should be to emphasize individual freedom of initiative, instead of authoritarian direction by a boss [...] synchronizing individual effort by a continuous give and take of its members."[5] Here Ward (at the time formulating an anarchist politics of children and playgrounds,[6] it should be noted), hoped to deploy the legacy of Gropius and the avant-garde to organize, synchronize, and reciprocate the autonomous desires of individuals and small groups with the liberation of society at large **(fig. 1)**. Avant-gardism ordinarily sought alliances with socialism, the better to take over the organization of life via the state. Yet a dialectic between socialism and anarchism—something like a political corollary of the tension between Apollonian reason and form, and Dionysian spontaneity and life, as identified by Enlightenment theories of play—was recognized by artists and designers from at least William Morris onwards.[7] And in its search for a just state (or, better, something superseding the state), vanguard play became incrementally more instrumental: this was implicit in Bauhaus experimentation in the 1920s, where a student's "innate" sense of materials and aesthetics prototyped new forms, and where theater suggested new social spaces, even as its *Neue Sachlichkeit* culture at large projected a utopian condition of Reason.

After the Second World War, legatees of the Bauhaus—like Black Mountain College in North Carolina from 1933 to 1957, or the Imaginist Bauhaus and Global Tools gatherings in Italy in the 1950s and 1970s—can be recognized as such much less by their aesthetic choices and curriculum than in their playful prefiguring of a free culture. Global Tools produced little that has entered history as iconic, and no figurative future utopia. Instead, the organizers explained in 1974, that "the school [...] proposes enhancement of the creative faculties in every individual human being, faculties that are presently stifled by specialization and the frenzy to achieve efficiency"[8]. Perhaps the closest that the "school" came to making architecture or any public product was, significantly, a game: Riccardo Dalisi's workshop with street children in Rione Traiano, Naples, from 1971 to 1975. The foregrounding of play is obvious when we draw a comparison between the sorts of post-War bricolage craft seen at the Imaginist Bauhaus and Global Tools, and its Arts and Crafts antecedents, which demonstrated a commitment to the betterment of the world through the patient acquisition of consummate technique. With the bricoleur, as Claude Lévi-Strauss noted in 1962, we find "someone who works with his hands and uses devious means compared to those of a craftsman.[9]"

Black Mountain, the Imaginist Bauhaus and Global Tools, as highly redolent as they were of the *art* of play, also corresponded with a mid-century, *scientific* concern with play as a mode of social and cognitive development. To be a fully perceiving and comprehending adult, one needed first to access the child within: "it would seem that to perceive the expanded world," explained György Kepes, in his art and science crossover role in 1956, "we need to return to our prior mode of perception, and, as children do, see interactions rather than things."[10] This revived the experiential learning demanded by the Pragmatism of George Mead and John Dewey, which by the 1970s would become educational doctrine; Dewey (who used children's building blocks as one analogy) was preparatory reading for Charles and Ray Eames as they devised toys in the 1950s.[11] In something like a revival of the Dionysian and Apollonian, Dewey claimed that creativity could be experienced only within a regime of imposed limitations.[12] The converse presumably was equally true—constraint without play would engender a sort of madness—as illustrated delightfully in the "metalogue" written in 1953 by cyberneticist and anthropologist Gregory Bateson, in the form of a conversation between himself and his young daughter. "If we both spoke logically all the time, we would never get anywhere," Bateson mused in his "About Games and Being Serious." "We would only parrot all the old clichés that everybody has repeated for hundreds of years."[13] "I play with [...] ideas," he goes on, "in order to understand them and fit them together. It's 'play' in the same sense that a small child 'plays' with blocks [...]. And a child with building blocks is mostly very serious about his play.'"[14]

Serious Games

At one level, then, the trope of games and play retained a sense of the carnivalesque of the early avant-garde. Marcel Duchamp, for instance, was instated as a game-loving, chess-playing scalawag by his Pop Art admirers in the 1950s and 1960s. But a strategic, cognitive and semiotic seriousness was imbued in games from the 1930s on, as though trying to recover a "deep structure" of organization during the ascent of so-called civilization, and all insisting, in various ways, on the productive tension between play and constraint. Tapping an unconscious mapped by Sigmund Freud, Surrealist games attempted to access a more profound order than that admitted by the bourgeois world: much more than just pleasure, the repetition and destruction afforded by play, Freud explained in 1920, allowed the human subject to compensate for difficulty, contain it, and adapt to it.[15] Existing in its demarcated spaces, play was functioning as nothing less than the prime mover of culture: the Dutch cultural historian Johan Huizinga contended in his 1938 thesis (read a little later by avant-gardes like the Situationists) that we are players before we are knowers or makers—that our species is *Homo Ludens* before it is *Homo Sapiens* or *Homo Faber*.[16] Psychologist Jean Piaget meanwhile identified children's play as a vital stage in epistemological and social development, and Roger Caillois's influential 1958 sociology, translated in 1961 as *Man, Play and Games*, expanded upon Huizinga's thesis by classifying games and interpreting social structures as elaborate forms of play.[17] Games allowed players to interact with new technological worlds, Caillois observed, or even encourage competition between the self and cultural norms, such that the player "avenges himself upon reality, but in a positive and creative way."[18]

Perhaps literally: games could be commandeered for revolutionary activity, or so at least hoped Guy Debord, a co-founder in the 1950s of the Situationist International, when he tried to popularize the military theories of Sun Tzu and Carl Von Clausewitz through his *Game of War* **(fig. 3)**.[19] Launched in 1977, Debord wondered whether his board game would be the achievement for which he would be most remembered, rather than his seminal cultural analysis, deconstructive films, and political organization. The economy itself had become the subject of the most popular board game of the century, *Monopoly* (1935), and economics was sincerely approached by mid-century economists as a type of game, especially in the US, where game theory's mathematical models of conflict and cooperation revolutionized the analysis of decision-making in fields from economy to diplomacy to biology to philosophy.

The projected organization of the world through games would be, then, both an end to utopianism, and a new beginning for utopianism, for modernists and anti-modernists alike. In her landmark studies of the 1960s, Jane Jacobs included the assimilation of children as one hallmark of a traditional and truly living city,[20] while Cartesian rationalism appeared moribund even to Le Corbusier from the 1930s on, as his murals become playful and his forms more ambiguous. Mid-century, no planned, principle-driven final state for the world seemed possible—no telos, or ultimate purpose, of the sort that made Le Corbusier's 1924 Ville Radieuse utopian, with its determinate form for the execution of the great Hegelian, rational and technological "laws" of history. His urbanism was anchored no longer by productivity but crowned, at the 1947-52 Unité d'Habitation, with a playground. Starting at the same time and stretching over the following three decades, architect Aldo van Eyck provided a widely-emulated interest in design for play and committed to designing hundreds of playgrounds for Amsterdam **(fig. 4)**. This was to be a golden age of playground building, cresting in the adventure playgrounds originally suggested in 1931 by the Danish landscape architect C.Th. Sørensen.[21] Nigel Henderson's 1950s street photography of children's games on the streets of East London became central to Alison and Peter Smithsons' *Urban Reidentification Grille* for CIAM in 1953 **(fig. 5)**; and the Smithsons's Robin Hood Gardens scheme, of 1964-1973, was organized around the play area at its center. "Take your pleasure seriously" the Smithsons's friend Charles Eames famously advised, as he and Ray Eames devised *The Toy* (1951) and the *House of Cards* game (1952), aids to lifelong learning for the child and adult alike. "Toys are not for children," one of the Eames's grandchildren told *Vogue* magazine in 1959. "They are for grandparents."[22]

John Maynard Keynes predicated in 1930 that the work week would decline to fifteen hours,[23] a forecast that seemed very possible in the post-War decades. More than just a way to fill out the hours of leisure freed by automation and by which to compensate (as Caillois suggested) for the bondage of work, recreation increasingly suggested a "counter-state," organizing nations and the planet from the inside-out rather than from the top down. French situationist Jacques Fillon, for instance, promised Marxist-anarchist "New Games!" in a 1954 manifesto (available in English by 1970 in as handy a format as Ulrich Conrads's *Programs and Manifestoes on 20th-Century Architecture*).[24] Life might be opened up to the operations of chance, which were central to the aesthetics of John Cage, and generalized by the deployment of one of Cage's tools, the *I-Ching*, throughout counterculture. The "zome" geometry of the iconic, bricolage buildings of the outlaw early-hippie settlement of Drop City in Colorado were part inspired by designer Steve Baer's observation of his wife, Holly Baer, manipulating a child's toy into semi-regular figures **(fig. 6)**. Baer and Drop City colleagues launched their Zomeworks structural products company with playground climbers, and in 1969-1970 patented the *Zometoy*, a ball-joint and strut system later used for modeling molecules in laboratories.[25] In *Playpower*, of 1970, Richard Neville documented the reinvention of the world by the Beats, by the Paris barricades of May 1968, and by the Hippie trail; counterculture devised elaborate socio-psychological games, like those choreographed by Lawrence and Anna Halprin, and documented in *The RSVP Cycles* (1969) as preliminary site surveys for a reinvented Northern California **(fig. 7)**. Cedric Price's and Joan Littlewood's early 1960s *Fun Palace* projects aimed to facilitate games directly through the deployment of technology as part of a campaign for democratic creativity.[26] In their wake, the Archigram group began by depicting the city itself as a "found" game at the *Living City* show of 1963, and the group's only completed building was a 1972 Adventure Play Centre for Calverton End, Milton Keynes **(figs. 8-9)**. Arguably the summary built icon of the post-War period, Piano and Rogers's Pompidou Center, completed 1977, positioned a sense of play as a value shared with the French state itself. Indeed, the idea for *Jeux sans Frontiers* ("Games without Frontiers," or *It's a Knockout*)—the famous pan-European television gameshow, with its architecturally-scaled sets and costumes, broadcast from 1965—reportedly came from French president Charles de Gaulle, who hoped to convert historic and bloody French and German rivalry into friendly play.[27]

But singer Peter Gabriel's 1980 hit record *Games Without Frontiers* surreally inverted *Jeux sans Frontiers* into a meditation on international relations—which had indeed become subject to game theory. The video accompanying the record included footage of crashing toy trains and cars, and excerpts from Leni Riefenstahl's 1938 film of the infamous 1936 Berlin Olympics: this creeping sense that play was rote, sanctioned, even a mandatory and manufactured sublimation of politics, helps date a post-War dystopian turn around the ludic ideal earlier glimpsed in the proxy diplomacy of games like cricket (propagating Empire through a class-specific sense of "fair play") and the Olympics, their German tragedy repeated in the bloodshed at Munich in 1972. Constant's 1959-74 *New Babylon* project, disowned by the sections of the Situationist International but an icon nonetheless of Situationism, revived the heroism of the inter-war Ville Radieuse as a post-war labyrinth that instituted Fillon's "New Games" as a permanent, apparently mandatory game **(fig. 10)**. The monumentalization of games and festivity, witnessed in the Olympics, *New Babylon* and the Pompidou Center, would occupy visions of the future too, in the surest sign that gaming was assuming an instrumentality. Rather than see anarchic play further reified and technically managed, then, 1968 handbills of British anarchists King Mob urged readers to "Occupy the Fun Palace" before Price and Littlewood could even build it.[28]

New Babylon, the *Fun Palace*, and the like were in turn antecedents for the immersion of contemporary gaming culture and of post-industrial citizenship, a cultural foray enacted by the British state in 2000 by the Millennium Dome, which drew upon the cream of UK design talent—much of which had been schooled in design's "game turn" of the 1950s, 60s and 70s—to create situations (like the world's largest table-football game, gathering strangers into teams) exploring the playful, competitive uncertainty welcomed by the Dome's corporate sponsors in banking and information technology.[29] This preparation for a fantastical, borderless, globalized interaction (for "war without tears," as Peter Gabriel's lyric put it) was prototyped in Stewart Brand's *New Games* tournaments, exported globally from California in 1973, which included games like "Slaughter," where two groups attempted to push a large ball, painted like the planet, over the other side's line, with no overt winners or losers, since rules allowed players on the winning side to switch to the losing side—saving the world.[30]

Such New Age game-playing modeled the *obligation* of global and civic citizenship. Brand (founder in 1968 of the hippie *Whole Earth Catalog*) had been an acolyte of Richard Buckminster Fuller ("a child is comprehensive," remarked Fuller in a 1972 book, *Buckminster Fuller to Children of Earth*: "he wants to understand the [...] Universe")[31] **(fig. 11)**. Fuller presented the entire global system as a World Game, his alternative to war games. "The use of the word 'game' [...] is [...] instructive," the Buckminster Fuller Institute has since explained: "it says a lot about Fuller's approach to governance and social problem solving. Obviously intended as a very serious tool, Fuller choose to call his vision a 'game' because he wanted it seen as something that was accessible to everyone, not just the elite few in the power structure who thought they were running the show."[32] *How to Play the Environment Game*, an exhibition which toured the UK from London's Hayward Gallery 1973, similarly suggested a social ecological model of resource allocation and decision making after the disappointment of modernist environmental planning **(fig. 12)**.[33]

These "games" still hewed to an ultimately rational program of citizenship and resource distribution, be that founded in social contracts, or in Malthusianism, or in cybernetics, or in communications theory. In 1965 Marshall McLuhan described games as a mass medium of social catharsis, and so as one of "the extensions of man."[34] But the logic and teleology of the global system-game was under increasing pressure in the 1960s and 1970s, with second-order cybernetics implying the impossibility of a overall governor for the global system, and as epistemology itself was successively impacted by second-order cybernetics and poststructuralism. "Daddy, do our talks have rules?," Bateson (a second-order cyberneticist) scripted his daughter asking him in his 1957 metalogue. "The purpose of these conversations is to discover the 'rules'", Bateson imagined himself responding. "It's like life—a game whose purpose is to discover the rules, which rules are always changing and always undiscoverable".[35] Over the next couple of decades, French structuralism too would discover a regime of free play in the making of meaning, rendering the universe an interpretive game. Jacques Derrida's 1966 essay "Structure, Sign, and Play in the Discourse of the Human Sciences" notoriously observed the absence of a center, of a presence, in the structure of meanings and of the humans who make them; freed of linear meaning, Roland Barthes noted in 1971 of the unlimited freedom afforded by semantic dislocation, readers become active co-producers of a writer's meaning (a postulate since become central to the design of video games and their "emergent stories").[36] As with meaning, so too with matter in the post-structuralism of Félix Guattari and Gilles Deleuze, the latter eventually drawing a celebrated analogy between transformations in the world and the playful Japanese art of origami.[37]

With no stable rules, the "game" of late- and post-modernism, from epistemology to finance to design, was open-ended—perhaps to the point of neurosis, or ecstasy. "Architecture," MIT's Nicholas Negroponte wrote in 1970, "unlike a game of checkers with fixed rules and a fixed number of pieces, and much like a joke, determined by context, is the croquet game in Alice in Wonderland, where the Queen of Hearts (society, technology, economics) keeps changing the rules."[38] While Negroponte reached this conclusion in quest for an "Architecture Machine," his postmodern colleagues were encouraging semiotic play, which would perhaps allow for the transgression of stable subjectivity itself, the culture of pleasure raised to the excess of *jouissance* (as Jacques Lacan suggested).[39] Architect Bernard Tschumi presented this possibility in "Ropes and Rules," one of his 1976-77 *Advertisements for Architecture*: "The game of architecture is an intricate play with the rules that you may break or accept. These rules, like so many knots that cannot be untied, have the erotic significance of bondage: the more numerous and sophisticated the restraints, the greater the pleasure."[40]

Gamed Gamers

Nonchalance about the rules and purposes of games are inconsequential when they are *just* games (even games at the scale of culture), but of course potentially dystopian if games are modes or metaphors for political organization. Consider, say, the ascent of the throwaway notecard as a device in design, from the Eames's *House of Cards* **(fig. 13)**, to the 5,000 Post-It notes affixed to a wall at the Millennium Dome (a metaphor of multi-tasking), to the deployment of Post-It notes as the key medium of contemporary "design thinking": by playfully seeking association, collaboration, and the ephemeral, the notecard seemingly naturalizes decision making, with little concern for the assumptions and agency underwriting it. Game theory was meanwhile hampered by its utilitarian assumptions, first in their petty limits (why not facilitate interactions beyond those of immediate, individual utility?), second in their casting of rational actors bereft of other forms of motivation (like custom, community and empathy).[41] And whereas anarchists fret about what is being prefigured in their actions,[42] and by whom—the better to defy domination (by capitalist, racist, militarist patriarchy)—the anarchic borrowings of the creative disciplines from situationism, libertarianism, poststructuralism, ecology, and direct action have presumed that creativity itself is the key heuristic, negating the need for guiding principles.

So we might ask: in its efforts to game the status quo, is creativity gamed by the status quo? Alongside tropes like self-help, self-organization and entrepreneurship, games potentially surrender the power to rationally redistribute the very power and resources necessary for new and better games, leaving only limited archipelagos of players unable or unwilling to invite new players (the high intellectual, geographical and social barriers for entry into the early 20th-century Parisian avant-garde are echoed a century later in Silicon Valley). Gamers might be playing a world whose rules they have not set: consider the possibility that Tactical Urbanists—whose temporary, often witty and surreal interventions pre-empting urban government (such as parklets, i.e. parking spaces requisitioned for the public or public-private realm)—might be gamed by neoliberal capitalism, which has already put the state's monopoly on planning politics in retreat, and encouraged "enterprise" in its stead.[43] Markets themselves became ever more game-like with the de-regulation of Wall Street and the digitization of exchange in the 1990s.[44] Vanguard games earlier in the century imagined subverting bourgeois order, but, as the architectural historian Manfredo Tafuri concluded in the 1970s, the organized chaos which this essay has presented in its guise as game culture was a bid by the bourgeoisie to make sense of the storm it unleashed as capitalist modernization.[45] Designers might be left wielding only "an editorial authority that sits somewhere between top-down and bottom-up to orchestrate a networked design process fit for the mechanics and mental theatre of the 21st century," as one critic characterizes the recent variant of the game phenomenon as "open source architecture."[46] And video gamers have developed skills useful to the military institutions which historically invested in simulation.

There were compelling epistemological, critical and creative reasons why utopianism all but disappeared after the mid-twentieth century, because utopianism boxed-in the future—both literally and figuratively, in the case of architecture. But with the scourge of over-prescription and over-design off the table, we are still seeking games sufficient for the collective and informed programming of the future (markets? Flash mobs? Reality television and its political pretenders? Apps? An ersatz direct democracy of "likes"?). As the future became a game without frontiers, fun could auger dystopia.

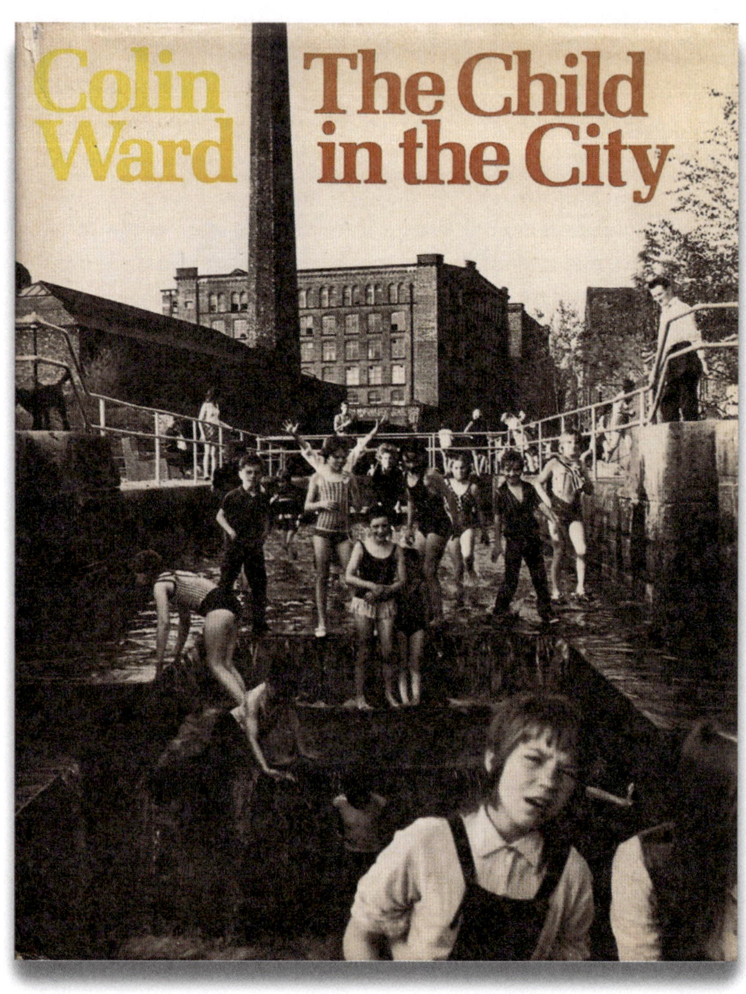

Fig. 1_ Colin Ward, *The Child in the City,* London: Architectural Press, 1978 (book cover).

Fig. 2_ Riccardo Dalisi, *Project for the Rione Traiano*, 1970.

Fig. 3_ *A Game of War,* after Guy Debord and Alice Becker-Ho, *Le jeu de la guerre*, Paris: Éditions Gérard Lebovici, 1987.

Fig. 4_ Aldo van Eyck, Playground in Laurierstraat, Amsterdam, 1965.

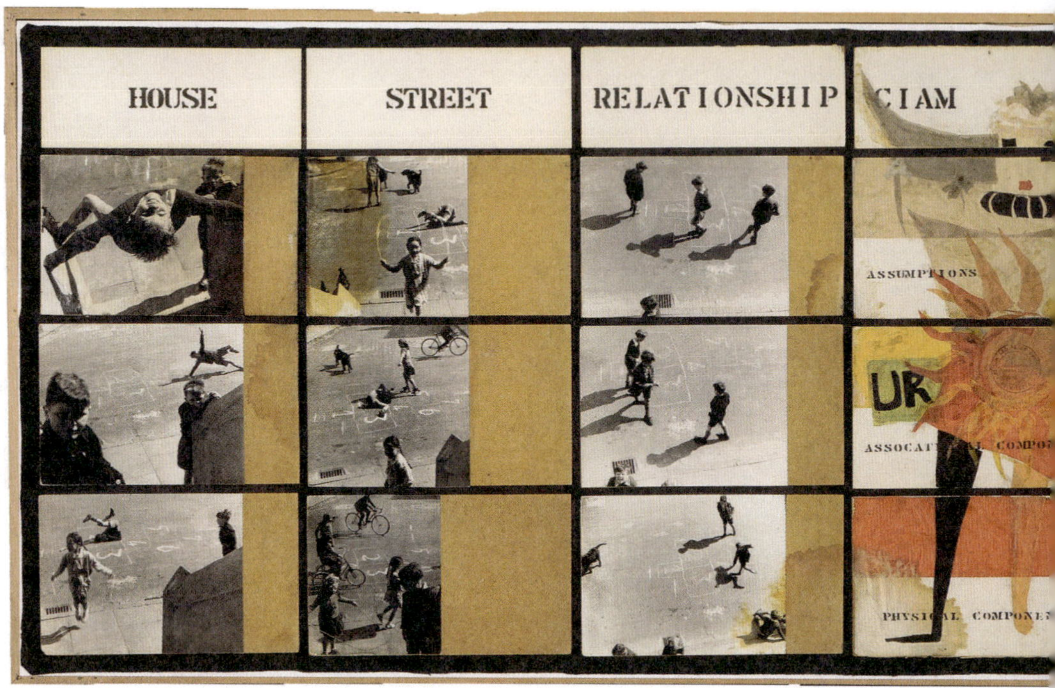
HOUSE
STREET
RELATIONSHIP
CIAM
ASSUMPTIONS
UR

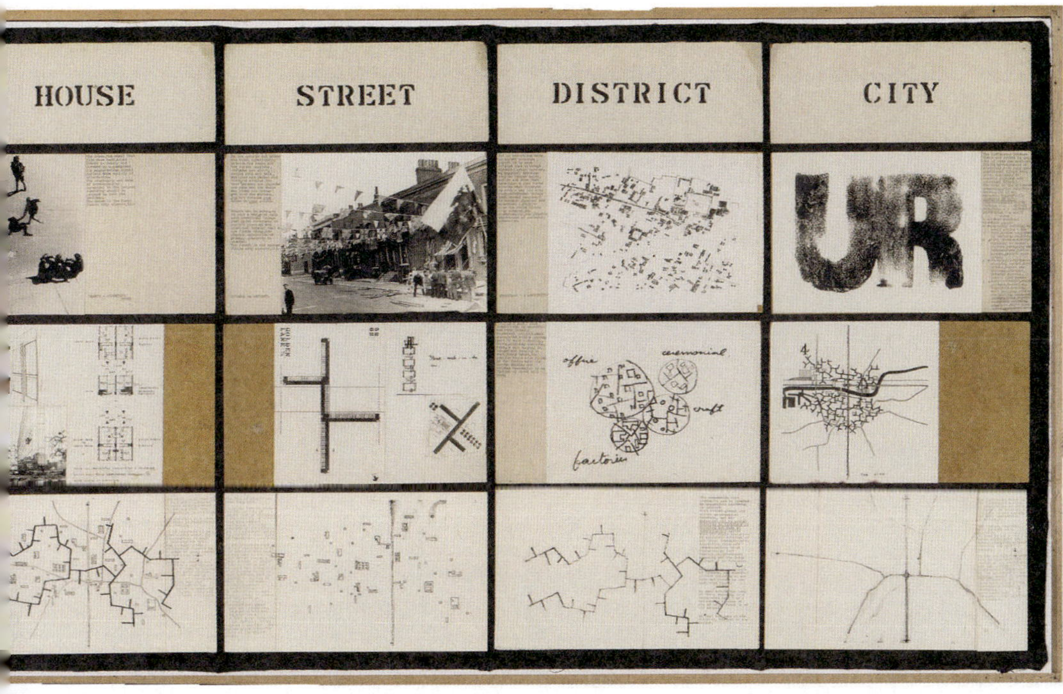

Fig. 5_ Alison and Peter Smithson, *Urban Reidentification Grille*, 1953.

Fig. 6_ Drop City, Colorado.

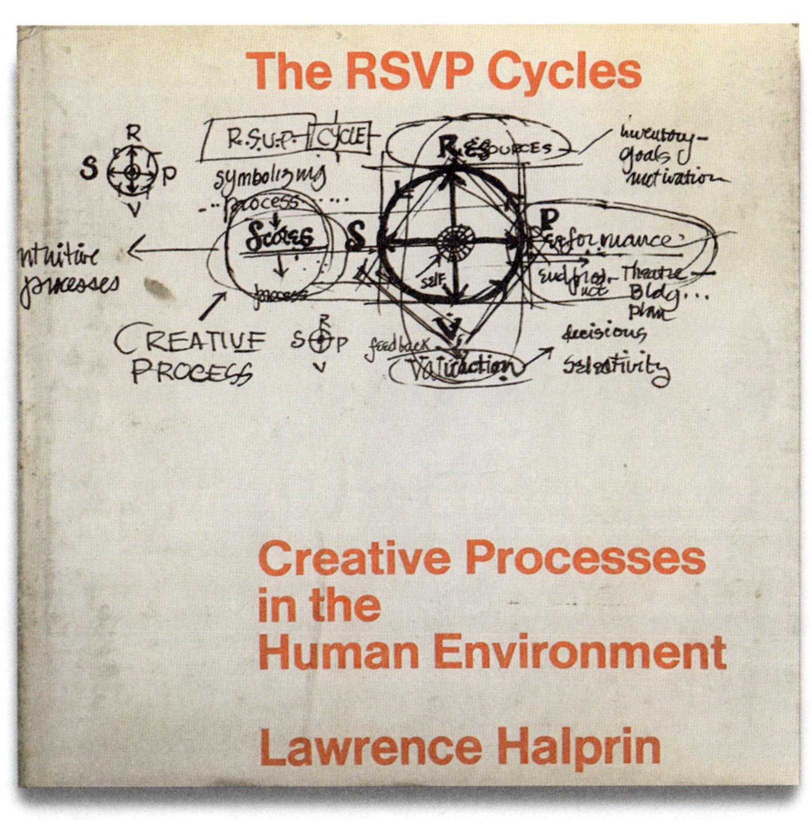

Fig. 7_ Lawrence Halprin, *The RSVP Cycles*, New York: G. Braziller, 1969 (book cover).

Fig. 8_ Archigram, Adventure Play Centre for Calverton End, Milton Keynes, 1972.

Fig. 9_ *Living City Exhibition: Various Views and Components*, from *Archigram*, edited by Peter Cook, London: Studio Vista, 1972.

Fig. 10_ Constant, *Klein Labyr*, Gemeentemuseum Den Haag, 1959.

Fig. 11_ Cam Smith, *Buckminster Fuller to Children of Earth*, New York: Doubleday, 1972 (book cover).

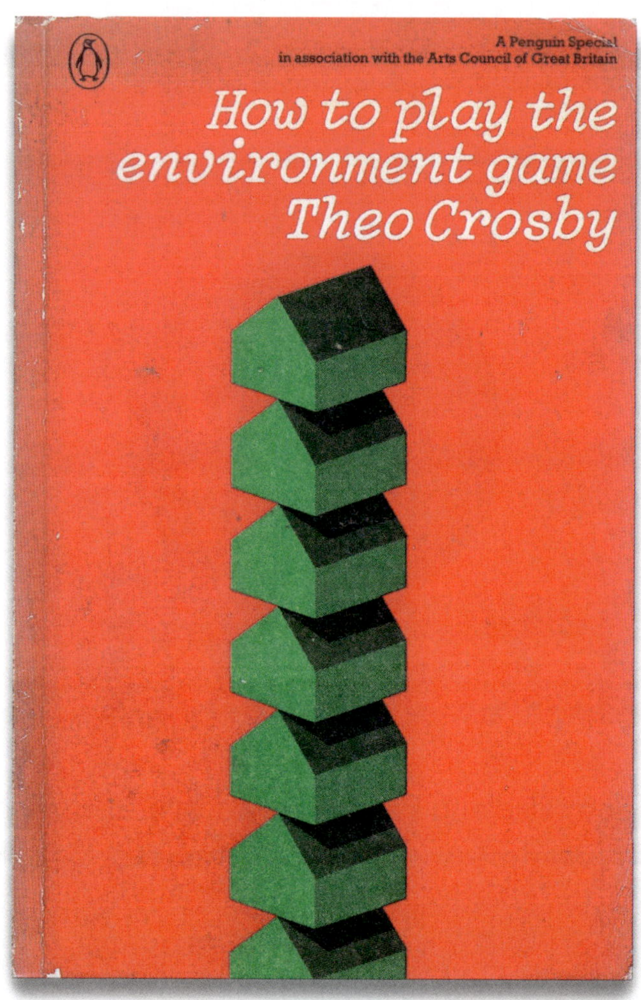

Fig. 12_ Theo Crosby, *How to Play the Environment Game*, Harmondsworth: Penguin/London: Arts Council of Great Britain, 1973 (book cover).

Fig. 13_ Charles Eames, Ray Eames, *House of Cards (Giant Size)*, Chicago: Tigrett Enterprises,1954.

Reality as Dystopia: Urban Contemporary Visions

Marco Biraghi

Why dystopia? Why interrogate this issue, nowadays? I think the question of dystopia answers some form of need, which goes beyond mere academic interest, with a power and urgency related to the present moment. Tafuri's thought, promulgated in the 1970s, focused on the idea of the end—and the impossibility—of utopia.[1] With great clarity Tafuri drew a route along which utopia was no longer practicable: in this almost ridiculous field theoretical debate was still possible but no longer with the intention to influence reality. Instead, utopia ran behind reality. Today, on the other hand, the query about dystopia stands in the face of our reality; if partly addressed to past and future, dystopia definitively and conclusively addresses the present. The present deals with many problems: complicated economic, political, and social ones; and global and local issues to be faced by appealing to equally complicated analysis and reflections. However, at this difficult moment I suggest an alternative approach to such issues: to give the image back its voice—through the work of contemporary artists—not to escape problems, but rather to approach them from a different point of view, attempting, somehow, to avoid extra complications.

Images, like any language, possess their own interior dialectic; their own rhetoric; and their own major, or minor, persuasive capacity. Despite a high degree of ambiguity, requiring interpretation (compared to other types of dialogue), images are absolutely immediate—easily accessible and comparable. When observing some images related to urban representation produced in the last few years, something new seems to emerge: a kind of innovation which, indeed, recalls something already known, but not exactly the same, as it always is when things come back. Some of these contemporary artists' works show a way to observe the city critically. The artist neither reproduces reality, nor celebrates it, as happened for the two decades before from the 1980s to about 2000. After the critical season of the 1960s and 1970s, art and architecture long abandoned any oppositional attitude, rather devoting themselves to the market. But recently the critical attitude has returned, and images in particular are silently communicating—or actually shouting as only they can do—something worthy of being heard. I would start this journey through images with something known and, at the same time very generic: a rendering of the Palazzo della Regione Lombardia in Milan, although any similar rendering or digital image could be used **(fig. 1)**. It deals with that way of looking at the city, to which we have become accustomed, through the filter of the most recent years of architecture. A "mellow" way but also a euphemistic way, where skies are always clear and blue (much more than you can imagine!), and where cities, in all their complexity, offer a break from the familiar disorder in which we used to place them—a break in which architecture triumphs. The context is realistic but altered at the same time, and this familiar effect reflects the difficulty of separating the real from the virtual. This optimistic vision is essentially an illusion instead of the real city.

In another historical moment—London of the 1960s—the problem was posed in different terms. For Archigram and Peter Cook the idea was a positive technological utopia **(fig. 2)**. Going totally beyond reality, and with the humor and lightness typical of that era, they proposed fascinating images which, however, did not deal with true problems. From the same era, *Monumento Continuo* by Superstudio, in apparent equilibrium between positive and negative, utopia and dystopia, actually presented a sense of threat.[2] A kind of "clash of civilizations" between something that still persisted and something new smashing through it totally without regard, creating an alienated and hostile effect **(fig. 3)**. Opposed to this emphasis on the megastructure, which never became a city, was Archizoom's *No Stop City* **(fig. 4)**, whose basic concept was to let capitalism fall beneath its own contradictions.[3] Adopting such models as the factory and the supermarket, Archizoom gathered inside the never-ending city the same spatial values that belonged to capitalism itself, throwing them against it, leading to unsustainable, contradictory extremes. All of this stands as reaction: the 1960s and the 1970s response to the effective mutations of reality that were happening then, projecting into the future the negativity of urban images.

The attitude adopted earlier in the 20th century was different. Regarding art and photography, that period's images had a definite critical position towards contemporary reality; through images, artists often criticized what was in front of their eyes. The streets of Berlin—so crowded in the aftermath of the First World War—deeply inspired George Grosz **(fig. 5)**.

His unrealistic representations, in the 19th-century sense of the term: reality is evidently deformed, but at the same time this is the true (real) city, the one that everyone could observe with his own eyes in that historical moment. A high negative charge electrified that city, made alarming by its overcrowding and the continuous "collisions" within it (the "psychic shocks" discussed by Walter Benjamin and most of the sociological literature of those years).[4] This was the season of Expressionism, in which places like Potsdamer Platz became new symbols of the urban impetuosity and metropolitan dynamism. We could find enlightening essays that could perfectly parse these images. But images speak for themselves; they are manifestos of a condition, of a mutation in the relationship between individual, society, and city. Afterwards, techniques changed but not the message. *Metropolis,* Bauhaus student Paul Citroen's famous 1923 collage, fully synthesizes that period **(fig. 6)**. Here are all the influences from the Dadaists, and the European avant-gardes, who invented the avant-garde technique *par excellence:* photomontage. They appropriated parts of reality and reassembled them into an unusual order (or disorder), emphasizing, exaggerating, and turning reality into something apocalyptic, while feeding off it. That the effect is too full, the image too saturated, is typical of this kind of vision. The same occurs in the poster illustration for a play by Walter Mehring, *Der Kaufmann von Berlin*; the analogies are particularly interesting since the technique becomes, somehow, the work's leading aspect, compared to its overt content—the awareness of crisis—foregrounding the critical attitude towards the city.

To the Bauhaus, again, belongs the 1926 collage by Marianne Brandt *Unsere irritierende Großstadt* (Our Unnerving City) whose title is still a statement, or a judgment **(fig. 7)**. Another example of urban collage is one of the posters realized for Fritz Lang's movie *Metropolis* (1927) by the Russian artist Boris Bilinsky. The movie, in this case, says something totally different from what had been seen previously. *Metropolis* restores a comforting utopia—of the type that would highly annoy Tafuri—where love overcomes all contradictions, mediating between the slave working class, living in the underground, and an aristocratic elite, living above, in Eden's garden: a falsified vision, completely erasing the conflictive dialectics between social classes. German Expressionism affirmed something quite precise: the civilization's discontent, in which men were engulfed by the whirling urban explosion. The evolution from city to metropolis registered not just as a change of name, but also as a formal mutation, which included not just enlarged dimensions but transformed social relations. Within this condition the individual constantly clashed with reality.

All of this is typical of an historic moment that has left few traces behind. Exploring the art world nearer to us, there are some artists trying to reflect the city in a similar way. One is Giacomo Costa, from Florence, who produced his first works in the 1990s **(fig. 8)**.[5] These are in some ways still naive: an echo of the overthrow of the Tower of Babel tower in the middle of Metropolis, where the city literally collapses into pieces. But those "pieces" are the real buildings of a still completely recognizable Italian city. Then the early naivety disappears, giving way to more "composed" images, not as a matter of technical skill, but to better express the artist's message or point of view **(fig. 9)**. Here he seems more conscious of what he wants to say: the urban context is no longer rejected as a negative factor, but instead a dialogue is established between man and the city, in a new kind of dialectical relation. In more recent years Costa has updated his techniques to fully join the age of digital images.[6] Thanks to this, he is able to realize a reverse operation in the creation of renderings, that is a more sophisticated simulation of "unreality." With this aviso: what is shown in his images is the process of our world and reality in decay. A vision arises of a kind of imminent new Middle Ages, among the ruins of civilization as we know it. Gradually Costa's images take on an ever more visionary nature: those defunct aqueducts typical of Piranesi transform themselves into relics of urban highways. Recently Costa started to elaborate some iconic architectural images: ruined buildings decomposing like bodies, and with them the rest of the city. Not a dream city, nor a sci-fi city, but, in some ways a real city: our city, just a little after its evolution and dissolution.

We next turn to an artist who works deeply inside that sensibility typical of German Expressionism, and recovers the theme of Kettelhut's *Babel Tower*. The Chinese artist Du Zhenjun's *Babel Towers* are made of fragments of real buildings, a sort of collage which doesn't talk about fragmentation or dispersion, but constructs buildings, or images of buildings, rising as threatening towers **(fig. 10)**.[7] Here images alone are persuasive: enough to notice that each strip, each floor of these huge towers has a distinct architectural treatment, finding typologies and elements to reuse. In some cases, we have exploding towers, collapsing on themselves. It is interesting to note how much we know of the different fragments: products of modernity, such as the never-ending *curtain wall*—always the same—this time rebelling against the same society that produced them. Human presence, here, is disturbing and alienating. The images described so far may tend to "interpret" too much, projected too far into the future. To get closer to the present we can look at the wonderful photographs of Michael Wolf, a German architect from Frankfurt, who presents a series of buildings in Hong Kong in his project *Architecture of Density* **(fig. 11)**: extraordinary pictures because of their stark realism. No collages are used to reinvent reality here.[8] It is already in front of us, you just need to be attentive and stare. In the last few years photography has accustomed us to similar experiences, extraordinary enough: images of existing places that nevertheless seem untrue.

Also dealing with the topic of possible urban visions is a kind of young neo-expressionist movement that has recently developed in Italy. An interesting artist, in this sense, is Vincenzo (Vins) Grosso, born in Sardinia in 1977. Grosso studied at the Accademia di Belle Arti in Florence, then moved to Berlin. His images are not realistic, in the sense that you could recognize the buildings represented **(fig. 12)**. However, at the same time, it is obvious that he presents absolutely familiar contexts for us: buildings that belong to our experience of the city—it could be Berlin or any other big European or American city. Like the Expressionists, Grosso fixes these urban scenes with a threatening feeling. There is something distorted in the reality painted here; there is no "future," no sci-fi evocation: the present itself is dystopic, our urban environment stares at us threateningly, and the artist—as if he were the most sensitive seismograph—simply stares at it in the same way. One of the most interesting effects is how Grosso, with his past experience as a street artist, paints his canvas with just a denticulated spatula: with these denticles he "caresses" the canvas, and the spatula leaves signs of color creating a kind of *curtain wall*. A seemingly easy technique, entirely gestural. The gesture immediately resolves any dialectical uncertainty: there is no more to say, nothing to add. As everything else in the field of aesthetics, signs pose a problem of taste: they may be liked or not. But here, beyond any other consideration, the gesture recreates an idea of the city as simultaneously real and negative: a reified negativity expressed by the black signs representing the buildings. An artist like Grosso takes a position on what he represents in his works. He doesn't just reproduce and reflect the reality, nor does he invent something new and different. He represents and cleverly reinterprets what is produced by the culture in which we live. His images of cities are sometimes characterized by strong color tones, reminding us again of 1920s Expressionism. Likewise the "explosion"—literally breaking out—of the architectural forms, as if the building were animate, not just a soulless object, but a subject with its own life. These are, moreover, the same movements we encounter in our metropolis.

Grosso's experience as a graffiti artist, like that of Francesco Barbieri, an artist born in Pisa in 1976, is fundamental. Before creating works on canvas, these artists blazoned their own tags directly on the city's walls. As a result, they experienced their work and their relation to the city not in an elitist way, but actually concentrating on its marginal and abandoned parts. There is a convergence between their own points of view on the city and the particular ones from which they physically represent it. This is particularly evident in Barbieri's work **(fig. 13)**. The subjects of his paintings are urban visions that, despite their contents' mundanity—or maybe exactly because of it—acquire a universal value: they really could be any city with an adequate urban structure, but they are also the portrait of a very specific, albeit generic, city.

Once again, the city is observed from a lateral point of view, but this marginality takes an unusually central role: the subject's. However this centrality has a new locus: the city is seen and interpreted through its outskirts, its eccentricities, its apparently "minor" parts. Like those districts in which railway intersections are located: infrastructure as the primary framework of contemporary cities. Here is where cities reveal their true nature, a nature embodied here in a more effective way than their much better-known public spaces. Today we must look at railway intersections with major interest: not for their actual beauty (as aesthetic concepts change over time), but for their density of meaning, however disturbing. In Barbieri's work these elements are recognizable in all their necessity and inevitability. It is not just a city portrait, but also our personal and collective portrait: like a deforming mirror which reflects what we really are inside the city and contemporary reality.

Fig. 1_ Pei Cobb Freed & Partners, *Project for Palazzo Lombardia*, 2010.

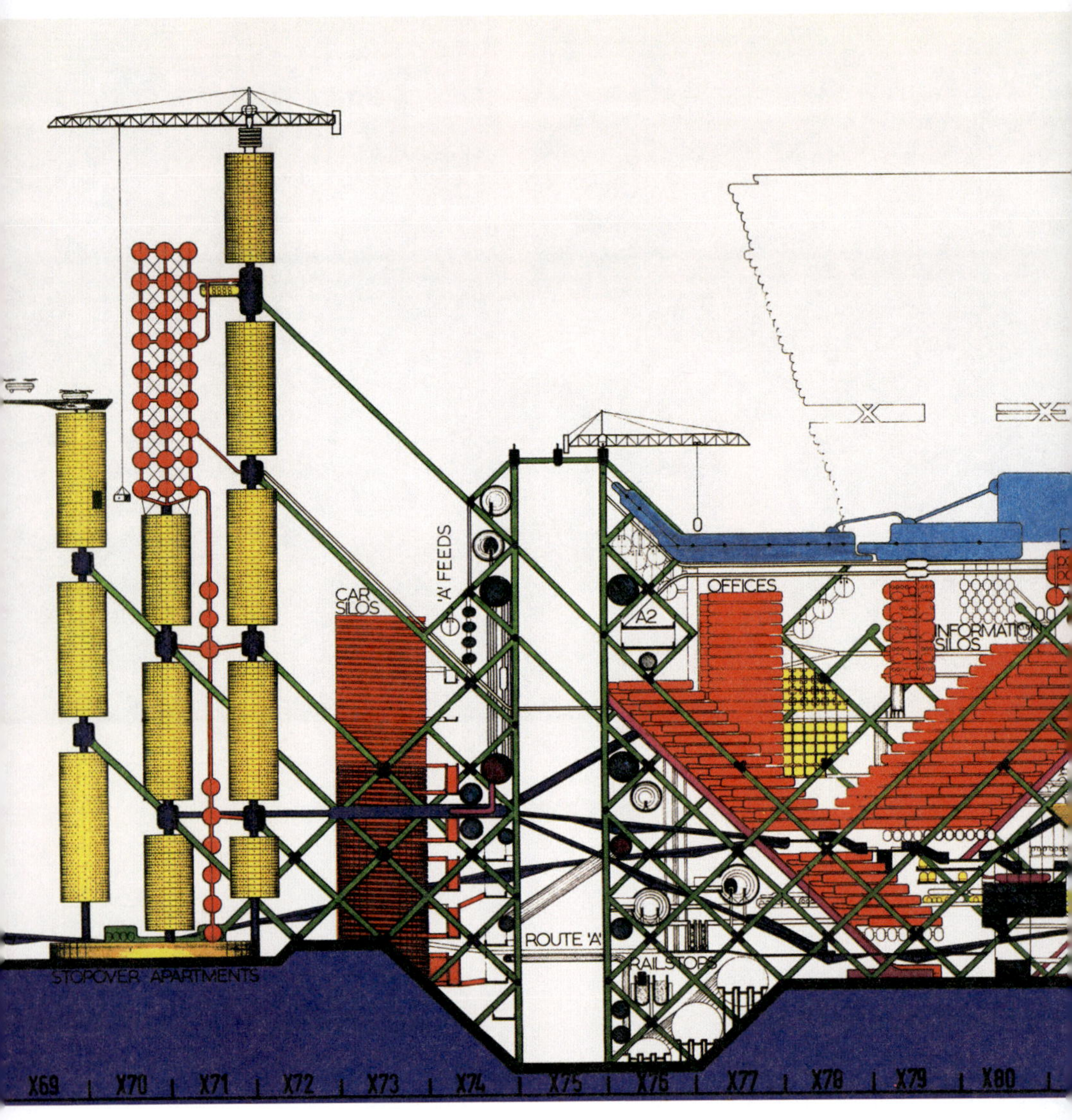
CAR SILOS
'A' FEEDS
OFFICES
A2
INFORMATION SILOS
ROUTE 'A'
RAILSTOPS
STOPOVER APARTMENTS
X69
X70
X71
X72
X73
X74
X75
X76
X77
X78
X79
X80

Fig. 2_ Archigram, *Plug-in City*, 1963.

Fig. 3_ Superstudio, *Monumento continuo*, 1969.
Fig. 4_ Archizoom, *No-Stop-City*, 1970.

Fig. 5_ George Grosz, *Der Leichenzug, Widmung an Oskar Panizza*, 1917-1918.

Fig. 6_ Paul Citroen, *Metropolis*, 1923.

Fig. 7_ Marianne Brandt, *Unsere irritierende Großstadt*, 1925.

Fig. 8_ Giacomo Costa, *Agglomerato n. 6*, 1997.

Following page:
Fig. 9 (Above)_ Giacomo Costa, *Atto n. 9*, 2007.
Fig. 10 (Below)_ Du Zhenjun, Tower of Babel, 1, 2003.

Fig. 11_ Michael Wolf, *Architecture of Density, 20*, 2009.
Fig. 12_ Vins Grosso, *Senza titolo*, 2014.

Fig. 13_ Francesco Barbieri, *Landscape n. 35*, 2013;
Milano Big City of Dreams Nothing Moves but the Money, 2014.

Notes

Architecture and Dystopia, or Negative Thinking as a Design Method
Dario Donetti

1 Manfredo Tafuri, Progetto e utopia: Architettura e sviluppo capitalistico (Bari: Laterza, 1973). English translation: Architecture and Utopia: Design and Capitalist Development (Cambridge MA: MIT Press, 1976). The book derived from the Tafuri's earlier notorious article "Per una critica della ideologia architettonica," Contropiano 1 (1969), 31–79.

2 Tafuri, *Architecture and Utopia*, ix.

3 Manfredo Tafuri, *L'architettura dell'umanesimo* (Bari: Laterza, 1969), a revised version of the encyclopedic entry "Rinascimento," in *Dizionario enciclopedico di architettura e urbanistica*, Paolo Portoghesi, ed. (Rome: Istituto Editoriale Romano, 1968–1969), V, 173–232; Manfredo Tafuri, *Ricerca del Rinascimento* (Torino: Einaudi, 1992). Some crucial critical issues were already anticipated in Manfredo Tafuri, *L'architettura del manierismo nel Cinquecento europeo* (Roma: Officina libraria), 3–9; cf. Andrew Leach, *Crisis on Crisis, or Tafuri on Mannerism* (Basel: Standpunkte 2017), 26–33.

4 Cf., this volume, Marco De Michelis, "Manfredo Tafuri and the Death of Architecture," 45-55.

5 Margaret Wood's celebrated dystopian novel, *The Handmaid's Tale* (Toronto: McClelland and Stewart, 1985), was turned into a 2017 television series, created by Bruce Miller and produced by Hulu. On the recent dystopian turn in fiction and cinematography, cf. Mark Bould, *Dulltopia*, in *Boston Review: Global Dystopias*, Junot Díaz, ed. (Cambridge MA: MIT Press, 2017), 191–206; Junot Díaz, *Editor's Note*, ibid., 5–6. One example of the political use of the term is the recent anthology of short stories, *Trump: Utopia or Dystopia?*, JF Garrard and Jen Frankel, eds. (Toronto: Dark Helix Press, 2017).

6 Cf. Antoine Picon, "Architecture and the Dystopian Trap," in *Utopia/Dystopia: A Paradigm Shift in Art and Architecture*, Pedro Gadanho, ed. (Milano: Mousse Publishing, 2017), 103–115.

7 Cf., this volume, Simon Sadler, "Games without Frontiers," 163-171, making the case for the pan-European television show *Jeux Sans Frontières* (1965–1999), and the more recent film *The Hunger Games* (2012), dir. Gary Ross.

8 Fredric Jameson, "Utopia as Method, or the Uses of Future," in *Utopia/Dystopia: Conditions of Historical Possibility*, Michael D. Gordin, Helen Tilley, and Gyan Prakash, eds. (Princeton: Princeton University Press, 2010), 42. For the definition of dystopia in literary and philosophical debate, cf. also Fredric Jameson, *Archeologies of the Future: The Desire Called Utopia and Other Science Fictions* (New York: Verso, 2005); and Raffaella Baccolini and Tom Moylan, eds., *Dark Horizons: Science Fiction and the Dystopian Imagination* (New York: Routledge, 2003).

9 Cf., as an example, the famous critique formulated by Karl R. Popper, *The Open Society and Its Enemies* (London: G. Routledge & Sons, 1945), particularly Vol. 1: "The spell of Plato".

10 This has been the case in Italy, with three major exhibitions on Superstudio organized in Milan, Rome, and Florence in the last three years, and the related publications: Andreas Angelidakis, Vittorio Pizzigoni, and Valter Scelsi, *Super Superstudio* (Cinisello Balsamo: Silvana Editoriale, 2015); Gabriele Mastrigli, ed., *Superstudio: Opere 1966–1978* (Macerata: Quodlibet, 2016); and Pino Brugellis, Gianni Pettena, and Alberto Salvadori, eds., *Utopie Radicali: Archizoom, Remo Buti, 9999, Gianni Pettena, Superstudio, UFO, Zziggurat* (Macerata: Quodlibet, 2017).

11 Cf., this volume, Antony Vidler "Utopia Rediviva, 1960–1972," 25-35.

12 The apt expression of Reyner Banham, *Theory and Design in the First Machine Age* (Cambridge MA: MIT Press, 1960), 10.

13 Cf., this volume, Marie Theres Stauffer, "Learning from No-Stop City: Archizoom's Utopia Revisited," 101-111.

14 Cf., this volume, Massimiliano Savorra, "Leisure in a Time of Utopia," 129-142.

15 Rem Koolhaas, "Bigness, or the Problem of Large,", in *S,M,L,XL*, Office for Metropolitan Architecture, Rem Koolhaas and Bruce Mau, eds. (New York: The Monacelli Press, 1995), 503-504.

16 Rem Koolhaas, *Delirious New York: A Retroactive Manifesto for Manhattan* (New York: Oxford University Press, 1978); Office for Metropolitan Architecture, Koolhaas, and Mau, *S,M,L,XL*; Rem Koolhaas, "Junkspace," *ANY* 27 (2000), [no pagination].

17 Michel Foucault, "Des espaces autres" (Conférence au Cercle d'études architecturales, 14 mars 1967), in *Architecture Mouvement Continuité* 5 (1984), 46–49.

18 Cf., this volume, Marco Biraghi, "Appendix: Reality as Dystopia: Urban Contemporary Visions," 189-194.

19 Cf., this volume, Dominique Rouillard, "Dystopia: A Positive Narrative for Architecture," 65-73; Maddalena Scimemi, "Architecture on Paper: Cedric Price and the Scientific Aesthetic of Diagrams," 85-91.

Utopia Rediviva, 1960-1972

Anthony Vidler

1 "Utopia Supplement," *Granta* LXIII, 1187 (1959), 19–39.

2 Nikolas Berdiaeff, cited in Aldous Huxley, *Brave New World* (London: Chatto & Windus,1935), 5.

3 Karl Popper, *The Open Society and its Enemies* (London: Routledge: 1945), I, 200.

4 Id., *The Poverty of Historicism* (London and New York: Routledge, 2002 [1937]), 58–69.

5 Bertrand Russell, cited in Bryan Magee, *Popper* (Oxford: Cass), 93.

6 Lewis Mumford, *The City in History* (New York: Harcourt, Brace and World, 1961), 176.

7 Karl Mannheim, *Ideology and Utopia: An Introduction to the Sociology of Knowledge*, trans. Louis Wirth and Edward Shils (New York: Harcourt & Brace, 1936), 262–263.

8 Robin Marris, "Utopia and Conviction," *Granta* LXIII, op. cit., 37–39.

9 Richard Layard, "News from Somewhere," ibid, 31–34.

10 Andre Schiffrin, "The Need for Utopia," ibid., 27–30.

11 Andre Schiffrin, "The Need for Utopia," *Granta* LXIII, op. cit., 27 citing Mannheim, ibid., 192.

12 Robert Taylor and Tom Steele, *British Labour and Higher Education, 1945–2000: Ideologies, Policies and Practice* (London: Continuum International, 2011), 67.

13 Edward P. Thompson, *William Morris: Romantic to Revolutionary* (London: Lawrence & Wishart, 1955).

14 Raymond Williams, *Culture and Society 1780–1950* (London: Chatto & Windus, 1958).

15 John Cornford, "Just Around the Corner," ibid., 35–37.

16 Günter Grass, *The Tin Drum*, trans. Ralph Manheim (New York: Pantheon Books, 1962).

17 Robin Marris, *How to Save the Underclass* (Basingstoke: Macmillan, 1996).

18 Trevor Smith, "James Cornford obituary," *The Guardian*, Wednesday October 5th, 2011.

19 Colin Rowe, "The Architecture of Utopia," *Granta* LXIII, op. cit., 20–26.

20 Cf. sup., note 9.

21 Popper's arguments will be summarized later: they bear on the development of Rowe's thought in the late 1960s and early 1970s, as well as on the specific critique of Plato.

22 Helen Rosenau, *The Ideal City in its Architectural Evolution* (London: Routledge, 1959).

23 Emil Kaufmann, *Von Ledoux bis Le Corbusier: Ursprung und Entwicklung der autonomen Architektur* (Wien/Leipzig: Verlag Dr. Rolf Passer, 1933); id., *Three Revolutionary Architects: Boullée, Ledoux, Lequeu* (Philadelphia: American Philosophical Society, 1952).

24 Id., *Architecture in the Age of Reason: Baroque and Post-Baroque in England, Italy, and France* (Cambridge: Harvard University Press, 1955).

25 Helen Rosenau, ed., *Boullée's Treatise on Architecture: A Complete Presentation of the "Architecture Essai sur l'Art" which Forms Part of the Boullée Papers (Ms. 9153) in the Bibliothèque Nationale, Paris* (London: Tiranti, 1953).

26 Aldo Rossi, "Emil Kaufmann e l'architettura dell'illuminismo," *Casabella-Continuità* 219 (1958), 32–35.

27 Hans Sedlmayr, *Verlust der Mitte* (Salzburg: Otto Müller Verlag, 1955).

28 Id., *Art in Crisis, the Lost Center*, trans. Brian Battershaw (London: Hollis & Carter, 1957).

29 B.F. Skinner, *Walden Two* (New York: Macmillan Co., 1948).

30 Leonardo Benevolo, *Le origini dell'urbanistica moderna* (Bari: Laterza, 1963); Françoise Choay, *L'urbanisme: Utopies et réalités* (Paris: Éditions du Seuil, 1965).

31 Liselotte Ungers and Oswald Mathias Ungers, *Kommunen in der Neuen Welt, 1740–1972* (Cologne: Kiepenheuer & Witch, 1972), with bibliography.

32 Raymond Ruyer, *L'utopie et les utopies* (Paris: Presses universitaires de France, 1950), XX.

33 André Canivez, "Introduction," in Georges Duveau, *Sociologie de l'utopie et autres essais* (Paris: PUF, 1961), 3.

34 Roger Mucchielli, "L'Utopie de Thomas Morus," in Jean Laneere, ed., *Les Utopies à la Renaissance. Colloque International (avril 1961)* (Bruxelles/Paris: Presses Universitaires de France, 1963), 101.

35 Jean Servier, *Histoire de l'utopie* (Paris: Gallimard, 1967).

36 Louis Marin, *Utopiques: Jeux d'espaces* (Paris: Éditions de Minuit, 1973).

37 Claude Lévi-Strauss, Anthropologie structurale (Paris: Plon, 1958).

38 Leo Strauss, *The City of Man* (Chicago: Rand McNally, 1964).

39 Plato, *The Republic*, trans. Allan Bloom (New York: Basic Books, 1968).

40 Robert Boguslaw, *The New Utopians: A Study of System Design and Social Change* (Englewood Cliffs: Prentice Hall, 1965). Servier, whose earlier work included studies of occultism, was deeply influenced by Marin Buber's vision of the kibbutz as a communal-utopian experiment in his *Paths in Utopia*, first published in Israeli in 1946.

41 Ibid., Extending his analysis to the history of utopias, Boguslaw claims, for example, that because of his mathematical theories, "Fourier's orientation was fundamentally that of a design engineer rather than that of a radical reformer." (Ibid., 12).

42 Tomàs Maldonado, *La Speranza Progettuale* (Turin: Einaudi, 1965), delivered as lectures at Princeton University between 1966 and 1970. English version: *Design, Nature, and Revolution: Toward a Critical Ecology*, trans. Mario Domandi (New York: Harper and Row, 1972).

43 Ibid., 72–73.

44 Colin Rowe and Fred Koetter, *Collage City* (Cambridge, Mass.: MIT Press,1978), 40.

45 Ibid., 40–41.

46 Cf. sup. note 5.

47 Manfredo Tafuri, *History of Italian Architecture 1944–1985*, trans. Jessica Levine (Cambridge, Mass.: MIT Press, 1989), 99. [need Italian reference]

48 Ibid., 99.

49 Emilio Ambasz, "I: The University of Design and Development"; "II: Manhattan: Capital of the Twentieth Century"; "III: The Designs of Freedom," *Perspecta* 13/14 (1971), 359–365: 362.

50 Louis Aragon, *Le paysan de Paris* (Paris: Gallimard, 1926).

51 Emilio Ambasz, ed., *Italy: The New Domestic Landscape: Achievements and Problems of Italian Design* (New York/Florence: Museum of Modern Art/Centro Di, 1972).

52 Manfredo Tafuri, "Design and Technological Utopia," ibid., 388–404.

53 Ibid., 398.

54 Manfredo Tafuri, "Per una critica della ideologia architettonica," *Contropiano* 1 (1969), 31–79.

55 Tafuri, "Design and Technological Utopia," op. cit., 400.

Manfredo Tafuri and the Death of Architecture
Marco De Michelis

1 This text has been presented for the first time, in Italian, on October 16, 2014, at the Kunsthistorisches Institut in Florenz – Max-Planck-Insitut, as the opening intervention of the conference *Architecture and Dystopia*.

2 Massimo Cacciari, *Quid Tum* (Venice: Istituto Universitario di Architettura, 1994). Also in *Casabella* 619–620 (1995), 168–169.

3 Jean-Louis Cohen, "Ceci n'est pas une histoire," *Casabella* 619–620 (1995), 48–53.

4 Joan Ockman, "Venice and New York," *Casabella* 619–620 (1995), 56–71.

5 Mark Wigley, "Manfredo Tafuri (1935–1994)," *Archis* 4 (1994), 6–7.

6 Marco Biraghi, *Progetto di crisi* (Milan: Christian Mariotti, 2005). English translation: *Project of Crisis* (Cambridge MA: MIT Press, 2013); Andrew Leach, *Manfredo Tafuri: Choosing History* (Ghent: A&S books, 2007).

7 Manfredo Tafuri, *Progetto e utopia: Architettura e sviluppo capitalistico* (Bari: Laterza, 1973). English translation: *Architecture and Utopia: Design and Capitalist Development* (Cambridge MA: MIT Press, 1976).

8 Manfredo Tafuri, "Per una critica della ideologia architettonica," *Contropiano* 1 (1969), 31–79. English translation: "Toward a Critique of Architectural Ideology," in *Architecture Theory since 1968,* K. Michael Hays, ed. (Cambridge MA: MIT Press, 2000), 6–35.

9 Aldo Rossi, *L'architettura della città* (Venice: Marsilio, 1966); Robert S. Venturi, *Complexity and Contradiction in Architecture* (New York: Museum of Modern Art, 1966).

10 Marc Antoine Laugier, *Essai sur l'Architecture* (Paris: Duchesne, 1753).

11 Citations are from Vittorio Ugo, "Presentazione," in Marc-Antoine Laugier, *Saggio sull'architettura*, (Palermo: Aesthetica Edizioni, 1987), 15.

12 Wolfgang Herrmann, *Laugier and the Eighteenth Century French Theory* (London: Zwemmer, 1962), 200–201.

13 Laugier, *Saggio sull'architettura*, 39 (author's translation).

14 Manfredo Tafuri, *G.B. Piranesi: L'architettura come "utopia negativa," Angelus Novus* 20 (1971), 89–127.

15 Quatremère de Quincy, "Architecture" in *Encyclopédie méthodique:* (Paris: Panckoucke, 1788–1825), I, 109. Quoted by Tafuri in *"Toward a Critique of Architectural Ideology,"* 10.

16 Cf. Kenneth Frampton, *Studies in Tectonic Culture: The Poetics of Construction in Nineteenth and Twentieth Century Architecture* (Cambridge MA: MIT Press, 1995); Marko Pogacnik, *La dissolution de la grande forme*, in *Faces* 57 (1999/2000), 14–23.

17 Manfredo Tafuri, *Teorie e storia dell'architettura* (Bari: Laterza, 1968), 112. English translation*: Theories and History of Architecture* (London: Granada, 1980).

18 Antony Vidler, *Histories of the Immediate Present: Inventing Architectural Modernism, 1930-1975* (PhD diss., Technische Universiteit Delft, 2005) 174.

19 Manfredo Tafuri and Francesco Dal Co, *Architettura Contemporanea* (Milano: Electa, 1976), 105.

20 Tafuri, "Toward a Critique of Architectural Ideology," 6.

21 Marco De Michelis, "Fin de Siècle," *Thesis: Wissenschaftliche Zeitschrift der Bauhaus-Universität Weimar* XLVI, 4/5 (2000), 160–167.

22 Tafuri and Dal Co, *Architettura contemporanea*, 368.

23 Ibid.

24 Tafuri, *Teorie e storia dell'architettura*, 252–253.

25 Manfredo Tafuri, *La sfera e il labirinto* (Torino: Einaudi, 1980) 323. English translation: *The Sphere and the Labyrinth* (Cambridge MA/London: MIT Press, 1987), xx.

26 Aldo Rossi, *Autobiografia scientifica* (Parma: Pratiche editrice, 1990), 22.

27 Massimo Scolari, "The New Architecture and the Avant-Garde [1973]," in *Architecture Theory since 1968*, Hays, ed., 131–132. First published as "Avanguardia e nuova architettura," in *Architettura razionale*, Aldo Rossi, ed. (Milano: Franco Angeli, 1980), 153–187.

28 Ibid.

29 Manfredo Tafuri, *Storia dell'architettura italiana 1944–1985* (Torino: Einaudi, 1986), 166.

30 Manfredo Tafuri, "L'architecture dans le boudoir [1974]," in *Architecture Theory since 1968*, Hays, ed., 155. First published as "L'Architecture dans le Boudoir," *Oppositions* 3 (1974) 37–62.

31 Pierluigi Nicolin, "Tafuri and the Analogous City," *ANY* 25/26 (2000), 17.

32 Manfredo Tafuri, "Ceci n'est pas une ville," *Lotus* 13 (1976), 10–13.

33 Tafuri, "L'Architecture dans le Boudoir," in *Oppositions, 38.*

34 Manfredo Tafuri, "Il 'progetto' storico," *Casabella* 429 (1977). 11–18. English translation: "The Historical Project," *Oppositions* 17 (1979), 55–75.

35 Carlo Ginzburg and Adriano Prosperi, *Giochi di pazienza: Un seminario sul "Beneficio di Cristo"* (Torino: Einaudi, 1975), 84.

36 Ibid.

37 Tafuri, *The Sphere and the Labyrinth*, 2–3.

38 Mark Wigley, "Post-Operative History," *ANY* 25/26 (2000), 47.

39 Tafuri, *The Sphere and the Labyrinth*, 3.

40 Ibid.

41 Michel Foucault, "Nietzsche, Genealogy, History," in *The Foucault Reader,* Paul Rabinow, ed. (New York: Pantheon, 1984), 88

42 Tafuri, *The Sphere and the Labyrinth*, 4–5.

43 Ibid.

44 Georg Simmel, "Zur Metaphysik des Todes [1910]," in *Das Individuum und die Freiheit* (Berlin: Klaus Wagenbach, 1984), 29–35 (author's translation).

45 Friederich Nietzsche, "Aurora," in *Opere,* Giorgio Ciolli and Mazzino Montinari, eds. (Milan: Adelphi, 1965), V, I, 40 (author's translation).

46 Tafuri, "Il 'progetto' storico," 14–15.

47 K. Michael Hays, "Tafuri's Ghost," *ANY* 25/26 (2000), 36.

48 Ibid., 37.

49 "For a historical history: Pietro Corsi interviews Manfredo Tafuri," *La rivista dei libri* 4 (1994), 10–12. Also published in *Casabella* 619–620 (1995), 144–151.

50 Anna Bedon, Guido Beltramini, and Howard Burns, eds., *Questo: Disegni e studi di Manfredo Tafuri,* (Vicenza: Centro Internazionale di Studi di Architettura Andrea Palladio, 1995).

Dystopia: A Positive Narrative for Architecture

Dominique Rouillard

1 This article makes no distinction between "counter-utopia" and "dystopia." Etymologically—the Greek *dys* meaning difficulty or evil—*dys*topia extends the notion of opposition ("counter-utopia") by adding a moral connotation to its already negative implication.

2 Jean Dethier and Alain Guiheux, eds., *La ville: Art et architecture en Europe*, 1870–1993, exhibition catalog (Paris, Centre G. Pompidou: 1994). For the 1960s, cf. Dominique Rouillard, "Archigram," ibid., 428–429; "Hans Hollein, Walter Pichler, Raimund Abraham, Friedrich Saint-Florian," ibid., 430–431; "Archizoom," ibid., 432–433; "Superstudio," ibid., 434–435; Rem Koolhaas and Elia Zenghelis: "1972: Exodus, ou les prisonniers volontaires de l'architecture," ibid., 436–437.

3 The controversy led to a libel suit against an architect's offending remarks in the journal *Architecture d'Aujourd'hui*. The case was won by Alain Guiheux.

4 Dominique Rouillard, *Superarchitecture: Le futur de l'architecture 1950–1970* (Paris: Éditions de La Villette, 2004).

5 R. Koolhaas, "Exodus/1972," *Architectural Design* XLVII, 5 (May 1977), 329. Archizoom and Superstudio, "Discorsi per immagini," *Domus* 481 (1969), 46–48, a publication, in the form of manifesto, of projects by the two Florentine groups.

6 Cf. sup., note 2.

7 Dominique Rouillard, "'Radical' Architettura," in *Tschumi, une architecture en projet: Le Fresnoy*, (Paris: Centre G. Pompidou, 1993), 89–112; id., "Radical architecture," in *Tschumi Le Fresnoy: Architecture In/Between,* Bernard Tschumi and Joseph Abram, eds. (New York: Monacelli Press, 1999), 119–134.

8 Hans Hollein, "What is Architecture?" in *Protokolle '66: Weiner Jahresschrift für Literatur, Bildende Kunst und Musik* (Wien–Munich: Jugend und Volk, 1966), XX–XX. While published in 1966, the text was first written in Chicago in 1958, then presented in a lecture titled "Zurück zur Architektur" (Wien, 1962), and republished as "Was ist Architektur?," *Bau* 2/3 (1969).

9 Le Corbusier used the same expression in 1933, "The Spirit of Truth," but with the exact opposite meaning: he stated that any object could borrow something from architecture's architectonic dimension in terms of proportion and order, while Hollein pretended that architecture could no longer claim to have its own conception or mode of fabrication for a project. Cf. Rouillard, *Superarchitecture,* 191–202.

10 H. Hollein, "Vive la Liberté!," *Domus* 481 (October 1969), 50.

11 Manfredo Tafuri, "Per una critica dell'ideologia architettonica," *Contropiano* 1 (January 1969), 31–79.

12 Manfredo Tafuri, "G. B. Piranesi: l'Architettura come utopia negativa," *Angelus Novus* 20 (1971), 89–127. In Tafuri's *Teoria e storia dell'architettura* (Bari: Laterza, 1968), Piranesi is approached only from the point of view of eclecticism. On this aspect, see Rouillard, *Superarchitecture*, 289–376.

13 "Radical architecture raises no hypothesis concerning the shape of the future city" [Andrea Branzi, "Radical Architecture," *Casabella* 386 (1974), 46–47]. The article ends with a reference to the theses introduced since 1968.

14 "I terroristi": the February, 1968 issue of the magazine *Panorama* made no mistake when it gave that title to a picture of Archizoom's members in neo-futuristic or neo-terrorist disguise, dressed in black and donning bowler-like hats, the pose of the Italian futurists.

15 Presented by Nathan Rogers to the members of Team Ten gathered at Otterlo in 1959 to bury the CIAM.

Architecture on Paper: Cedric Price and the Scientific Aesthetic of Diagrams

Maddalena Scimemi

1 Antoine Picon, "Architecture, Science and Technology," in Peter Galison and Emily Thompson, eds., *The Architecture of Science* (Cambridge MA/London: MIT Press, 1999), 310.

2 I am borrowing this definition from Catherine Jolivette, "Science, Art and Landscape in the Nuclear Age," *Art History Journal of the Association of Art Historians* 35 (2012), 253–269; see also Catherine Jolivette, ed., *British Art in the Nuclear Age* (Farnham: Ashgate, 2014).

3 Herbert Matter, *Arts and Architecture* 45 (1945). The cover was recently republished by Jeffrey Head, ed., *Herbert Matter: Modernist Photography and Graphic Design*, exhibition catalogue (Stanford: Stanford University Libraries, 2005).

4 Designed by André Waterkeyn and André and Jean Polak, the *Atomium* pavilion was modelled on the enlargement of an elementary iron crystal. On the topic of architecture at the Expo '58, cf. Rika Devos and Mil De Kooning, eds., *L'Architecture moderne à l'Expo 58. 'Pour un monde plus humain'* (Bruxelles: Fonds Mercator/Dexia, 2006). On the Underwater City, cf. "Metropolis Issue," *Archigram* 5 (1965); see also Simon Sadler, *Archigram: Architecture Without Architecture* (Cambridge MA: MIT Press, 2005), 120.

5 On the cylindrical tower by Pei see Philip Jodidio, ed., *I.M. Pei Complete Works* (New York: Rizzoli International, 2008), 21,23. On the biological grounds of the Japanese Metabolists, cf. Tobias Cheung, "Kurokawa Metabolic Space," in Kirsten

Wagner, Jasper Cepl, eds., *Images of the Body in Architecture: Anthropology and Built Space* (Tübingen/Berlin: Ernst Wasmuth Verlag, 2014), 131–165, note 90. On Kahn's ideas for Philadelphia, cf. Louis I. Kahn, "Toward a plan for Midtown Philadelphia," *Perspecta* 2 (1953), 10–27; Louis I. Kahn, "Order in Architecture," *Perspecta* 4 (1957), 58–65. See also Anne Griswold Tyng, "Geometric Extensions of Consciousness," *Zodiac* 19 (1969), 160: "[Biology] is a field dealing with the physical aspects of man, with its animal origins, aspects of which are involved in the shadow archetype."

6 Peter Collins, *Changing Ideals in Modern Architecture 1750–1950* (London: Faber & Faber, 1965).

7 Banister Fletcher, *A History of Architecture on the Comparative Method* (London: B.T. Batsford/ New York: C. Scribner's Sons, 1896 [London: University of London/The Athlone Press, 1961]).

8 On the application of morphological criteria to the science of architecture, cf. Alfred Neumann, "Morphologic Architecture," *Zodiac* 19 (1969), 136–140.

9 Philip Steadman, *The Evolution of Designs: Biological Analogy in Architecture and the Applied Arts* (Cambridge: Cambridge University Press, 1979 [London/New York: Routledge, 2008]).

10 Another lineage of biological analogy in architecture, clarifying Gottfried Semper's and Viollet-le-Duc's contribution, is the one proposed by Caroline van Eck, *Organicism in Nineteenth-century Architecture: An Inquiry into Its Theoretical and Philosophical Background* (Amsterdam: Architectura & Natura Press, 1994), 228–240; see also Caroline van Eck, "What was Revolutionary about the Romantic Pensionnaires: The Role of Biology in the Work of Labrouste, Vaudoyer and Reynaud," in *L'architecture, les sciences et la culture de l'histoire au XIXe siècle* (Saint-Étienne: Publications de l'Université de Saint-Étienne, 2001), 83–98.

11 On the question of the diagram and its ambiguity as a design method, cf. Anthony Vidler, "Diagrams of Utopia: The Activist Drawing," *LOTUS International* 123 (2004), 28–41. On architectural diagrams of the twentieth-century, cf. the monographic issues of *OASE* 48 (1998), *ANY* 23 (1998), *Daidalos* 74 (2000), *LOTUS International* 127 (2006). Focused on the US context of the 1920s and 1930s, cf. Hyungmin Pai, *The Portfolio and the Diagram. Architecture, Discourse, and Modernity in America* (Cambridge MA: MIT Press, 2002). On diagrams in the British post-World War II context, cf. Maddalena Scimemi, "The Other History of English Modernism," *Daidalos* 74 (2000), 14–21.

12 D'Arcy Wentworth Thompson, *On Growth and Form* (Cambridge: Cambridge University Press, 1917 [1942]); Patrick Geddes, *Cities in evolution* (London: Williams & Norgate, 1915 [1949, with a new introduction by Lewis Mumford]); Matyla Glyka, *The Geometry of Art and Life* (London: Sheed and Ward, 1946).

13 László Moholy-Nagy, *Vision in Motion* (Chicago: Hillison & Etten, 1947). Cf. Maddalena Scimemi, "The Ethics of the Perception in the 'Machine Ages,'" in Gerd Zimmermann and Norbert Korrek, eds., *Medium Architektur. Zur Krise der Vermittlung, 9. Internationales Bauhaus-Kolloquium* (Weimar: Bauhaus Universität, 2003), Vol. 1, 168–176.

14 Complementary to the topic of Le Corbusier and diagrams, is the essential discussion on Le Corbusier's books by Catherine de Smet, *Vers une architecture du livre. Le Corbusier: édition et mise en pages 1912–1965* (Baden: Müller, 2007).

15 The work of Patrick Geddes was a favourite topic of the post-war CIAM. The new edition of *Cities in Evolution* followed a tiny book by the secretary of Sigfried Giedion (disciple of Geddes): Jaqueline Tyrwhitt, *Partick Geddes in India* (London: Lund Humphries, 1947). Cf. Michael Darroch and Janine Marchessault, "Anonymous History as Methodology: The Collaborations of Sigfried Giedion, Jaqueline Tyrwhitt, and the 'Explorations' Group (1951–55)," in Andreas Broeckmann and Gunalan Nadarajan, eds., *Place Studies in Art, Media, Science and Technology* (Weimar: VDG, 2008), 9–27. On the role of Tyrwhitt cf. Ellen Shoshkes, *Jaqueline Tyrwhitt: A Transnational Life in Urban Planning and Design* (London: Routledge, 2016); see also Paola Zanotto, *Backstage Chronicles: Jaqueline Tyrwhitt's Contributions in Three Emerging Issues of the Contemporary City: Interdisciplinarity, Media Networks and Sustainability* (PhD diss., Università Iuav di Venezia, 2015).

16 Others include Patrick Abercrombie, Maxwell Fry and Jane Drew, Jaqueline Tyrwhitt, Ernö Goldfinger, Arthur Korn, and Berthold Lubetkin. Cf., among others, Maxwell Fry, "Arthur Korn and the English MARS Group," in Dennis Sharp and Walter Bor, eds., *Planning and Architecture* (London: Barrie & Rockliff, 1967), 127-128; Peter Coe and Malcom Reading, *Lubetkin and Tecton: Architecture and Social Commitment* (Bristol: University of Bristol Unit., 1981); John R. Gold, "The MARS Plans for London, 1933–1942: Plurality and Experimentation in the City Plans of the Early British Modern Movement," *The Town Planning Review* 3 (1995), 243–267; Alan Powers, *Modern: The Modern Movement in Britain* (London: Merrell, 2005).

17 Several studies on the IG "young rebels," inspired by Reyner Bahnam, *The New Brutalism, Ethic or Aesthetic?* (Stuttgart/Bern: Karl Krämer Publishers, 1966), have recently enriched the state of the research. Cf., among others, Lisa Tickner and David Peters Corbett, eds., "British Art and the Cultural Field, 1939–69," monographic issue, *Art History* 35 (2012); Claire Zimmerman and Mark Crinson, eds., *Neo-avant-garde and Postmodern: Postwar Architecture in Britain and Beyond* (New Haven: Yale University Press, 2010). See also

Claude Lichtenstein and Thomas Schregenberger, eds., *As Found: die Entdeckung des Gewöhnlichen/ The Discovery of the Ordinary* (Baden: Springer Science & Business Media, 2001); Anne Massey, *The Independent Group*, Manchester/New York: Manchester University Press, 1995); David Robbins, ed., *The Independent Group: Postwar Britain and the Aesthetics of Plenty* (Cambridge MA: MIT Press, 1990).

18 Lancelot Law White, "On the Frontiers of Science: This Hierarchical Universe," *Architectural Design* 10 (1972), 611: "Now what is a 'hierarchy'? Since I am now entering the realm of Science, I must stress that I am speaking as a frontiersman without the authority of Science. A structural hierarchy may be define as a spatial system, displaying a sequence of stable structures. It is a system of subsystems, from larger and more complex to simpler ones."

19 Lancelot Law Whyte (1896–1972) was a major figure in science and philosophy who brought his approach into the living community of art historians, artists and architects in London during the 1950s. He had served as Director of Statistical Enquiries in the Ministry of Supplies during World War II. Among his books are: *The Unitary Principle in Physics and Biology* (London: The Cresset Press, 1949); *Aspects of Form: A Symposium on Form in Nature and Art* (London: Pellegrini & Cudahy, 1951); *Internal factors in evolution* (New York: G. Braziller, 1965).

20 Further publications on Hamilton's contribution to the exhibition are in Jolivette, "Science, Art and Landscape in the Nuclear Age," 254–255, note 15.

21 This is one of Lasdun's first autonomous projects after years of practicing with Wells Coates (1935–1937), and with Tecton (1937–1938), becoming partner in 1946. See William Curtis, *Denys Lasdun: Architecture, City, Landscape* (London: Phaidon, 1999), 42. Denys Lasdun taught at Architectural Association in London from 1953–1959 while Cedric Price was attending his diploma (1957). For more about Price, cf. later in this essay.

22 Alison and Peter Smithson, "Cluster City," *The Architectural Review* 730 (1957), 333–336; Alison and Peter Smithson, *Urban Structuring* (London: Studio Vista, 1967); Alison and Peter Smithson, *Ordinariness and Light, Urban Theories 1952–1960* (London: Faber & Faber, 1970). On the cluster frame, cf. Banham, *The New Brutalism*, 73-75. See also Maddalena Scimemi, "An Open Work by the Smithsons at Bad Karlshafen," *Casabella* 726 (2004), 6–21; on Berlin, cf. Johannes Warda, *Keeping West Berlin "As Found." Alison Smithson, Hardt-Waltherr Hämer and 1970s Proto-Preservation Urban Renewal*, in Ákos Moravánszky, Torsten Lange, Judith Hopfengärtner, Karl R. Kegler, eds., *East West Central. Rebuilding Europe 1950–1990, Re-framing identities* (Basel: Birkhäuser, 2017), Vol. 3, 275–288.

23 György Kepes, *Language of Vision* (Chicago: Theobald, 1948); György Kepes, *The New Landscape in Art and Science* (Chicago: Theobald & Co., 1956); James R. Killian, *György Kepes: The MIT Years 1945–1977. Paintings, Photographic Work, Environmental Pieces, Projects at the Center for Advanced Visual Studies* (Cambridge MA: MIT Press, 1978).

24 Following Wittkower's steps, his disciple Colin Rowe applied diagrams in comparing works by Palladio and Le Corbusier, and by Michelangelo and the Dutch painter Mondrian. Cf. Colin Rowe, "The Mathematics of the Ideal Villa," *The Architectural Review* 603 (1947), 101–104; Colin Rowe, "Mannerism and Modern Movement," *The Architectural Review* 641 (1950), 289–300; Colin Rowe, "Dominican Monastery of La Tourette – Eveux sur Arbresle, Lyons," *The Architectural Review* 772 (1961), 401–410; Colin Rowe, and Robert Slutzky, "Transparency: Literal and Phenomenal – Part 2," *Perspecta* 13/14 (1971), 286–301. See also Nicholas Bullock, *Building the Post-War World. Modern Architecture and Reconstruction in Britain*, (London & New York: Routledge, 2002), 106-109.

25 Kenneth Frampton, "The Mutual Limits of Architecture and Science," in Galison, Thompson, eds., *The Architecture of Science*, 358. On Banham's influential role, see also Todd Gannon, *Reyner Banham and the Paradoxes of High Tech* (Los Angeles: The Getty Research Institute, 2017).

26 On the professional practices of Ove Arup and Felix Samuely, and in particular on the younger engineers Ronald S. Jenkins, Peter Rice and Frank Newby, cf. Andrew Saint, *Architect and Engineer. A Study in Sibling Rivalry* (New Haven: Yale University Press, 2007), 365–370, 386–394; see also Maddalena Scimemi, "English Thoughts: Peter and Alison Smithson/Hunstanton Secondary Modern School (1949–1954)," *Casabella* 750–751 (2006–2007), 28–41.

27 Cf. Peter Murray, ed., "CP Supplement," *Architectural Design* 10 (1970), 507-522. This was the first section of five serialized surveys of the work of Cedric Price. See *Architectural Design* 1, 6, 10 (1971) and 1(1972).

28 Stanley Mathews, *From Agit-Prop to Free Space: The Architecture of Cedric Price* (London: Black Dog Publishing, 2007); Hans Ulrich Obrist, *Cedric Price – The Conversation Series 21* (Köln: Walther Konig, 2009); Samantha Hardingham, *Cedric Price, Works 1952–2003: A Forward-minded Retrospective* (Montreal/London: Canadian Centre for Architecture/Architectural Association, 2016).

29 On the first phase of the *Fun Palace Pilot Project*, cf. Mathews, *From Agit-Prop to Free Space*, 84.

30 Ibid., 73.

31 First used by Fumiko Maki, *Investigations in Collective Form* (The School of Architecture, Washington University: Saint Louis, 1964), the term "megastructure" became a book by Reyner Banham, *Megastructures: Urban Futures*

for Recent Past (London: Thames & Hudson, 1976). On Price's *Fun Palace*, cf. ibid., 84-88.

32 On June 18, 1956 Banham left the I.C.A. and was replaced by Colin St. John Wilson and Lawrence Alloway. In 1958, the I.C.A. featured a lecture by Buckminster Fuller and the projection of the film of Charles and Ray Eames *The Information Machine* (1958), both attended by Price. Cf. Mathews, *From Agit-Prop to Free Space*, 34.

33 ICA Building materials are to be found in the archive of the Canadian Center for Architecture (Cedric Price fonds, Centre Canadien d'Architecture/ Canadian Centre for Architecture, Montreal, no. DR1995:0208:001–004). See also Hardingham, *Cedric Price, Works 1952-2003*, vol. "Projects", 165.

34 See the Ham Common Flats, Richmond (1955–1958) and the tower for Administration in Leicester University Engineering Building, Leicester (1959–1963). On these "simple diagrams" see Anthony Vidler, ed., *James Frazer Stirling, Notes from the Archive* (Montreal/New Haven: Canadian Center for Architecture/Yale Center for British Art, 2011), 116-118 and 126-138. In the same years Price would involve Frank Newby, the consultant engineer for Leicester's structural work, in holding the Aviary job at the London Zoo (1962–1965). Cf. Peter Reyner Banham, "Aviary, London Zoological Gardens," *Architectural Design* 6 (1965), 263.

35 Banham, *The New Brutalism*, 134. See also Alvin Boyarsky, "Stirling 'Dimostrationi'", *Architectural Design* 10 (1968), 454-455.

36 Cf. Martin Meade, *Il Mechanics Institute, un precedente ambiguo delle case del popolo*, in Marco De Michelis, ed., *Case del popolo* (Venezia: Marsilio, 1984), 3–24.

37 Sarah Williams Ksiazek, *Critique of Liberal Individualism: Louis Kahn's Civic Projects 1947–57*, in *Assemblage* 31 (1997), 56–79, and Sarah Williams Goldhagen, *Louis Kahn's Situated Modernism* (New Haven: Yale University Press, 2001), 33-37.

38 Starting from the Centre Pompidou by Rogers and Piano, inaugurated in 1977 in Paris, and ending with the bankrupt "Cloud" or EUR Convention Center by Massimiliano Fuksas in Rome of 2016.

39 James Stirling, *On Drawing*, in *James Stirling*, exhibition catalogue (London: RIBA Publications, 1974). On Stirling's diagrams and transparency, cf. Laurent Stalder, Moritz Gleich and Jill Denton Source, "Stirling's Arrows," *AA Files 72* (2016), 57–67.

40 "No architectural high jinks, no applied whoopee styling; nothing to shield one from the uncomfortable necessity of judging whether the building was a human answer to the occupants' needs. Humankind cannot bear too much reality" (Stephen Mullin, "Cedric Price or Still Keeps Going When Everything Else Has Stopped," *Architectural Design* 5 (1976), 287.

41 Vidler, "Diagrams of Utopia: The Activist drawing," 38.

42 Cedric Price, *Fun Palace Project, Services Towers*, 1963 (Cedric Price fonds, Centre Canadien d'Architecture/Canadian Centre for Architecture, Montreal, no. DR1995:0188:010).

43 Significantly in 1963 Focillon's book on Piranesi had just been reprinted: Henri Focillon, *Giovanni-Battista Piranesi 1720–1778* (Paris: Henri Laurens, 1918 [1963]). The work of Piranesi was part of the education of the London schools of architecture and topic of discussion by the most considerable art historians across the ocean; cf. Rudolf Wittkower, *Piranesi as Architect*, in Robert O. Parks, ed., *Piranesi*, exhibition catalogue (Northampton MA: Smith College Museum of Art, 1961). See also *Archigram* 5 (1965), where one finds among other visionary urban sets the "Imaginary Prisons" by Piranesi.

Learning from No-Stop City: Archizoom's Utopia Revisited
Marie Theres Stauffer

1 Archizoom, "Discorso per immagini," *Domus* 481 (1969), 46–48.

2 Cf. Marie Theres Stauffer, *Figurationen des Utopischen, Theoretische Projekte von Archizoom und Superstudio* (Munich: Deutscher Kunstverlag, 2008); Roberto Gargiani, *Archizoom associati, 1966–1974: Dall'onda pop alla superficie neutra* (Milan: Electa, 2007); Dominique Rouillard, *Superarchitecture: Le futur de l'architecture 1950–1970* (Paris: Hazan, 2004); Peter Lang, and William Menking, *Superstudio: Life without Objects* (Milan: Skira, 2003); Gianni Pettena, ed., *Superstudio 1966–1982: Storie, figure, architettura* (Florence: Electa, 1982).

3 Cf. Archizoom, "Archizoom, Gazebi," *Pianeta Fresco* 1 (1967): [s.p.]; Archizoom, "Le stanze vuote e i gazebi," *Domus* 462 (1968), 51–53; Archizoom, "Stand Archizoom alla XIV, Triennale," *Domus* 466 (1968), 35; Archizoom, "Il teatro impossibile," *Pianeta Fresco* 2–3 (1968), [s.p.]; Archizoom, "New York 7000 Km [Concorso per la Fortezza da Basso a Firenze]," *Casabella* 336 (1969), 33; Archizoom, "[Intervento sul] Dibattito sulla Triennale del 1968," *Casabella* 333 (1969), 44–45; Archizoom, "Architettonicamente," *Casabella* 334 (1969) 36–41.

4 The term "architecture of the city" is a deliberate reference to Aldo Rossi's *L'architettura della città* (Padua: Marsilio, 1966).

5 A further reconstruction of the historic center also took place after the Second World War, particularly in the area of the Ponte Vecchio. While the bridge was preserved, immediately adjoining streets were destroyed in 1944 by the retreating German troops to delay the pursuing Allied forces. This situation cannot be discussed here in detail, but it should be mentioned that the newly erected buildings surrounding the Ponte Vecchio have

been rebuilt in a style combining old and modern designs, with varying degrees of success.

6 On this point, cf. for example Amedeo Belluzzi and Claudia Conforti, *Architettura italiana 1944–94* (Rome: Laterza, 1994).

7 Andrea Branzi in conversations with the author in December 2002 and April 2007.

8 Ibid.

9 A few exceptions to this were the model estates erected under special conditions, such as the INA-Casa residential complexes. On these, cf. Stephanie Zeier Pilat, *Reconstructing Italy: the Ina-Casa Neighborhoods of the Postwar Era* (Farnham: Ashgate, 2014), and numerous articles published in Italian architecture journals such as *Domus, Casabella,* among others.

10 Archizoom, "Città, catena di montaggio del sociale, Ideologia e teoria della metropoli," *Casabella* 350–351 (1970), 43–52; Archizoom, "Archizoom," *Architectural Design* 7 (1970), 330–331; Archizoom, "Firenze: Università," *Casabella* 358 (1971), 12–13; Archizoom, "Utopia della qualità, utopia della quantità," *In* 1 (1971), 30–35; Archizoom, "No-Stop City, Residential Parkings, Climatic Universal Sistem [sic]," *Domus* 496 (1971), 49–55; Archizoom, "La distruzione degli oggetti," *In* 2–3 (1971), 4–13; Archizoom, "[Intervento]," in *52 Interventi sulla proposta di comportamento di Enzo Mari*, Lea Vergine, ed., *NAC* 8–9 (1971), 9–11; Archizoom, "Distruzione e riappropriazione della città," *In* 5 (1972), 3–23; Archizoom, "La città amorale," *In* 7 (1972), 27; Archizoom, "Progetto per il concorso per l'Università di Firenze," *Domus* 509 (1972), 10–12.

11 Only the best known architectural journals are listed here. Further publications are cited in Stauffer, *Figurationen des Utopischen*, 25–43.

12 Cf. in particular Archizoom, "No-Stop City," 51.

13 In addition to Archizoom, *architettura radicale* was also associated in Florence with the architectural groups Superstudio, U.F.O., Zziggurat, and 9999, as well as Gianni Pettena und Remo Buti; in Milan with Ugo La Pietra, Alessandro Mendini, Gaetano Pesce, Franco Raggi, and Ettore Sottsass Jr.; in Turin with the groups Libidarch and Strum; and in Naples with Ricardo Dalisi. However, *architettura radicale* was never an organized movement; instead, it is more of a conceptual association thought to have been developed by art historian Germano Celant. around 1972. Cf. Germano Celant, "Radical Architecture," in Emilio Ambasz, ed., *Italy: The New Domestic Landscape* (New York: Museum of Modern Art, 1972), 380–388; Germano Celant, "Senza titolo," *In* 2–3 (1971), 76–81.

14 Archizoom, "Città, catena di montaggio",43–44.

15 Ibid.

16 Ibid., 43–52. In fact, Archizoom adopted these systems with particular intentions (to be discussed in a further article).

17 Ibid.

18 This version of *No-Stop City* was submitted for a competition for the new home of the Università di Firenze in 1971. Moreover, Archizoom documented a whole series of modern propositions for housing estates in their article "Architettonicamente," *Casabella* 334 (1969), 36–41.

19 Archizoom, "Città, catena di montaggio," 43–52; Archizoom, "Archizoom," 330–331; Archizoom, "Firenze: Università," 12–13; Archizoom, "Utopia della qualità," 30–35; Archizoom, "No-Stop City," 49–55; Archizoom, "La distruzione degli oggetti," 4–13.

20 Important members of Team 10 included Alison and Peter Smithson, Georges Candilis, Shadrach Woods, Jacob Bakema, Aldo van Eyck, Giancarlo De Carlo, and Stefan Wewerka. It should also be emphasized that the postwar CIAM congresses often involved revision of earlier work.

21 In Italy, Manfredo Tafuri was the most important theorist denouncing modern architecture's complicity with capitalism. Cf. Manfredo Tafuri, *Teoria e storia dell'architettura* (Bari: Laterza, 1968); Manfredo Tafuri, "Per una critica dell'ideologia architettonica," *Contropiano* 1 (1969), 31–79.

22 In fact, "*la nuova dimensione*" was one of the fashionable topics among the faculty of architecture of the University of Florence. The first design for a large-scale construction can be traced to Paolo Deganello, later a member of Archizoom. In 1963, he had designed an "urban structure" extending from Florence to Prato that could provide living and working space for 70,000 inhabitants (Deganello, in conversation with the author, Milan, October 2001; Carlo Chiappi and Paolo Marliani collaborated on the project, and Gilberto Corretti confirmed these facts in Florence in November 2001). This was followed in 1964 by a design for a megastructure drawn up by a group including the later Archizoom members Branzi, Corretti, and Morozzi, and the later Superstudio member Cristiano Toraldo di Francia, along with four other students). Cf. *Gilberto Corretti: Professione designer* (Florence: Alinea, 1993), [s.p.]; Lara Vinca Masini, "Archifirenze," *Domus* 509 (1972), 40; Paola Navone and Bruno Orlandoni, *Architettura radicale* (Milan: Segrate, 1974), 19; Bruno Orlandoni and Giorgio Vallino, *Dalla città al cucchiaio* (Turin: Studio Forma, 1977), 16–19; Cristina Rattazzi, *Andrea Branzi, Militanza tra teoria e prassi* (Milan: Angeli, 1997), 65.

23 On this point, cf. for example Mathias Listl, "Gegenentwürfe zu Moderne, Paradigmenwechsel" *in Architektur und Design, 1945–1975* (Cologne: Böhlau, 2014); Ingo Bohning, *"Autonome Architektur" und "partizipatorisches Bauen": zwei Architekturkonzepte* (Basel: Birkhäuser, 1981).

24 Archizoom, "Città, catena di montaggio," 44: "Solo così si può interrompere la continuità dei processi e dei legami, facendo impazzire il Cervello del Sistema."

25 Ibid.: "L'Utopia però che noi utilizziamo è solo strumentale: essa rappresenta se stessa, ma non come prefigurazione di un Modello Diverso del Sistema (che non esiste Metropoli Operaia) [...] come [...] Ipotesi critica sul Sistema stesso."

26 Archizoom, "Utopia della qualità," 30: "Tale Modello Urbano non rappresenta però l'alternativa alla realtà attuale, ma piuttosto rappresenta la realtà attuale ad un livello di Coscienza Critico nuovo."

27 Cf. Stauffer, *Figurationen des Utopischen,* 103–122.

28 Cf. also Beda Alleman, *Ironie und Dichtung* (Pfullingen: Neske, 1969); Ernst Behler, *Klassische Ironie. Romantische Ironie, Tragische Ironie* (Darmstadt: Wissenschaftliche Buchgesellschaft, 1972); Ernst Behler, *Ironie und literarische Moderne* (Munich: Schöningh, 1997); Uwe Japp, *Theorie der Ironie* (Frankfurt am Main: Klostermann, 1992).

29 In conversations with the author, Gilberto Corretti and Paolo Deganello independently mentioned that Superstudio founder Adolfo Natalini had introduced Pop Art into their circle. However, Natalini was not the only person to combine architectural studies with an interest in visual art. Instead, this dual attitude—or synthetic design approach—is reflected in several of the careers of the Archizoom and Superstudio architects: Andrea Branzi received art training from the Florentine painter Piero Vignozzi; cf. Franco Fioretti, *Archizoom e Superstudio, Protagonisti dell'architettura radicale, Firenze 1966–1972* (PhD diss., University of Venice 1999/2000), xxiv. Archizoom architects Corretti and Bartolini also had ambitions to become artists when in their teens. The latter, at least, returned to art after several years practicing as a designer and has been active as an object artist since the 1980s; cf. Dario Bartolini, *Acque, meridiane* (Pistoia: Maschietto & Musolino, 2001), catalogue of an exhibition at the Galleria d'Arte Moderna di Palazzo Pitti. In general, however, it is true for all the Archizoom architects that their engagement with art—British and American Pop Art in particular—was a central topic during their studies and in their initial years as practicing architects. On Archizoom's references to Pop Art cf. also Stauffer, *Figurationen des Utopischen*, 149–181.

30 Conversations of the author with former members of the Archizoom group, November and December 2001.

31 Cf. also Stauffer, *Figurationen des Utopischen,* 204–205.

32 Archizoom, "Utopia della qualità," 30: "Da una parte l'Architettura cessa di essere Naturale, e dall'altra la Natura cessa di essere Cultura."

33 Cf. Archizoom, "Città, catena di montaggio," 51.

34 Archizoom "No-Stop City. Residential Parkings. Climatic Universal Sistem (*sic*)." Cf. Archizoom, "No-Stop City," 49.

35 I am grateful to Marco De Michelis for drawing my attention to specific aspects of Graham's project.

36 Philippe Vergne, "Dan Graham," in *Bits & Pieces Put Together to Present a Semblance of a Whole: Walker Art Center Collections,* Joan Rothfuss and Elizabeth Carpenter, eds. (Minneapolis, MN: Walker Art Center, 2005), 244.

37 Cf. also Stauffer, *Figurationen des Utopischen,* 217–222.

38 Thomas More, *Libellus vere aureus nec minus salutaris quam festiuus de optimo reipublicae statu deque nova insula Utopia* (Louvain: Martinus, 1516); see also *Thomas Morus: Utopia,* George M. Logan and Robert M. Adams ed. and trans. (Cambridge EN: Cambridge University Press, 2002). The title was a neologism created by More meaning "no-place." However, the concept of utopian qualities, in the sense of an ideal contrasted with a defective reality, goes back to antiquity: one of the earliest examples is Plato's *Republic* (Πολ⊠τεία). Cf. Plato, *The Republic,* Chris Emlyn-Jones and William Preddy, ed. and trans.(Cambridge MA: Harvard University Press, 2013). More also refers to Plato's *Politeia* in his *Utopia;* cf. Ulrich Dierse, "Utopie," in *Historisches Wörterbuch der Philosophie*, Joachim Ritter, Karlfried Gründer, and Gottfried Gabriel, eds. (Basel: Schwabe & Co., 2001), 11, 510.

39 This definition is given in Wolfgang Biesterfeld, ed., *Utopie* (Stuttgart: Reclam, 1985), 139. A comprehensive overview of the history of debates over utopia is provided by Wilhelm Vosskamp, *Utopieforschung* (Frankfurt am Main: Suhrkamp, 1985).

40 Miriam Eliav-Feldon, *Realistic Utopias: The Ideal Imaginary Societies of the Renaissance 1516–1630* (Oxford: Clarendon Press, 1982), [1].

41 Archizoom, "Città, catena del montaggio," 44: "[Non] si tratta di una 'alternativa,'" "[non è] prefigurazione di un Modello Diverso del Sistema."

42 On utopia as an anticipation of the future, cf. for example Hanno-Walter Kruft, *Städte in Utopia: Die Idealstadt vom 15, bis 18, Jahrhundert zwischen Staatsutopie und Wirklichkeit* (Munich: Beck, 1989). On utopia as a better state that is genuinely possible, cf. Ernst Bloch, *The Principle of Hope*, Neville Plaice, Stephen Plaice, and Paul Knight, trans. (Cambridge, MA: MIT Press, 1986 [1959]).

43 Archizoom, [Intervento], 9: "Di fatto l'elaborazione utopica, proprio perché tesa a contribuire alla risoluzione degli squilibri e delle contraddizioni dello sviluppo, (in altri termini tesa al superamento dell''anarchia del capitale', e concentrato quindi non tanto sulla produzione capitalistica, ma sulla inefficacità della distribuzione capitalistica)

viene ad assumere sempre più il ruolo di ipotesi avanzata del futuro praticabile del capitale".

44 For example, the Florentine group of architects Superstudio wrote in 1972: "Solo nell'orrore è la speranza. Ed il Potere ha sempre conosciuto la forza di esso e con esso ha creato innumerevoli Inferni da protendere come spade contro i propri nemici nascosto dietro gli scudi delle proprie utopie." Cf. Superstudio, "Utopia Antiutopia Topia," *In* 7 (1972), 42.

45 Mario Tronti was co-founder of the Marxist journal *Quaderni rossi* and founder of the workers' movement journal *Classe operaia*, an important source for Archizoom. Massimo Cacciari had a brief affiliation with *Potere operaio*, a radical left-wing Italian political group, and he wrote for *Classe operaia* until 1968. Regarding Archizoom's *No-Stop City*, Cacciari's writing *Sulla genesi del pensiero negativo* (1968) seems relevant.

46 Marco Biraghi, "Manfredo Tafuri (1935–1994)," *The Architectural Review*, June 9, 2014, accessed December 19, 2015: http://www.architectural-review.com/rethink/reputations/manfredo-tafuri-1935-1994/8663417.

47 Cf. Tafuri, "Per una critica dell'ideologia architettonica" 31–79; Manfredo Tafuri, *Progetto e utopia: architettura e sviluppo capitalistico* (Bari: Laterza, 1973). Although Archizoom and Tafuri had comparable views, the later strongly criticized projects such as *No-Stop City.* Cf. Tafuri, "Design and Technological Utopia," in *Italy: The New Domestic Landscape*, Emilio Ambasz, ed., 398; Tafuri, *Progetto e utopia,* 130.

48 Cf. Friedrich Engels, "Ernst Moritz Arndt, Von F. Oswald (1841)," in Institut für Marxismus–Zentralkomitee der Kommunistischen Partei der Sowjetunion, Institut für Marxismus-Leninismus beim Zentralkomitee der Sozialistischen Einheitspartei Deutschlands, eds., *Marx-Engels-Gesamtausgabe* 1/3 (Berlin: Dietz, 1972), 210–222, 218; Karl Marx, "Ökonomische Manuskripte (1857/58)," in *Marx-Engels-Gesamtausgabe* 2/1.1, 171–172; Karl Marx, "Zur Kritik der Hegelschen Rechtsphilosophie, Einleitung (1844)," in *Marx-Engels-Werke* 1, Manfred Kliem et. al., eds. (Berlin: Dietz 1959–1971), 378–391, particularly 388. Cf. also Karl Marx, and Friedrich Engels, "Ökonomisch-philosophische Manuskripte (1844)," in *Marx-Engels-Gesamtausgabe* 1/2, 845; Karl Marx and Friedrich Engels, "Die heilige Familie (1945)," in *Marx-Engels-Werke* 2, Manfred Kliem et. al., eds., 3–223, particularly 212.

49 Max Horkheimer and Theodor Wiesengrund Adorno, *Dialektik der Aufklärung* (Frankfurt am Main: Fischer, 1986), 196. English translation: Alfred Schmidt and Gunzelin Schmid, eds., *Dialectic of Enlightenment*, trans. John Cumming, (New York: Herder & Herder, 1972); cf. also Max Horkheimer, "Die Utopie," in *Gesammelte Schriften,* 2 (Frankfurt am Main: Fischer, 1985–1996), 179–268, particularly 237–251; Theodor W. Adorno, *Negative Dialectics,* trans. E.B. Ashton (New York: Seabury Press, 1973).

50 Archizoom, "Città, catena di montaggio," 44; and Archizoom, "Utopia della qualità," 30: "L'utopia che noi utiliziamo è quindi soltanto *linguaggio Critico più generale*, che permette la Comunicazione più immediata e plefficace [*sic*]." A more detailed presentation of what is meant is given in Archizoom's article "[Intervento]," 9, op. cit.: "Unica utopia possibile, quindi capace di essere funzionale ad un programma più generale di eliminazione del modo capitalistico di produrre e della società che ne deriva, è l'utopia critica, cioè la visualizzazione esasperata delle contraddizioni della società, e l'indicazione alternativa che questa lettura critica impone. Cosí l'utopia esce dal campo delle manifestazioni creative, delle genialità formali, per diventare pura informazione, formazione di coscienza come condizione e preparazione al rifiuto".

51 Id. Archizoom, "[Intervento]," 10: "[La nostra UTOPIA] non ha valore definitivo e ideologico, ma semplicemente strategico e quindi continuamente e indefinitamente aggiornabile."

Leisure in a Time of Utopia

Massimiliano Savorra

1 The present work looks back to and enlarges upon: Massimiliano Savorra, "Ricerche sull'architettura del loisir: Cellule modulari, megastrutture e visioni utopiche per il turismo di massa tra anni Sessanta e Settanta," in *Architettura e paesaggi della villeggiatura in Italia tra Otto e Novecento,* Fabio Mangone, Gemma Belli, and Maria Grazia Tampieri, eds. (Milano: Franco Angeli, 2015), 51–72. I would like to thank especially Fabio Mangone for encouraging me a few years ago to take on this research and Dario Donetti for accepting this paper for the collection presented at the Florence symposium of 2014. I also wish to thank all those, in Italy and in France, who helped with bibliographical and archival material, as well as those who helped with primary information and printed sources. This essay is dedicated to the memory of my mother, who was fond of holiday villages.

2 Michel Ragon, *Où vivrons-nous demain?* (Paris: Robert Laffont, 1963), 23.

3 Ulrich Conrads and Hans G. Sperlich, *Fantastic Architecture* (Stuttgart: Verlag Gerd Hatje, 1960). Cf. also Larry Busbea, *Topologies: The Urban Utopia in France, 1960–1970* (Cambridge MA/London: MIT Press, 2007).

4 Massimiliano Savorra, "Ideologie, emozioni e design: Il 'Tempo libero' alla Triennale di Milano del 1964," *ASUP* 3 (2015 **[sic]; actually published 2016/17), 75–85.**

5 Georges Hourdin, *Une Civilisation des loisirs* (Paris: Calmann–Lévy, 1961). Cf. also Tom McDonough, ed., *Guy Debord and Situationist International: Texts and Documents* (Cambridge MA/London: MIT Press, 2002).

6 Cf. the renowned study by John Kenneth Galbraith, *The Affluent Society* (Boston: Houghton Mifflin, 1958).

7 Cf. Henri Lefebvre, *Critique de la vie quotidienne* (Paris: Grasset, 1947).

8 Georges Candilis, *Planen und Bauen für die Freizeit/ Recherches sur l'architecture des loisirs/Planning and Design for Leisure* (Stuttgart: Karl Krämer Verlag, 1972 [Paris: Editions Eyrolles, 1973]), 11.

9 Dirk Van den Heuvel and Max Risselada, eds., *Team 10: 1953–81: In Search of a Utopia of the Present* (Rotterdam: NAi Publishers, 2005). The list of the archives of the leading members of Team 10 may be consulted at: http://www.team10online.org.

10 Candilis, *Planen und Bauen für die Freizeit*, 5.

11 In France, between the end of the 1950s and the 1960s, building for tourism was part of a national program of planning policies. In particular, it envisaged the radical transformation of the Mediterranean coast, from the Camarque to the Spanish border: this shoreline of Languedoc-Roussillon constituted a complex of over 180 kilometers of beaches, which was expected to receive over half a million holidaymakers. Abel Thomas, a government commissioner, asked Candilis to chair a group of architects charged with studying and creating favorable conditions for the development of tourism in what was to be a "nouvelle Côte d'Azur." To that end five "tourist units" were created, of which four were built, each under the responsibility of one architect with total freedom of action: Jean Balladur designed la Grande-Motte; Jean Le Couteur devised the structure for Cap d'Adge; Edouard Hartanné and Raymond Gleize built the unit at Gruissan; Henri Castella and Pierre Lafitte worked on the area in Aude; and Candilis envisaged, in collaboration of Diwi Dreysse, Fernando Montez, Anja Blomstedt, Panayotis Frangouilis, Mario Bonilla, and Maria Kandreviotis, the complexes at Leucate-Barcarés. For a full report cf. Georges Candilis, *Bâtir la vie: Un architecte témoin de son temps* (Gollion CH: Infolio éditions, 2012), 271–280. Cf. also Claude Prelorenzo and Antoine Picon, *L'aventure du balnéaire, La Grande Motte de Jean Balladur* (Marseille: Éditions Parenthèses, 199, 23–42; Tom Avermaete, "Travelling Notions of Public and Private, The French Mass Tourism Projects of Candilis-Josic-Woods," *OASE* 64 (2004), 16–45; Bruno Vayssière, "L'originalità del caso francese negli anni Sessanta, le sue origini e i suoi problemi oggi," in *Paesaggi in verticale, Storia, progetto e valorizzazione del patrimonio alpino*, Guido Callegari, Antonio De Rossi, and Sergio Pace, eds. (Venezia: Marsilio Editori, 2006), 135–147; Bénédicte Chaljub, *Candilis Josic Woods* (Gollion CH-Paris: Infolio-Éditions du patrimoine Centre des monuments nationaux, 2010); Richard Klein, "Le bord de mer pour tous: Nouveaux programmes et villes nouvelles (1930-1975)," in *Tous à la plage! Villes balnéaires du XVIIIe siècle à nos jours*, Bernard Toulier, ed. (Paris: Lineart éditions: 2016), 73–97; Massimiliano Savorra, "Il Mediterraneo per tutti: Georges Candilis e il turismo per il Grande Numero," in *Immaginare il Mediterraneo: Architettura, arti, fotografia*, Andrea Maglio, Fabio Mangone, and Antonio Pizza eds. (Napoli: Artstudiopaparo, 2017), 235–245.

12 Bernard Toulier, "Nascita ed evoluzione delle città balneari in Francia XVIII–XX secolo," in *Milano Marittima 100: Paesaggi e architetture per il turismo balneare*, Valentina Orioli, ed. (Milano: Bruno Mondadori, 2012), 69–82.

13 Jos Bosman, "I CIAM del dopoguerra: un bilancio del Movimento Moderno," in "Gli ultimi CIAM," Dario Matteoni, ed., *Rassegna* 52 (1992), 6–21.

14 Bénédicte Chaljub, *Alexis Josic: Architectures, trames, figures* (Paris: Éditions L'Œil d'or, 2013), 67–80.

15 Following the same design principles, Pierre Raoux with Guy Guntz, Jean Claude Perrier, and Dimitri Augoustinos also built the *Les Baronnets* holiday complex at Le Grau du Roi. Cf. Giampiero Aloi, *Complessi turistici/Tourist complexes* (Milano: Hoepli, 1980), 97–102.

16 Tom Avermaete, *Another Modern: The post-war architecture and urbanism of Candilis-Josic-Woods* (Rotterdam: NAi Publishers, 2004), 334–378.

17 Julien Donada, *Bulles: Conversation avec Pascal Häusermann* (Bruxelles: Facteur humain, 2010).

18 Fulvio Irace, "Apologia e critica dell'idea megastrutturale," in *Utopia e crisi dell'antinatura: Momenti delle intenzioni architettoniche in Italia: Immaginazione megastrutturale dal Futurismo a oggi*, Enrico Crispolti, ed., exhibition catalog (Milano: Edizioni La Biennale di Venezia-Electa, 1978), 10.

19 On the ordering criteria of the Milanese event, cf. Savorra, "Ideologie, emozioni e design." On the Italian section, reflecting the debate on the coastal tourism developed in the preceding years, cf. Chiara Baglione, "La corsa al mare, La 'creazione del paesaggio' e la questione dello sviluppo turistico delle coste italiane," in *Ernesto Nathan Rogers 1909-1969*, Chiara Baglione, ed. (Milano: Franco Angeli, 2012), 112–121.

20 Umberto Eco and Vittorio Gregotti, "Sezione introduttiva a carattere internazionale," in *Tredicesima Triennale di Milano, 12 giugno–27 settembre 1964* (Milano: Triennale di Milano 1964), 14.

21 Cf. David Monteyne, *Fallout Shelter, Designing for Civil Defense in the Cold War* (Minneapolis-London: University of Minnesota Press, 2011); Chiara

Baglione, in "Come sopravvivere alla bomba. Architettura e protezione civile nell'America della Guerra fredda," in *Senza Pericolo! Costruzioni e sicurezza, Triennale di Milano, 3 maggio–1 settembre 2013,* Federico Bucci, ed. (Bologna: Editrice Compositori, 2013), 191–197.

22 Cf. Roberto Gargiani, *Dall'onda pop alla superficie neutra: Archizoom associati 1966–1974* (Milano: Electa, 2007); Marco Wolfler Calvo, *Archigram/ Metabolism: Utopie negli anni Sessanta* (Napoli: Clean, 2007); Roberto Gargiani and Beatrice Lampariello, *Superstudio* (Roma-Bari: Laterza, 2010); Rem Koolhaas and Hans Ulrich Obrist, *Project Japan: Metabolism Talk...* (Köln: Taschen, 2011); Beatriz Colomina and Craig Buckley, eds., *Clip Stamp Fold: The radical architecture of little magazines 196X to 197X* (Barcelona/Basel/ New York: Actar-Media/Modernity Program, Princeton University 2010); Peter Lang and William Menking, *Superstudio: Life without Objects* (Milano: Skira, 2013); Patrizia Mello, *Neoavanguardie e controcultura a Firenze: Il movimento Radical e i protagonisti di un cambiamento storico internazionale* (Firenze: Angelo Pontecorboli Editore 2017).

23 *Yona Friedman: Une utopie réalisée*, exhibition catalog (Paris: Editions du Musée d'Art Moderne, 1975); cf. also Manuel Orazi, "The Erratic Universe of Yona Friedman," in *Yona Friedman: The Dilution of Architecture,* Nader Seraj, ed. (Zurich: Park Books, 2015), 269–540. Justus Dahinden, *Structures urbaines de demain, analyses, thèse, projets* (Paris: Editions du Chêne, 1972).

24 Cf. contributions by Arata Isozaki, Hugh Hardy, Malcom Holzaman, Norman Pfeiffer, Aldo van Eyck, George Nelson, Archigram and others in *Quattordicesima Triennale di Milano: Esposizione internazionale delle arti decorative e industriali moderne e dell'architettura moderna, 30 maggio–28 luglio 1968*, exhibition catalog (Milano: Triennale di Milano, 1968). Cf. also Paola Nicolin, *Castelli di carte: La XIV Triennale di Milano, 1968* (Macerata: Quodlibet, 2011).

25 Giampiero Aloi, *Complessi turistici*; Marie Wozniak, "Sneeuwschepen: Franse alpen, 1960–2000," *OASE* 64 (2004), 47–77; Francine Glière, ed., *Archives professionnelles de Michel Bezançon: Architecte-urbaniste 1952–1985* (Chambery: Archives Departementales de Savoie, 2011).

26 Paolo Riani, "Dreamland di Yamagata presso Tokio," *L'architettura: Cronache e storia* 150 (1968); 804–808; Paolo Riani, "La città come trasformazione biologica," *Casabella* 327 (1968), 19.

27 In collaboration with Gengo Matsui, Kikutake had built in 1966 the *Pacific* complex at Chigasaki, a resort less than an hour away from Tokyo, which saw experimentation on a smaller scale with the idea of a recreational center complete with hotel, swimming pool, and amusements areas. Cf. Giampiero Aloi, *Hotel Motel* (Milano: Hoepli, 1970), 1–8.

28 Cf. Eric Mumford, *The CIAM Discourse on Urbanism, 1928–1960* (Cambridge MA/ London: MIT Press, 2000), 258–265.

29 "Utopia e realtà nell'urbanistica," *Edilizia Moderna* 82–83 (1964), 199.

30 Ludovico Quaroni and Helio Piñón, *Architetture di Julio Lafuente* (Roma: Officina, 1982), 96–97.

31 Franco Raggi, "Storia del pensiero negativo nella pratica del Radical Design dal '68 ad oggi: Il ruolo delle avanguardie tra evasione e impegno disciplinare," in *Utopia e crisi dell'antinatura: Momenti delle intenzioni architettoniche in Italia, Topologia e morfogenesi*, Lara Vinca Masini, ed., exhibition catalog (Milano: Edizioni La Biennale di Venezia-Electa, 1978), 20–24.

32 Reyner Banham, *Megastructure: Urban Futures of the Recent Past* (London: Thames & Hudson, 1976; Italian translation: *Le tentazioni dell'architettura: Megastrutture* (Roma-Bari: Laterza, 1980), 75–90. The text by Huizinga appeared in German in Amsterdam in 1939 and was translated soon after the war into a number of languages. In Italy it was published in 1946. Cf. also Umberto Eco, *"Homo ludens oggi,"* in Johan Huizinga, *Homo ludens* (Torino: Giulio Einaudi editore, 1973), vii–xvii.

33 Nicolas Schöffer, "Nouvelles structures pour l'avenir: la ville cybernétique," in Jean Balladur, Yona Friedman, Walter Jonas, Paul Maymont, Michel Ragon, and Nicolas Schöffer, *Les visionnaires de l'architecture* (Paris: Robert Laffont éditeur, 1965), 22–23. Cf. also Nicolas Schöffer, *La ville cybernétique* (Paris: Tchou, 1969).

34 Massimiliano Savorra, "La X Triennale e la casa prefabbricata," in *Casa per tutti: Abitare la città globale*, Fulvio Irace, ed., exhibition catalog (Milano: La Triennale di Milano-Electa, 2008), 115–121. Cf. also Eve Roy, "La question de la mobilité dans les représentations et experimentations architecturales en Europe de 1960 à 1975," *Rives méditerranéennes: Jeunes chercheurs* (2008), accessed October 9, 2013: http://www.rives.revues.org.

35 Pietro Natale Maggi, Luigi Morra, *Coordinazione modulare: Documentazione su studi e ricerche, Metodi, procedure e strumenti applicati all'edilizia abitativa industrializzata* (Milano: Franco Angeli, 1975).

36 Robert Kronenburg, *Houses in Motion: The Genesis, History and Development of the Portable Building* (Chichester: Wiley Academy, 2002); Véronique Willemin, *Maison mobiles* (Paris: Editions Alternatives, 2004); Arnt Cobbers and Oliver Jahn, *Prefab Houses* (Taschen, Köln 2010).

37 Paul Maymont, "L'urbanisme flottant a la conquête des espaces," in Balladur, Friedman, et al., *Les visionnaires de l'architecture*, 96–108.

38 Giovanni Klaus Koenig, "L'esecutivo dell'utopia," *Casabella* 347 (1970), 16–27; Manfredo Nicoletti,

Continuità Evoluzione Architettura (Bari: Dedalo, 1978), 48–65. Cf. also Manfredo Nicoletti, "Flash Gordon and the Twentieth Century Utopia," *Architectural Review* (1966), 87–91; Manfredo Nicoletti, "L'utopie du présent," *Architecture d'Aujourd'hui* 148 (1970), xiv; Manfredo Nicoletti, "The End of Utopia," 13/14 (1971), 268–279.

39 "Rudolph in sospensione," *L'architettura: Cronache e storia* 154 (1968), 320–321. A similar system was devised in 1978 by Vittorio Giorgini; cf. Marco Del Francia, ed., *La natura come modello: Vittorio Giorgini* (Firenze: Angelo Pontecorboli Editore, 2000), 68–69.

40 Blake Gopnick, "Casa dolce Habitat," in Blake Gopnick and Michael Sorkin, *Moshe Safdie: Habitat '67, Montreal* (Torino: Testo & Immagine, 1998), 19–23.

41 Banham, *Le tentazioni dell'architettura*, 121.

42 G. Mario Oliveri, "Industrializzazione dell'edilizia," *Casabella* 301 (1966), 22–33. On lab practice in schools of architecture, see the case of the University of Ulm, with its in-depth research on cells and polygonal grids, their linking, and their progressive transformation, aggregation, and juxtaposition. Cf. Giovanni Anceschi, ed., "Il contributo della scuola di Ulm," *Rassegna* 19 (1984).

43 Manfredo Tafuri, "La nuova dimensione urbana e la funzione dell'utopia," *L'Architettura: Cronache e storia* 124 (1966), 680–683.

44 Alan Hess, *Googie Redux: Ultramodern Roadside Architecture* (San Francisco: Chronicle Books, 2004).

45 "Inventaire des maisons en matières plastiques," *L'Architecture d'Aujourd'hui* 3 (1971), 34–35.

46 "La Maison tout en plastiques," *Arts Ménagers* 79 (1956), 44–47. Cf. also Gérard Monnier, ed., *Les Années ZUP: architectures de la croissance 1960–1973,* (Paris: Picard, 2002).

47 Claude Parent and Ionel Schein, "Essai pour un habitat individuel évolutif," *L'Architecture d'Aujourd'hui* 49 (1953), 4–5. Cf. also Silvia Berselli, *Ionel Schein: Dall'habitat evolutivo all'architecture populaire* (Mendrisio/Milano: Mendrisio Academy Press/Silvana Editoriale, 2015).

48 Arthur Quarmby, *The Plastics Architects* (London: Pall Mall Press, 1974), 44–45.

49 Reyner Banham, "A Clip-on Architecture," *Architectural Design* 35 (1965), 534–535. Cf. also Zygmunt Stanislaw Makowski, "Les applications structurales des plastiques dans l'industrie du bâtiment," *Plastiques bâtiment* 122 (1968), 9–10; Zygmunt Stanislaw Makowski, "Les structures en plastiques de Renzo Piano," *Plastiques bâtiment* 126 (1969), 10–17.

50 On the concept of "cluster," cf. also Dominique Rouillard, *Superarchitecture: Le futur de l'architecture 1950–1970* (Paris: Éditions de la Villette, 2004), 44–73.

51 Marco Vidotto, A+P Smithson: Pensieri, progetti e frammenti fino al 1990 (Genova: Sagep, 1991), 20.

52 Jean-Louis Chanéac, *Architecture interdite* (Paris: Éditions du Linteau, 2005), 31–34.

53 Cf. Georges Candilis, "L'Hexacube, Kunststoffraumzellen," *Bauen + Wohnen* 4 (1973), 144–145; Paul-Henri David, "Maisons Mobiles: Architecture Modulaire," *Technique et Architecture* 99 (1973), 57, 75.

54 P. Joly, "Habitations préfabriquées en matiéres plastiques en France," *L'Architecture d'Aujourd'hui* 117 (1965), LII; "Celulle préfabriquée en matiére plastique," *L'Architecture d'Aujourd'hui* 124 (1966), 102; Pascal Häusermann and Patrick Le Merdy, "Les Domobiles," *Techniques et Architecture* 292 (1973), 82.

55 The cells were produced in 1971 and sold by Bungalows International of Milano. They were first called *3L-tre letti*, then *la Tana,* and finally *BANGA*, and were used in some tourist complexes in Sicily and the Punta Lunga village at Vieste on the Gargano.

56 Extensive cataloging in Pamela Voigt, *Die Pionierphase des Bauens mit glasfaserverstärkten Kunststoffen (GFK) 1942 bis 1980* (PhD diss., Fakultät Gestaltung der Bauhaus Universität Weimar, 2007).

57 Philippe Bancilhon, *Jean Benjamin Maneval: La Bulle six coques* (Paris: Jousse éditions, 2004), 10–11.

58 The "Bulle trois coques" prototype was perfected in 1966. Cf. Jean Maneval, "Bâtiplastique," *L'Architecture d'Aujourd'hui* 137 (1967), 90.

59 The 1971 Fair also saw the exhibition of the prototypes of *Unità Algeco "2002"* and of *Habitat 3H Design*, built out of Styrofoam, PVC, phenol resin, polyurethane, and polyester. Among the advantages of these modules was the ease of transport, which could take place in liquid form.

60 Marko Home and Mika Taanila, eds., *Futuro: Tomorrow's House from Yesterday* (Helsinki: Desura Oy, 2002).

61 Cf. Vittorio Gregotti, *Il disegno del prodotto industriale, Italia 1860–1980* (Milano: Electa, 1986), 329.

62 Cf. William Katavalos, *Organics* (Hilversum: de Jong, 1961).

63 Cf. Mario Scheichenbauer, "Progettare con le materie plastiche," *Casabella* 313, (1967), 42–49. This inaugurated a series of articles by Scheichenbauer published up to issue 320 of the same magazine, which in those years paid special attention to new materials and experimentation with prefabricated elements.

64 Cf. Heinrich Klotz, ed., *Vision der Moderne: Das Prinzip Konstruktion*, exhibition catalog (München: Prestel-Verlag, 1986).

65 In addition to the catalog of the exhibition curated by Ambasz, cf. also Franco Raggi, "Italy: The New Domestic Landscape," *Casabella* 366 (1972), 12–26, which presented, among others, the models of cell-cabin by Colombo, Sottsass, Zanuso, and Rosselli. Cf. also the articles in the magazine *Abitare*, July–August 1972.

66 "Utopia," *Edilizia Moderna* 89–90 (1966), 218. This short article quoted the February 1966 issue of the magazine *Architectural Design*, dedicated to the architecture of the future.

67 Luigi Pellegrin, *Un percorso nel potenziare il mestiere del costruire* (Milano: Silvana Editoriale, 2003), 72–73, 88–90.

68 "Taormina 1968: Villaggio turistico, Fabrizio Carola," entry no. 8, *Casabella* 332 (1969).

69 Dante Bini, *A cavallo di un soffio d'aria: L'architettura autoformante* (Milano: Guerini e Associati, 2009).

70 *Architectures expérimentales 1950–2000* (Orléans: collection du FRAC Centre, HYX, 2003).

71 Mauro Scionti, "La fine dell'utopia," *Parametro* 87 (1980), 25–51.

72 Carlo Guenzi, "Concorso per l'euro-kursaal," *Casabella* 299 (1965), 63.

73 *Ibid.*

74 Pietro D. Patrone, *Daneri* (Genova: Sagep, 1982), 166–168; Guido Montanari, *Architettura tra ricostruzione e transizione: Progetti e realizzazioni di Sergio J. Hutter* (Milano: Edizioni Lybra Immagine, 2004), 182–187.

75 This work by Marcello D'Olivo (1921–1991), the *Gusmay*, included fifteen hotels arranged around a large ring road, from which a number of roads arced out along the ridges with houses arranged in "clusters." Cf. Ferruccio Luppi, "Manacore (1959–64)," in *Marcello D'Olivo, Architetture e progetti 1947–1991*, Guido Zucconi ed. (Milano: Electa, 1998), 51–57.

76 The ENI complex was designed by a team including, among others, Gianemilio (1920–2002), Pietro (1922–1990) and Anna (1923–) Monti, and Ignazio Gardella (1905–1999). Cf. Dorothea Deschermeier, *Impero ENI: L'architettura aziendale e l'urbanistica di Enrico Mattei* (Bologna: Damiani, 2008), 95.

77 "Due insediamenti turistici nel Mezzogiorno: 1. Albergo-villaggio a Marina di Ostuni, Brindisi; 2. Albergo-villaggio a Isola Capo Rizzuto, Catanzaro: Architetti Luisa Anversa Ferretti, Gabriele Belardelli. Coordinatori Lucio Barbera, Claudio Maroni, Vieri Quilici, con la consulenza dell'Ufficio Tecnico Valtur," *L'Architettura: Cronache e storia* 175 (1970), 6–17. [Interviews with the author and other archtiects.]

78 Claudia Conforti, "Roma, Napoli, la Sicilia," in *Storia dell'architettura italiana: Il secondo Novecento*, Francesco Dal Co, ed. (Milano: Electa, 1995),195.

79 "Due insediamenti turistici nel Mezziogiorno," 20–29 (see note 77 above); "Hotel-villaggio Valtur a Brucoli, Siracusa: Architetti Luisa Anversa, Lucio Barbera, Gabriele Belardelli, con la consulenza di Jean Weiler e dell'Ufficio Tecnico Valtur," *L'Architettura: Cronache e storia* 230 (1974), 494–505.

80 The Valtur company was constituted with the aim of encouraging tourism in the Mediterranean area, through the creation and management of a series of integrated tourist centers of large dimensions and on vast extensions of ground. In the space of a few years, Valtur had built villages in Apulia, in Calabria, and in Sicily. Notable among them is the complex at Pollina (1973–75), by Antonio Foscari with Francesco Doglioni.

81 "Consuntivo di un'esperienza di progettazione: dialogo con i protagonisti," *L'Architettura: Cronache e storia* 175 (1970), 18–19.

82 *Ibid.*

83 *Ibid.*

84 *Ibid.*

85 *Progettare in Costa: Disegni, spazi e architetture nella Gallura del secondo Novecento*, exhibition catalog (Olbia: Soprintendenza per i Beni Architettonici il Paesaggio e il Patrimonio Storico Artistico Etnoantropologico per Sassari e Nuoro-Ordine degli Architetti, Pianificatori, Paesaggisti e Conservatori della provincia di Sassari, 2005).

86 Cesare de Seta, *Città, territorio e Mezzogiorno in Italia* (Torino: Giulio Einaudi Editore, 1977), 131–133.

87 In some cases, these activities were more than theoretical. For instance, the "Festivals of proletarian youth" promoted by *Re Nudo*, one of the leading counter-cultural and counter-information magazines, one of whose slogans was "let's turn free time into freed time." These festivals took place in different locations (Ballabio, Lecco in 1971; Zerbo, Pavia in 1972; Alpe del Vicerè, Como in 1973; and Milan in 1974–76). The Milan meetings took place at Parco Lambro and saw the participation of thousands. On Situationism, cf. Mirella Bandini, *L'estetico, il politico: Da Cobra all'Internazionale situazionista 1948–1957* (Roma: Officina edizioni, 1977); Leonardo Lippolis, *La nuova Babilionia: Il progetto architettonico di una civiltà situazionista* (Milano: Costa & Nolan, 2007); **Éric Brun, *Les situationnistes: Une avant-garde totale, 1950–1972* (Parigi, CNRS, 2014)**; Frances Stracey, *Constructed Situations: A New History of the Situationist International* (London: Pluto Press, 2014); Anna Trespeuch-Berthelot, *L'Internationale situationniste: De l'histoire au mythe*, 1948–2013 (Paris: Presses universitaires de France, 2015).

88 Cf. Mary Louise Lobsinger, "Cybernetic Theory and the Architecture of Performance: Cedric Price's Fun Palace," in *Anxious Modernisms, Experimentation in Postwar Architectural Culture,* Sarah Williams

Goldhagen and Réjean Legault, eds. (Montréal/Cambridge MA/London: Canadian Centre for Architecture/MIT Press, 2000), 119–139.

89 Andrea Mecacci, *L'estetica del Pop* (Roma: Donzelli editore, 2011).

90 Reyner Banham, "Who is this 'Pop'," *Motif* 10 (1963), 3–13; republished in *Pop,* Mark Francis, ed. (London: Phaidon, 2005), 222–224.

91 Guy Rottier, "Città degli svaghi da bruciare dopo l'uso," in *Complessi turistici/Tourist complexes,* Giampiero Aloi, ed. (Milano: Hoepli, 1980), 134. Cf. also Guy Rottier, *Architecture libre* (Paris: Editions Alternatives, 1986): the 4th volume is dedicated to "L'architecture de loisirs."

Games without Frontiers
Simon Sadler

1 I wish to thank the Kunsthistorisches Institut in Florenz for inviting me to take part in its symposium "Architecture and Dystopia" in October 2014, under the gracious guidance of Dario Donetti and his colleagues. I presented an earlier version of this essay at "1945–1975: British Culture for Architecture International Working Seminar," May 23–24, 2014, Canadian Center for Architecture, Montréal.

2 For further discussion of this Enlightenment dialectic of play, cf. Mihai I. Spariosou, *Dionysus Reborn: Play and the Aesthetic Dimension in Modern Philosophical and Scientific Discourse* (Ithaca: Cornell University Press, 1989); also cited in Tamar Zinguer, *Architecture in Play: Intimations of Modernism in Architectural Toys* (Charlottesville: University of Virginia Press, 2015), 10.

3 On the avant-garde interest in toys, cf. *Toys of the Avant-Garde*, exhibition at the Museo Picasso Málaga, Oct. 2010–Jan. 2011.

4 On cubism and anarchism, cf. for instance Patricia Leighten, *Re-Ordering the Universe: Picasso and Anarchism, 1897–1914* (Princeton: Princeton University Press, 1989). On the use of puns in cubism, including abbreviations of "jouer" (to play), cf. Robert Rosenblum, "Picasso and the Typography of Cubism," in *Picasso 1881–1973* (London: Paul Elek, 1973), 49–75.

5 Colin Ward, "Anarchism as a Theory of Organization," in Leonard I. Krimerman and Lewis Perry, eds., *Patterns of Anarchy* (New York: Anchor Books, 1966), republished online and accessed June 7, 2016: http://www.panarchy.org/ward/organization.1966.html.

6 Ward's most influential book was *The Child in the City* (London: Architectural Press, 1978), and the seventh edition of his journal *Anarchy* (1961) was dedicated to the adventure playground as "a parable of anarchy."

7 For Morris's tentative negotiations with anarchism, cf. for instance William Morris, "Socialism and Anarchism," letter in *Commonweal* (May 5, 1889), republished online and accessed June 8, 2016: https://www.marxists.org/archive/morris/works/1889/sa/sa.htm. For a sense of the struggle between socialism and anarchism for the political consciousness of the avant-garde, note that in 1944 Picasso famously threw in his lot with the French Communist Party (like Andre Breton before him, from 1927 to 1935, before breaking in protest at Stalinism).

8 Global Tools, "Bulletin No. 1" (1974), in Valerio Borgonuovo and Silvia Franceschini, eds., *Global Tools 1973–75* (Istanbul: SALT/Garanti Kültür AŞ), republished as an ebook and accessed June 8, 2016: http://saltonline.org/tr#!/tr/1195/global-tools-1973-1975.

9 Claude Lévi-Strauss, *The Savage Mind* [1962] (Chicago: University of Chicago Press, 1966), 12, quoted in Tamar Zinguer, *Architecture in Play: Intimations of Modernism in Architectural Toys* (Charlottesville: University of Virginia Press, 2015), 204.

10 György Kepes, *The New Landscape in Art and Science* (Chicago: Paul Theobald, 1956), 204-205, quoted in Zinguer, *Architecture in Play*, 208.

11 Cf. Zinguer, *Architecture in Play*, 189.

12 Cf. John Dewey, *Art as Experience* (New York: Minton, Balch & Company, 1934), and the exegesis offered in Zinguer, *Architecture in Play*, 193. On the larger tension between rules and freedom in design, cf. for instance Jonathan Hughes, Simon Sadler, eds., *Non-Plan: Essays on Freedom, Participation and Change in Modern Architecture and Urbanism* (Oxford: Architectural Press, 2000).

13 Gregory Bateson, "Metalogue: About Games and Being Serious", *ETC.: A Review of General Semantics*, X, (1953), reprinted in Gregory Bateson, *Steps to an Ecology of Mind* (New York: Ballantine, 1972), 24-30, 25.

14 Ibid., 27.

15 Cf. Sigmund Freud, *Beyond the Pleasure Principle* (London/Vienna,: The International Psycho-Analytical Press, 1922); and in relation to games of architecture, cf. Zinguer, *Architecture in Play*, 200.

16 For further analysis on the relationship of Huizinga to game and toy design, see Zinguer, *Architecture in Play*, 10, and Hector Rodriguez, "The Playful and the Serious: An Approximation to Huizinga's *Homo Ludens*", *Game Studies: the International Journal of Computer Game Research* 6:1 (2006), accessed June 8 2016: http://gamestudies.org/0601/articles/rodriges.

17 Caillois identified four main kinds of play: *agôn* (competition), *alea* (chance),

mimicry (simulation or role playing), *ilinx* (vertigo—spinning, rollercoasters, etc.).

18 Roger Caillois, *Man, Play and Games* (Urbana: University of Illinois Press, 2001), 32, quoted in Zinguer, *Architecture in Play*, 203.

19 On the *Game of War*, see for instance Benjamin Noys, "Guy Debord's Time-Image: *In girum imus nocte et consumimur igni*" [1978], *Grey Room* 52 (2013), 94-107. Debord, and the Situationists, drew in turn on the long vanguard heritage of play, including anarchism, Dada, Surrealism, Huizinga, and the Imaginist Bauhaus. Cf. for instance Sadie Plant, *The Most Radical Gesture: The Situationist International in a Postmodern Age* (London: Routledge, 1992); Simon Sadler, *The Situationist City* (Cambridge MA: MIT Press, 1998).

20 See "The uses of sidewalks: assimilating children", fourth chapter of Jane Jacobs, *The Death and Life of Great American Cities* (New York: Vintage, 1961).

21 Carl Th. Sørensen, *Parkpolitik i Sogn og Købstad* [*Park Politics in Parish and Town*] (Copenhagen: I Kommission hos Gyldendalske Boghandel, 1931). Cf. too the New York playgrounds of architect Richard Dattner and landscape architect Paul Friedberg, in James Trainor, *Steal This Playground: New York City and the Radical Playground Movement, 1961–1976* (New York: Metropolis, 2017).

22 *Vogue* August 15 (1959), 127, quoted in Zinguer, *Architecture in Play*, 146. The Eames also released a short movie, *Toy Trains*, in 1957.

23 John Maynard Keynes, "Economic Possibilities for our Grandchildren" [1930], reprinted in *Essays in Persuasion* (New York: W. W. Norton, 1963), 358-373.

24 Ulrich Conrads, ed., *Programs and Manifestoes on 20th-Century Architecture* (Cambridge MA : MIT Press, 1971).

25 Cf. Simon Sadler, "Drop City Revisited", *Journal of Architectural Education* 58:1 (2006), 5-14, 11.

26 Cf. for instance Stanley Mathews, *From Agit Prop to Free Space: The Architecture of Cedric Price* (London: Black Dog, 2007).

26 The formation of *Jeux sans Frontiers* is pieced together at the dedicated Wikipedia page, accessed June 8 2016: https://en.wikipedia.org/wiki/Jeux_Sans_Frontières.

28 See Britt Eversole, "Occupy the Fun Palace", *Thresholds* 41 (2013), 32-45.

29 See Simon Sadler, "Spectacular Failure: The Architecture of Late Capitalism at the Millennium Dome, 2000 CE", in Peggy Deamer, ed., *Architecture and Capitalism: 1845 to the Present* (New York: Routledge, 2014), 189-201.

30 Cf. for instance Fred Turner, "Why Study New Games?", *Games & Culture* 1:1 (2006) 1-4; "New Games movement", accessed June 8 2016: http://rationalwiki.org/wiki/Main_Page.

31 Cam Smith, *Buckminster Fuller to Children of Earth* (New York: Doubleday, 1972).

32 Buckminster Fuller Institute, "About Fuller: World Game," accessed June 8 2016: http://bfi.org/about-fuller/big-ideas/world-game.

33 Cf. Simon Sadler, "Theo Crosby's Environment Games, 1956-1973", in Eeva-Liisa Pelkonen, ed., *Exhibiting Architecture: A Paradox?* (New Haven: Yale School of Architecture, 2015), 99-106. In June 1961 Crosby had convened the UIA's London Conference, which climaxed with Fuller's speech on 'The Architect as World Planner."

34 See Marshall McLuhan, "Games: The Extensions of Man," in *Understanding Media: The Extensions of Man* (New York: McGraw-Hill, 1965), 234-245.

35 Bateson, "Metalogue: About Games and Being Serious", 29-30. "For a systems analysis of play, participation and playgrounds, see Tim Stott, *Play and Participation in Contemporary Arts Practices* (London: Routledge, 2015). On play in contemporary design, see Thomas Lee, "Too Much Fun: Contemporary Aesthetic Theory and Design," *Design and Culture*, 9:3, 2017, 301-315.

36 See Jacques Derrida, "Structure, Sign and Play in the Discourse of the Human Sciences" [1966], in *Writing and Difference*, trans. Alan Bass (London: Routledge, 1978), 278–294; Roland Barthes, "From Work to Text" [1971], in Stephen Heath, ed. and trans., *Image-Music-Text* (London: Fontana, 1977), 155-164. On the correlation with game design, see for instance Mark Filipowich, "From Game to Play: Roland Barthes, Videogames and Criticism", *Bigtallwords* (11/29/16), accessed June 9 2016: https://big-tall-words.com/2013/11/29/from-game-to-play/.

37 See Gilles Deleuze, *The Fold: Leibniz and the Baroque*, trans. Tom Conley (Minneapolis: University of Minnesota Press, 1992).

38 Nicholas Negroponte, *The Architecture Machine: Toward a More Human Environment* (Cambridge MA: MIT Press, 1970), 3.

39 Lacan's use of the term has been traced to a 1958 lecture (cf. for instance Nestor A. Braunstein, "Desire and Jouissance in the Teachings of Lacan", in Jean-Michel Rabate, ed., *The Cambridge Companion to Lacan* [Cambridge: Cambridge University Press, 2003], 102-115).

40 Bernard Tschumi, "Ropes and Rules," archived at Bernard Tschumi Architects, accessed June 8 2016: http://www.tschumi.com/projects/19/#.

41 See Raul P. Lejano, Francisco Fernandez de Castro, "Norm, Network, and cCommons: The Invisible Hand of Community", *Environmental Science & Policy*, 3:6 (2014), 73–85.

42 Contemporary anarchism insists on a prefigurative politics, in which life is lived in the here and now in a way that prefigures the society desired. For a summary of prefigurative politics, see for instance Uri Gordon, *Anarchy Alive!: Anti-authoritarian Politics from Practice to Theory* (London: Pluto, 2008), 34 ff.

43 Cf. for instance the implicit critique of Neil Brenner, "Is 'Tactical Urbanism' an Alternative to Neoliberal Urbanism?", accessed June 8 2016: http://post.at.moma.org/content_items/587-is-tactical-urbanism-an-alternative-to-neoliberal-urbanism.

44 As Robert Nozick influentially announced of his revival of the social contract theory of John Locke and libertarian revision of anarchism, the new, partial, minimally-regulated market order of the 1970s and beyond should be that of *Anarchy, the State and Utopia* (New York : Basic Books, 1974). Interestingly this was his response to another influential "game", the thought experiment of John Rawls's *A Theory of Justice* (1971).

45 Cf. Manfredo Tafuri, *Architecture and Utopia: Design and Capitalist Development* (Cambridge MA.: MIT Press, 1979), 139 ff.

46 Troy Conrad Therrien, "Prometheus Unbound", *The Architect's Newspaper* (February 3, 2016), 22-23, 22, reviewing Carlo Ratti with Matthew Claudel, *Open Source Architecture* (London: Thames & Hudson, 2016).

Reality as Dystopia: Urban Contemporary Visions

Marco Biraghi

1 Cf. Marco Biraghi, *Project of Crisis. Manfredo Tafuri and Contemporary Architecture*, trans. Alta Price, (Cambridge MA/London: MIT Press, 2013), 27-49, 145-172.

2 Superstudio, "Il Monumento Continuo: Storyboard per un film," *Casabella*, 358 (1971), 19-22

3 Archizoom, "No-Stop City, Residential Parkings, Climatic Universal Sistem [sic]," *Domus* 496 (1971), 49–55.

4 Cf. Walter Benjamin, "The Work of Art in the Age of Mechanical Reproduction" [1936], in *Illuminations* Hannah Arendt, ed., trans. Harry Zohn (New York, Schocken Books, 1968), 217-254.

5 *Giacomo Costa: Land(E)scape*, exhibition catalogue (Milan: Photology srl, 1999).

6 Luca Beatrice, *Giacomo Costa: The Chronicles of Time* (Bologna: Damiani, 2008).

7 "Du Zehnjun: Babel World," *Hanix*, 15 (2013), 48-55.

8 Michael Wolf, Natàsha Egan, and Emest Chui, *Architecture of Density* (Hong Kong/Berlin: Asia One/Peperoni Books, 2009).

Index of Names

Image Credits

Dario Donetti – Figs. 1: Manfredo Tafuri, *Progetto e utopia: architettura e sviluppo capitalistico,* (Bari: Laterza, 1973); 2: *Film Architecture: Set Designs from Metropolis to Blade Runner*, edited by Dietrich Neumann (Munich/London/New York: Prestel, 1999), 159; 3: *Italy: The New Domestic Landscape: Achievements and Problems of Italian Design*, edited by Emilio Ambasz, (New York/Florence: Museum of Modern Art/Centro Di, 1972), 259; 4: *Archigram*, edited by Peter Cook (London: Studio Vista, 1972), 53; 5: Courtesy Fondazione MAXXI and Galleria d'Arte Moderna, Milano; 6: Courtesy of Andrea Branzi; 7: Roberto Gargiani, *Rem Koolhaas/OMA: The Construction of Merveilles* (EPFL Press/Routledge: Lausanne/London and New York, 2008), 8; 8: Francesco Dal Co, *Renzo Piano* (Milano: Electa, 2014), 35.

Anthony Vidler – Figs. 1: *Granta* LXIII, 1187 (1959), cover; 2: Emil Kaufmann, *Von Ledoux bis Le Corbusier: Ursprung und Entwicklung der autonomen Architektur*, (Wien/Leipzig: Verlag Dr. Rolf Passer, 1933), cover; 3: Emil Kaufmann, *Architecture in the Age of Reason: Baroque and Post-Baroque in England, Italy, and France*, (Cambridge MA: Harvard University Press, 1955), cover; 4: Hans Sedlmayr, *Art in Crisis, the Lost Center*, (Chicago: H. Regnery Co., 1958), cover; 5: *Utopie: Sociologie de l'urbain*, 1 (1967), cover; 6: Plato, *The Republic*, translated by Allan Bloom, (New York: Basic Books, 1968), cover; 7: *Italy: The New Domestic Landscape: Achievements and Problems of Italian Design*, edited by Emilio Ambasz, (New York/Florence: Museum of Modern Art/Centro Di, 1972), cover; 8: Courtesy of Cristiano Toraldo Di Francia.

Marco De Michelis – Figs. 1, 5: Archive of the author; 2: *Casabella* 619–620 (1995), cover; 3: Pier Vittorio Aureli, Marco Biraghi, Franco Purini, *Peter Eisenman. Tutte le opere* (Milano: Electa, 2007), 22; 4: James Stirling, Michael Wilford and Associates, *Buildings & Projects 1975-1992* (London: Thames and Hudson, 1994), 54; 6: ‹http://venturiscottbrown.org/projects/›; 7: *Lotus international*, 13 (December 1976), 4; 8: *Questo. Disegni e studi di Manfredo Tafuri*, edited by Anna bedon, Guido Beltramini, Howard Burns (Vicenza: Centro Internazionale di Studi di Architettura Andrea Palladio, 1995), 50.

Dominique Rouillard – Figs. 1-6.a, 9: © Private collection; 6.b: Courtesy of Abraham Archives; 6.c, 8: © Superstudio Archives; 7: © Archizoom Archives; 10: Courtesy of Jean Nouvel, Emmanuel Cattani & Associés.

Maddalena Scimemi – Figs. 1: *Arts and Architecture* 45 (1945), cover; 2: *A Decade of New Architecture*, edited by Sigfried Giedion, (Zurich: Girsberger, 1951), 204›; 3: William Curtis, *Denys Lasdun: Architecture, City, Landscape* (London: Phaidon 1994), 42; 4: *Architectural Review* CXVIII, 707, (November 1955), 284; 5: James Stanley Mathews, *From Agit-Prop to Free Space: The architecture of Cedric Price* (London: Black Dog Publisher, 2007); 6: Canadian Center for Architecture, Cedric price Fonds, DR1995:0208:001; 7: ‹https://brutalistconstructions.com/2015/02/07/leicester-university-engineering-building-leicester/›; 8: Canadian Center for Architecture, Cedric price Fonds, DR1995:0188:010; 9: Bibliotheca Hertziana, Photographic Collection, no. bh119919.

Marie Theres Stauffer – Figs. 1-6, 10, 14, 16: © Archivio Andrea Branzi, Milano; 7, 8, 9, 11: © Centro Studi e Archivio della Comunicazione (CSAC), Parma; 12: Ed(ward) Ruscha, *Thirtyfour Parking Lots in Los Angeles*, 2nd edition, (Hollywood: E. Ruscha, 1974); 14: Ed(ward) Ruscha, *Some Los Angeles Apartments*, 2nd edition (Hollywood: E. Ruscha, 1965); 15: in *Arts Magazine* 41, 3 (1966-1967), 21-22.

Massimiliano Savorra – Figs. 1: Michel Ragon, *Où vivrons-nous demain?* (Paris: Robert Laffont, 1963), cover; 2: Jean Balladur, Yona Friedman, Walter Jonas, Paul Maymont, Michel Ragon, Nicolas Schöffer, *Les visionnaires de l'architecture* (Paris: Robert Laffont, 1965), cover; 3: Georges Candilis, *Planen und Bauen* für die *Freizeit/Recherches sur l'architecture des loisirs/Planning and Design for Leisure* (Stuttgart: Karl Krämer Verlag, 1972), cover; 4, 5, 15, 19, 20: Giampiero Aloi, *Complessi turistici/Tourist Complexes* (Milano: Hoepli,

1980), 11, 61, 73, 135, 136; 6: Ludovico Quaroni, Helio Piñón, *Architetture di Julio Lafuente* (Roma: Officina, 1982), 96; 7, 12: ‹http://astudejaoublie.blogspot.it/›; 8: Manfredo Nicoletti, *Continuità Evoluzione Architettura* (Bari: Dedalo, 1978), 55; 9: ‹http://www.citechaillot.fr/ressources/expositions_virtuelles/vegetal/03-theme05-sstheme01-doc27.html›; 10: Shadrach Woods, *Candilis-Josic-Woods: A Decade of Architecture and Urban Design* (Stuttgart : Krämer, 1978), 126-127; 11: © Fonds Candilis. SIAF/Cité de l'architecture et du patrimoine/Archives d'architecture du XXe siècle; 13: Arnt Cobbers, Oliver Jahn, *Prefab Houses* (Köln: Taschen, 2010), 151; 14: Casabella 299 (1965), 65; 16: *L'Architettura: Cronache e storia* 175 (1970), 6; 17, 18: *L'Architettura: Cronache e storia* 230 (1974), 500, 496.

Simon Sadler – Figs. 1: Colin Ward, *The Child in the City* (New York: Pantheon Books, 1978), cover; 2: *Riccardo Dalisi: In-Arch* (Firenze: Centro DI, 1977), 9; 3: Guy Debord, Œuvres, edited by Jean-Louis Rançon (Paris: Gallimard, 2006), 1746 ; 4: Aldo van Eyck, *The Playgrounds and the City*, edited by Liane Lefaivre (Rotterdam: Nai Publishers, 2002), 51; 5: Family Archive – Smithson Family Collection; 6: Courtesy of Clark Richard; 7: Lawrence Halprin, *The RSVP Cycles* (New York: G. Braziller, 1969), cover; 8: Simon Sadler, *Archigram: Architecture without Architecture* (Cambridge MA: MIT Press, 2005), 166; 9: *Archigram*, edited by Peter Cook (London: Studio Vista, 1972), 19; 10: *Constant – New Babylon: To Us, Liberty*, Edited by Laura Stamps (Ostfildern: Hatje Kantz), 157; 11: Cam Smith, *Buckminster Fuller to Children of Earth* (New York: Doubleday, 1972), cover; 12: Theo Crosby, *How to Play the Environment Game* (Harmondsworth: Penguin/London: Arts Council of Great Britain, 1973), cover; Fig. 13: Charles Eames, Ray Eames, *House of Cards – Giant Size* (Chicago: Tigrett Enterprises, 1954).

Marco Biraghi – Figs. 1: ‹http://www.regione.lombardia.it/wps/portal/istituzionale/HP/istituzione/regione/palazzo-lombardia/storia-del-progetto-palazzo-lombardia›; 2: © Peter Cook; 3Courtesy Fondazione MAXXI; 4: Courtesy of Andrea Branzi; 5: © Staatsgalerie Stuttgart; 6: © 2018 Paul Citroen/Artist Rights Society (ARS), New York/Pictoright, Amsterdam; 7: *Tempo, tempo! Bauhaus-Photomontagen von Marianne Brandt*, edited by Elizabeth Otto (Berlin: Jovis, 2005), 44; 8, 9: © Giacomo Costa; 10: © Du Zhenjun; 11: © Michael Wolf; 12: © Vins Grosso; 13: © Francesco Barbieri.

Architecture and Dystopia
Published by
Actar Publishers, New York, Barcelona
www.actar.com

Edited by
Dario Donetti

Graphic Design: Actar D

With contributions by
Marco Biraghi
Marco De Michelis
Dario Donetti
Dominique Rouillard
Simon Sadler
Massimiliano Savorra
Maddalena Scimeni
Marie Therese Stauffer
Anthony Vidler

Copy editing and proofreading
Kurt Klein
Antonina Tetzlaff

Printing and binding
Gràfiques Campàs

Distribution
Actar D, Inc. New York, Barcelona.

New York
440 Park Avenue South, 17th Floor
New York, NY 10016, USA
T +1 2129662207
salesnewyork@actar-d.com

Barcelona
Roca i Batlle 2-4
08023 Barcelona, Spain
T +34 933 282 183
eurosales@actar-d.com

Indexing
English ISBN: 978-1-945-150-94-4
PCN: Library of Congress Control Number: 2017962246

Printed in Barcelona

Publication date: July 2019

This publication has been realized with the support of the Kunsthistorisches Institut in Florenz - Max-Planck-Institut.

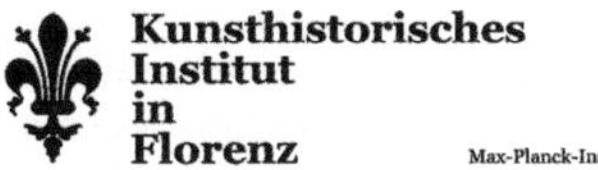